All About Jill

The Life and Death of
Jill Dando

All About Jill

The Life and Death of Jill Dando

DAVID JAMES SMITH

timewarner
books

A *Time Warner* Book

First published in Great Britain in 2002 by Time Warner Books

Copyright © David James Smith 2002

Extract on page 314 from 'If' by Rudyard Kipling, quoted with kind
permission of A. P. Watt Ltd, on behalf of the National Trust
for Places of Historical Interest or Natural Beauty.

A CIP catalogue record for this book
is available from the British Library.

ISBN (hbk) 0 316 85938 9
ISBN (pbk) 0 7515 3281 9

Typeset in Perpetua by M Rules
Printed and bound in Great Britain
by Clays Ltd, St Ives plc

Time Warner Books UK
Brettenham House
Lancaster Place
London WC2E 7EN

www.TimeWarnerBooks.co.uk

For my daughters
Sitira, Kitty, Orealla
and for my newborn son
Mackenzie

I strain my heart, I stretch my hands,
And catch at hope.

CHRISTINA ROSSETTI
'De Profundis', 1881

Jill Dando lived for 37 years and 169 days.
She was born on 9 November 1961.
She died on 26 April 1999.
11.30 am.

One

Jill Dando was baptised on the first Sunday of December 1976, a month after her fifteenth birthday. She had attended classes in preparation and had been interviewed by senior members of the Church to ensure her readiness for the event.

'Do you acknowledge Jesus as your personal lord and saviour?'

'I do.'

'Do you promise to serve him for ever in the Church and in the world?'

'I do.'

'On your profession of repentance towards God and faith in our Lord Jesus Christ, I baptise you in the name of the Father, the Son and the Holy Spirit.'

Jill was wearing a white robe. She stood in the baptismal pool and the minister, Philip Gathercole, eased her back so that her body and her face were submerged in the water. In that moment she was buried with Christ. A symbolic death. Then she was rocked forward, emerging from the pool, raised in the newness of life, resurrected with Jesus, joined to the fellowship of Milton Baptist Church in Weston-Super-Mare in Somerset.

Baptists believe that when you have died and been reborn through this ritual, death no longer holds the same significance for you. At least, that is the theory.

Philip Gathercole left Milton some time later and was replaced as minister by Roger Collins, who got to know Jill and her mother, Jean, very well. He observed the intensity of their closeness, as did everybody who knew them. He gave support when Jean became ill, remembered how he practically had to blackmail Jean into disclosing the seriousness of her condition. She had sworn him to secrecy, not wanting Jill to know, not just yet. He could not remember Jean or Jill ever using the word leukaemia, though this is what it was. He remembered the haemorrhages, Jean in the hospital bed in Bristol, wads of cotton wool in her mouth to staunch the bleeding from her gums. In the end, Jean had wanted to die. Let me go. Let me go home.

As ministers do, Roger Collins had gleaned the family history. He had heard that Jill had been a blue baby and had survived a heart operation which might have killed her. He noted how she always used to wear her blouses buttoned up to hide the scar which had resulted from that operation.

Roger considered that you could not be close to death and be untouched by it. He thought that proximity gave Jill depth, a knowledge which not everyone shared, layers way below the surface.

He gave the address at Jean's funeral and had been expecting to officiate at Jill's wedding. It had been a running joke between them for years: 'Do I need to book some time? Should I be keeping August free?'

'No, not yet, Roger.' And then, finally, 'Yes!'

Instead he found himself giving the address at Jill's funeral, too.

In that speech he described the symbolism of the baptism by full immersion, alluded to the idea of Jill's death as a natural part of life's cycle – death and resurrection – according to the Baptist faith. He believed it himself but still he could not get over the loss of expectation; the expectation of happiness that Jill had, right up to the moment, 11.30 am or thereabouts on Monday 26 April 1999.

There was another white robe. An 11.30 appointment at the Bridal Department of Harrods on 9 March, six months before the wedding, forty-eight days before her death.

Jill was a few minutes early and had already begun examining the dresses when Jenny arrived.

Jenny Higham was Jill's best friend and it had already been decided, at an earlier lunch, that Jenny would support Jill through her wedding. 'I really need you now, Jen. I haven't got my mum and I need somebody sensible to say, "That's a good idea, that's a bad idea."' Jill's mother had been her best friend; now her best friend was, so to speak, becoming her mother.

Jill had also asked Jenny to be her chief bridesmaid, a role she would share with Jill's cousin Judith. According to a long-standing routine between them, Jill would never have Jenny or anyone as a bridesmaid who posed the slightest threat or risk of outshining her on her day. Jenny knew that, deep down inside Jill, this was not entirely a joke. She always feared being eclipsed, one way or another. Jenny reminded her of it. 'Oh no, no, silly isn't it,' Jill had said, 'I've thought about it and I really want you to do it.'

The joke was based on an old acquaintance of Jenny's who had once been asked to be a bridesmaid. The bride had later said to her,

'Well, looking the way you do, there's no way you could outshine me on the day.'

At that lunch, Jill had begun dressing Jenny in her mind's eye. 'What about something nice in black? Yes, black with puffed sleeves, purple ribbons round the top of the sleeves, just like a Teletubby.' Much laughter between them.

Naturally, Jill had been dressing herself in her mind's eye, too. She was really only using Harrods as a try-out, having already decided to have a dress made by the designer Lindka Cierach. Jill was not about to buy an off-the-peg wedding dress, even from Harrods at £2,500 or £3,000.

Cierach was best known for having made the dress that Sarah Ferguson wore when she married Prince Andrew, which was not necessarily the best omen. Cierach had been widely quoted as saying she had designed the Duchess-to-be's dress in the middle of the night, in the middle of a dream: 'I woke up, and that was it.' Mmm, yes, Lindka Cierach, Jenny had thought to herself. Who's she? But then, it wasn't her wedding.

Jenny found Jill in the Bridal Department, beyond the evening dresses on the first floor. A powder-blue room with gold-leaf architraving, Jill foraging in the alcoves where gowns were arranged on cushioned, white satin hangers. They picked out maybe a dozen dresses and went through to the mirrored fitting room, where Jenny sat on a chair while Jill undressed to her underwear and begin a litany of self-criticism. 'Oh God, I'm so fat. I've got to lose this.' She tugged at the sides of her midriff. 'Don't worry, this will be all gone by the wedding.'

Jill wanted what Jenny suspected most mature brides wanted in a wedding dress: something simple, straight, not too fussy. Jenny, however, thought this was fine if you were Twiggy or Kate Moss and wore a size 8 but not if you were remotely normal or voluptuous. Jill's size fluctuated, but although she had lost some weight in the initial flurry of excitement of her relationship with Alan, she was now fairly stable at 12. Jill would've liked something sleeveless, but that, again, was not the kind of thing you could get away with in your mid- to late thirties.

So they tried everything, more or less. Some of the dresses were merely held up, others she got only half on, before they came off. It took about fifteen minutes to do one up properly, with the buttons, and they didn't have all day. Eventually, they returned to one particular dress and decided to go for the full fitting, accessories and all.

This dress was the polar opposite of Jill's desires. 'Ridiculous,' she had said when she first saw it. She'd never wear anything like that. Detachable sleeves, a long train; a princessy, meringuey, classic wedding dress. It was not an exact fit and had to be pinned back, which took even longer. They went back out and mulled over the options for accessories – tiara, veil, shoes – and finally, they put the whole thing together. The Harrods assistant was patient and meticulous and when Jill stood back they all agreed that she looked magnificent. All except Jill. 'Oh, I look all right.' She took a few steps forward and did a turn. She looked herself over very carefully in the mirror. Jenny thought it was fantastic and realised in that moment what a glorious bride her friend was going to be; felt privileged to have seen her at this early dress rehearsal, the first time she had ever worn a wedding dress. Absolutely out of this world.

Jill undressed and changed back into her day clothes and they went for a cappuccino and a sandwich in one of the cafés in Harrods. Jenny was going back to work and Jill was going into the BBC for yet another meeting about her new contract, which was still up in the air. Fed up with the BBC, she was still half-heartedly considering an attractive offer from ITV.

Most of all, she was hurt and humiliated by the knock-back she had received, not getting the job as the new main presenter of the *Six O'Clock News*. The public spin put about by her agent, Jon Roseman, was that Jill had withdrawn from competition for the role because of the BBC's dithering. The truth was that she had been rejected for a job she dearly wanted and thought herself eminently capable of doing.

With Jenny, there was no disguising her unhappiness and annoyance, or her uncertainty about the future of her career, and they talked about this for a while before they parted.

Jenny was glad later that she had not had another opportunity to encourage Jill to buy that particular dress, much as she had liked it. Jenny saw a photograph of Emma Noble's marriage to James Major, son of the former prime minister, John Major. Jill had been dead a month by this time. Emma, a former television game-show hostess, had worn a dress that was almost identical to the one Jill had tried on that day at Harrods, only without the sleeves. Jill would've hated that. The dress would've been straight out of the window and Jenny would've felt terrible.

Still, Jenny could not get out of her mind the thought that she had seen something no one else would ever see. Ridiculous though it might sound, she knew how distressed Jill would have been if she had known she was going to be deprived of the opportunity to be a bride. It would have been one of the things of which she would have felt most robbed or cheated.

Jenny missed the smell of Jill, the familiarity of her presence. She mentioned this to Alan. 'I know it sounds weird,' she said. But it did not sound weird to Alan; he understood. He gave Jenny a scarf that Jill had worn in the week before she died, and which had remained where she left it, draped over the banister in Alan's home in Chiswick.

The scarf was comforting to Jenny. She could not describe the smell of Jill with any precision. It was floral, feminine – very, very feminine – suffused with a mixture of scents from her various perfumes (she was not especially loyal to one), her deodorant, her make-up, her hair.

In her grief and in the highly public aftermath of Jill's death, Jenny was quite unable to comprehend that her best friend had been murdered. She felt lost, too, and somewhat marginalised, the media attention focused on Jill, the celebrity, and on Alan, her husband-to-be.

Jenny had given a brief television interview to the BBC on the day Jill died and another friend of Jill's said later that she didn't know how Jenny could have done that, when others had been too grief-stricken to speak. This comment played on Jenny's mind. She thought it was a rather bitchy thing to have said, yet at the same time – a trick of bereavement – she began to doubt the validity of her friendship with Jill.

In need of reassurance and confirmation, and still possessed by that vision of Jill in the fitting room at Harrods in the dress, Jenny walked out of work one day and travelled back to the store, up to the powder-blue room on the first floor. The sympathetic staff looked up the record of that fitting – 11.30, Jill Dando – in their appointments book.

The assistant who had pinned and buttoned Jill was off work that day, but another member of staff helped Jenny to find the dress that Jill had worn, and Jenny touched the dress and admired it again, and then left, feeling a bit better. Well, gosh, she thought. Jill really must have thought a lot of me, otherwise she wouldn't have included me in this, would she? A reality check, Jenny called it.

Two

It was a very Fulham morning in and around Gowan Avenue, that morning of 26 April 1999. Not the kind of morning on which anything seemed likely to happen. It rained lightly, early on. A very ordinary morning, clouded and drizzly. No ominous portents, except maybe, with hindsight. The character of the place betrayed by its particularities.

I had lived in Fulham for fifteen years or so but had never met or known Jill Dando, and had no idea that she lived there too. My children went to a nursery on Munster Road, not much more than a hundred yards from Gowan Avenue, but if she was ever passing I had never noticed her.

In truth, Jill was already leaving Fulham and, in a few weeks, would have been gone altogether. She had recently exchanged contracts on the sale of her house. Alan was selling his place, too, and they were pooling their resources to buy a new £1.5 million home, a marital home, a family home, in Warwick Avenue, Maida Vale.

She had bought 29 Gowan Avenue at the beginning of 1995, in the latter phase of her long relationship with Bob Wheaton, who had been her editor at *Breakfast News*. She had needed independence then, a place of escape, quite the opposite of what she needed or desired now. The house had paved the way for her separation from Bob, and for the year or so that followed, in which she had lived the life of a single woman, of dates, dinners, dalliances, flirtations, the criss-crossing relationships.

Cliff Richard had once been to a late supper at 29 Gowan Avenue, still wearing full make-up from his appearance, which had ended minutes earlier, as Heathcliff up the road at the Apollo Hammersmith. One or two boyfriends had stayed the night there (though certainly not Cliff, however much Jill might have wished it) in those free-agent, out-on-the-town days before she met Alan.

She had spent her last night in Gowan Avenue, with Alan, a week earlier, and had been away ever since, travelling with her work or staying with Alan in Chiswick. She had been back briefly on Saturday and had noticed the fax wasn't working. She would buy a new cartridge for the machine that Monday morning, stopping off at the house to replace it on her way to the Lanesborough Hotel.

People who know the place only by reputation tend to think of Fulham as a sub-Chelsea, uniformly middle-class, inner-London suburb. In reality it is a mixed area, where widespread gentrification has not yet eroded the traditional, working-class population. With some exceptions, the residents of any one street might span the entire social scale, with rows of elegant houses perhaps overshadowed by nearby low- or high-rise council estates.

That process of gentrification might be visible in the pubs, bars and restaurants of the Fulham Road and the New King's Road, where boisterous young Hoorays still bray their way through Friday and Saturday nights as they have done since the mid-eighties. But it is most evident in the constant extending and refurbishing of Fulham houses. For the most part, Fulham is dense with late-Victorian terraces which, according to taste, are always ripe for either ripping apart and modernising or recreating in their original form.

The houses are generally quite narrow, the gardens rarely longer than forty feet. The only scope for increasing size is upwards, into the loft – extra bedroom with en-suite bath or shower room – or downwards into the cellar (kitchen or breakfast room, children's playroom), or filling in the side return. Builders make fortunes in Fulham and loft-conversion specialists are never out of work.

Jill Dando did not have a loft conversion – she didn't need it. Hers was not a family home. But many of her neighbours had one, or, no doubt, planned one, or hoped to have one if and when they could afford it.

In this way, the houses got bigger and more expensive, and ever more inaccessible to all those except the more affluent. It was an evolving landscape, a community constantly in a state of change. The new Fulham was not the most neighbourly of places. You could wait around to kill somebody and go virtually unseen. You could be shot on your doorstep and lie there unnoticed. You could be doing the ordinary and be quite oblivious to the extraordinary in your midst. That was how it was in this street on that day.

Three minutes to seven. The exact same time every morning, not a minute later or earlier, Susan Mayes leaves for work. Head down, umbrella up, on her way to the underground station at Parsons Green. Lives at number 73, walks as always down the odd-numbered side of the road, the south side.

Sees a car double-parked in the road outside number 28, opposite number 29. A Ford Sierra perhaps – she's no good on cars – maroon in colour. She has been living in Gowan Avenue for nine months, after six years in nearby Munster Road. She has never seen a car double-parked like this, at this time of the morning, parked there in the road, practically blocking it, the road was so narrow. Very Fulham that, the narrow road, the pressure of parking.

But this car is double-parked next to an empty space. It could have parked at the kerb but it didn't. She notes that the engine is switched off, then sees a man she assumes is the driver, standing in front of it. She first thinks he must be the chauffeur, then decides he is too scruffy to be a chauffeur. He looks thuggish. A minicab driver, maybe, though no sign of his customer, his fare.

As she draws level he looks down, begins wiping the windscreen with his left hand, not watching what he's doing. She sees his face momentarily, has about three glances at him in total, five to six seconds at most. He is five foot nine, five foot ten in height, clean shaven, Mediterranean-looking with a hint of an olive complexion, collar-length, straight, dark hair, swept back. He is slightly overweight, rather untidy, wearing a dark suit with an open-necked shirt and no tie. And no coat.

A few minutes later, Keila Hartingan is taking her regular Monday and Friday thirty-minute walking exercise round Fulham with a friend. As she goes south on Munster Road, crossing Gowan Avenue, she sees a blue Range Rover parked on the southern corner of Gowan Avenue, facing towards her. The engine is off. The driver looks and nods as they pass.

At 7.15, Vanessa Walduck comes out of her flat at 17 Gowan Avenue to begin loading files into the boot of her car for the drive to work. She arrived home late the previous night and drove round the block in search of a parking place before deciding to squeeze into the small space outside number 29. Now she kept a careful watch on it as she made three journeys from the house to the car with her work papers. She saw nothing – no maroon-coloured car, no olive-coloured man. She drove off.

Richard Hughes' wife left for work at eight o'clock, cycling to the primary school where she taught. She saw nothing. Richard and Fiona, at 31 Gowan Avenue, had been Jill Dando's immediate neighbours since they moved there five and a half months earlier, in mid-November. Jill had called in to introduce herself and welcome them to the street. The couple had sometimes taken in deliveries of flowers for Jill, particularly after the announcement of her engagement to Alan at the end of January. Richard Hughes worked from home, and would be at home all that morning.

Half an hour later a black cab pulled up immediately opposite, outside number 30, delivering the Upfill-Browns, Geoffrey and Philippa, home from Heathrow. They had just arrived back from a holiday in South Africa. They carried their cases indoors, saw nothing.

Rosa Rodriguez, the cleaner at number 26, turned up at about 9.10 am, walking down Gowan Avenue from Fulham Palace Road. She saw nothing unusual, either, noticing only a blonde-haired woman with two children who passed her as she entered the house.

Across the road at number 25, Julia Grimwade returned from taking her daughter to school and then popped out again to the dry cleaner on Fulham Palace Road. On the way she called in at number 55 and asked her friend Charlotte de Rosnay if she would be free for coffee later. Coming back, she met another friend, Emma Cooper, the Upfill-Browns' niece, and chatted with her a while before going into her house to begin tidying up the bedrooms, making the beds and picking up her children's clothes. From the window of the front bedroom, she could see Rosa cleaning the front bedroom of number 26.

Emma Cooper had gone to the Upfill-Browns' to take her aunt shopping. They chatted for a while before going out to Emma's car for the drive to Sainsbury's by Wandsworth Bridge.

Down the road, at number 55, Charlotte de Rosnay was standing in the front bedroom with her mother-in-law, Stella. Charlotte, a former catwalk model, her husband Alexis and their two small children had not long since moved to the house from a flat in the same street. Alexis worked in the City, as did many a young Fulham man, though there were not so many who could claim a baronial heritage. Stella, who had been visiting that weekend from Paris, had her own entry in *Debrett's Distinguished People of Today*, as Baroness Joel de Rosnay, the Hon. Stella Candida.

Stella was visiting the house for the first time and trying to get the measure of the place, and of the lives her son and daughter-in-law led in Fulham.

She looked out of the window and saw someone and said to Charlotte, 'Look, that could be Alexis, going to work.' He appeared, to Stella, like a City man, a bona fide banker. Five ten, heavy build, aged thirty-five to forty, dark brown hair, tidy and straight, a round head, a pinkish, high-coloured complexion, a dark grey suit which might have been double-breasted, a tie. Alexis, her son, was five foot ten to six feet, but he was fit. Stella said to Charlotte, 'This man isn't nearly as fit, he's more portly.'

Charlotte looked too. She was more familiar with the local nuances. The man she saw was a couple of rungs down the ladder from Alexis, more like an estate agent than a banker. There are plenty of those in Fulham, too. The man was walking along the north side of Gowan Avenue but crossed the street in front of them, almost breaking into a jog as he passed diagonally to the near side.

He was, to Charlotte, five foot eleven, aged between thirty-two and thirty-seven, clean shaven with a full face, pale skin, his hair dark, almost black, wearing a dark suit with a blue shirt and tie. She was sure later that he had been wearing a tie – she was sure she would have noticed if he wasn't. Even so, he wasn't City-smart, and had a five-o'clock shadow which gave him a Desperate Dan appearance.

The de Rosnays went out not long afterwards, at about 9.50 am, Charlotte and Stella, with Charlotte's two children and Stella's other two grandchildren, heading for the Thomas Cook by the street market on North End Road. They did not see the suited man again and thought no more of him for a long while. They met Julia Grimwade outside number 25, and Charlotte introduced her to the baroness.

Three street cleaners, Messrs Bennett, Barker and Smith, had just finished their breakfast in the café at Fulham Cross and were on their way to complete their duties in Gowan Avenue, known to them as one of the streets on Beat 574. They entered Gowan Avenue from Munster Road and took fifteen to twenty minutes to reach the other end, leading to Fulham Palace Road. It was an unmemorable shift for them.

The postman, Terence Griffin, had been given a lift from his depot to Gowan Avenue and began his delivery down the evens from Munster Road. He had not got far when a friend of his sister's came along in her estate car. She called out to him and he had a little joke with her, a bit of banter about her kids and his kids, and then another car drove up behind her. She said goodbye and Terence continued his round. He passed the window cleaner, who was on his way to number 26, carrying a bucket with a cloth in it.

Charles Taylor, the window cleaner, was let into the house by Rosa. He worked his way up through the house, and when he got to the top, to the en-suite bathroom in the loft conversion, he stopped and had a smoke out of the Velux window. He could see practically the whole street from there, across to the back gardens of the houses opposite. He saw a man in the street using his mobile phone, a smart-looking man, like an estate agent, he thought. But it turned out that this was the gas man, phoning through his meter reading from number 28.

Terry Normanton at number 93 had a ten o'clock embroidery class on Filmer Road, on the other side of Munster Road, and left home some ten minutes earlier. She lived at home with her mother, Lady Annabel Normanton. Her father had been the conservative MP for Cheadle for seventeen years until his retirement in 1987. When Sir Tom died in 1997, his obituary in the *Daily Telegraph* noted that he had been a passionate advocate of the return of hanging and of corporal punishment. He had once blocked a Private Members' Bill which sought to ban the physical punishment of 'handicapped' children, seeing no reason why they should be given any special legal protection.

Terry, his only daughter, herself suffered from a medical condition that made her slow to articulate her thoughts. She often walked around the area with her dog, and couldn't help but notice on her travels the increasing use of mobile phones in the street these days. This morning was no exception. As she crossed Gowan Avenue at the junction with Kimbell Road, there was a man with a mobile phone to his right ear. And as she progressed, nearing number 29, she saw another, standing in the road by a black car, phone to his right ear. He was actually talking, though she couldn't hear what he was saying. He was under six feet tall and had dark skin – he was either of Mediterranean origin or very suntanned. He had thick, dark eyebrows and an oval face, a dark suit but no tie, a bracelet, which could have been a watch bracelet, and that phone in his hand, which had a rounded shape. The man seemed to be looking at the houses, and in particular at number 29.

Terry noticed the window cleaner on the other side of the road, cleaning windows, and ahead, near the doctor's surgery at number 21, she passed a blonde woman and another woman with a pram. The blonde was Charlotte, though Terry did not know her at the time.

A few minutes later, the postman was making his way down the odd-numbered side of the street. He stopped at number 29 – he knew it was Jill Dando's home – and delivered some mail. As he returned to the pavement he noticed a man standing in the road, watching him, a few houses down, towards number 17, about forty feet away.

Terence wondered why the man was watching him, wondered if he was 'after nicking some work from my trolley', as he explained later. As he watched him, briefly, the man saw Terence looking at him and shot behind a grey van. Terence described the man as being about five foot ten in height with straight, black, collar-length hair, a medium to large build and a Mediterranean complexion – slightly tanned skin.

Collecting a bundle of mail from his barrow, Terence realised he had forgotten to deliver a package to number 43. He turned to retrace his steps and forgot all about the man he had seen and never looked back and never saw him again.

Outside the surgery he saw the 'lady' from number 61, who he'd known for twenty years – he'd grown up with her son. Then the 'lady', from number 15 came along on her bike. 'Any mail?' she inquired. 'Not today.' The 'coloured lady' from number 3 asked the same thing. She didn't have any post, either.

At about 10.15, a traffic warden was about to issue a ticket to a blue Range Rover which was illegally parked back down the road. She thought the car was empty, but as she began to enter its details she suddenly noticed the driver waving at her, as he talked on a mobile phone. It made her jump, seeing the man, and then she was embarrassed so she stopped writing the ticket and carried on walking.

A woman crossing Munster Road in her car to enter Gowan Avenue noticed a pedestrian walking across the road in front of her. He seemed to have something wrong with his lower lip. Driving on down Gowan Avenue she became aware of a Range Rover behind her, on her tail as she approached Fulham Palace Road and continued on down Doneraile Street. The Range Rover, which had two occupants, followed her all the way to the end of the road where it parked on Stevenage Road, by Fulham Football Club.

At the bottom of Fulham Palace Road, just the other side of Putney Bridge, a driver watched a Range Rover jump the lights and head north across the bridge towards Fulham at some speed. This Range Rover had two men in it, and one was of Mediterranean appearance.

Corrinne Leguay, Jill Dando's neighbour at number 27, arrived back in Gowan Avenue at about eleven o'clock after a big shop at Waitrose on the King's Road. She made several journeys from car to house, unloading the shopping. She saw nothing unusual and when she had put her food away she began cooking a chicken stew.

A woman who had been visiting a house in Gowan Avenue for reflexology treatment left about this time. She had been parked in a space right outside number 29. When Julia Grimwade opened her front door to put out some rubbish, she noticed that parking space and thought how unusual it was, at this time of day, to see such a big space.

The de Rosnays returned from North End Road with the four children. As they passed number 29, Charlotte said, 'This is where Jill Dando lives', and Stella noted the house.

Emma Cooper and Philippa Upfill-Brown arrived back from Sainsbury's and Emma double-parked outside number 30 while they unloaded their shopping. Emma went home because her baby was ready for a sleep.

It had been a busy morning at the surgery at number 21. Dr Gossain had seen eleven patients and four or five people had called in to collect prescriptions. At 11.25, after the rush had ceased, the doctor went out to see a friend, another doctor, at his surgery on Lillie Road. He turned right out of the surgery, in the opposite direction to number 29, saw nothing unusual as he walked away.

Rosa Rodriguez was still cleaning at number 26. She took a break at about 11.20, sitting in the kitchen at the back of the house with the radio on, eating the sandwiches she had brought with her. Then she went outside and began cleaning the front door. She spent two or three minutes there and noticed nothing. Then she went back inside.

Charlotte de Rosnay's friend Vida Saunders arrived for coffee, parking her seven-year-old blue Range Rover not far from number 55. Stella would soon be leaving to return to Paris. A minicab had been booked for 11.30 to take her to Waterloo, where she would board the Eurostar train. About ten minutes before it was due, Stella went outside and took some photographs of the house and of the street. The street she photographed was deserted. Or at least, there was no one you could see.

Families, mothers and fathers, sons and daughters, had lived and died on Gowan Avenue for a century. There were other photographs of the avenue taken in the 104 years since it had been built.

Here it was, circa 1906, photographed westwards from Munster Road in drab monochrome, plain brick houses, unpainted façades on an unmade road, heavily cambered. There is no street lighting, no decorative trees, and the houses are separated from the pavement by low walls and fences. Curls of smoke rise from the chimneys.

There are no unpainted houses in Gowan Avenue now. They are all delicately coloured in pastel shades, whites and creams and blues and yellows. Trees now line the pavement and at certain times of the year the cherry blossom flowers and scatters in the wind, smothering the parked cars.

From the mid-seventeenth until the mid-nineteenth century, the area had consisted of orchards and meadows and market gardens, known broadly as Fulham Fields, dotted with grand estate houses owned by the families who would later give the streets their names. Nurseries reared plants and seeds for others to grow. There were strawberry fields and rows of tulip-trees. In 1872, Fulham was especially noted for its asparagus. The land that Gowan Avenue came to occupy was on the upper edge of the Colehill House estate, on Horseshoe Field.

Horseshoe Field was bisected by a walkway which ran from Munster Road to Fulham Palace Road. This was known as Devil's Alley, so named, according to the historian C. J. Feret, writing in 1900, after 'an unhappy mortal who, "possessed of the devil", withdrew to this retired spot where he was found one morning in the "sparrow grass" with his throat cut. The alley is reputed to be haunted and several strange incidents are said to have occurred in it.' The alleyway ran directly along the northern boundary of Gowan Avenue. It closed in 1894 to make way for Wardo Avenue.

Fulham developed rapidly in the second half of the nineteenth century. The underground came and new industry sprang up along the river. The fields gave way to houses and the nurseries closed. In 1881, the *Gardener's Chronicle* mourned the passing of one of the more prominent nurseries: 'The swallows that but last summer used to glide over the shrubs of Dancer's nursery, Fulham, will either have to take themselves to fresh feeding grounds or shape their flight over the chimney pots that have sprung up as if by magic.'

Christine Bayliss had worked at the Hammersmith and Fulham Archives and Local History Centre for thirty-eight years, with a mission to create a complete pictorial record of every street in the borough. She had photographed Gowan Avenue on 2 December 1976 and, it so happened, had singled out number 29. The brickwork was still unpainted, even then.

After she had taken *her* photographs, Stella went back inside number 55 to wait for her minicab. When it had not arrived at 11.30 Charlotte phoned the cab company to chase them up.

Jill's next-door neighbour, Richard Hughes, had been at home all morning, trading on the markets from a computer screen in his living room. He had been up at about seven to begin trading, as usual, and had gone upstairs at around 11.15 to shower and change, as usual. This was a quiet time, a lull in his working day.

Sometime after 11.30, between 11.30 and 11.45, he thought, he was in the front bedroom and heard the sound of a car alarm being set. He recognised this as Jill's car alarm because she had exactly the same soft-top BMW as his wife, Fiona.

Richard had seen Jill a couple of times in recent weeks but had not spoken to her since March, when they had talked about a *Holiday* programme she'd made featuring the Bahamas – a place Richard had planned to visit at Easter, until Jill said it would be better to go later in the year.

Hearing the alarm was perfectly normal. In his experience, Jill often came home on a Monday morning. He then heard her footsteps on the front path, which was also a familiar sound and then, after twenty or thirty seconds, he heard a scream: which he guessed came from Jill. It was not a worrying scream, so much as the scream of a person who had been surprised by somebody playing a joke. Perhaps somebody hiding behind the door, somebody Jill knew, Richard thought.

A few seconds later he heard the clang of Jill's gate as it closed. He went over to the window and looked through the shutters and saw a man walking away, going west past Richard's house towards Fulham Palace Road. The man looked respectable; more than respectable, like a man who might be Jill's friend, which Richard assumed him to be.

The man turned his head slowly to look back as he walked away, his face fleetingly reminding Richard of someone he had seen on television, a presenter called Bob Mills. His face was full, jowly, thick-set and his build was heavy, like the build of a soldier or a rugby player. The man was wearing a Barbour-type waxed over-coat, with lapels of a different material from the rest of the coat, which was dark brown in colour. It was difficult for Richard to say how tall the man was, though he was taller than Richard himself who was just over five foot seven and a quarter. He had a thick, black mop of straight hair. He was carrying what Richard took to be a mobile phone in his right hand.

When the man glanced back it seemed as if he might be looking to see that Jill's front door was shut. This rested Hughes' case, so to speak, that nothing untoward was happening, though he began to move quite briskly. The thought was reinforced when Richard noticed that his opposite neighbour, Geoffrey Upfill-Brown, was coming out of his house and did not show any sign of being startled or concerned. Richard turned away from the window and prepared to take his shower.

Geoffrey Upfill-Brown was on his way to the post office on Fulham Road and then to the chemists'. He thought it was about 11.30. Later he would retrace his steps with the police, with a chemists' till receipt timed at 11.42 (the till was one minute slow). The police would conclude that he must have left home no later than 11.26.

As he came down his path Geoffrey immediately noticed a man running away from him along the opposite side of the road, heading westwards. The run was somewhere between a jog and a sprint. Geoffrey did feel that something was wrong and made every mental note he could of everything he saw in the expectation that he might have to describe it later.

The man stopped running after about twenty yards, about the length of a cricket pitch, which is twenty-two yards. He turned and looked at Geoffrey, and then moved off again, this time at a slow trot, disappearing out of view behind a builder's lorry. That was the last Geoffrey saw of him.

Geoffrey described the man as being five feet eight tall and thick-set, with a mass of long, black curly hair that Geoffrey thought could have been a wig. He was aged between thirty-five and forty. He was clean shaven, his complexion was pale and he wore a long, dark, loose-fitting coat, baggy trousers that were also dark and loose-fitting, and black shoes.

Geoffrey turned left towards Munster Road, then right out of Gowan Avenue towards the Fulham Road.

At about 11.30, Nigel Jenkins at number 40 also heard a scream. To him, too, it sounded like the scream of a woman who had been surprised. Or perhaps of a woman in pain.

Stella's minicab arrived two or three minutes later and the entire household went out into the street to see her off. Stella and the two grandchildren she was taking home got into the back of the car, and Charlotte and her friend Vida stood waving as they drove away. Vida was carrying Charlotte's youngest child on her hip. Then Charlotte led the way back into her home. Vida was the last in, glimpsed by another friend, Helen Doble, as Helen entered Gowan Avenue on her way to the copy shop. As the minicab drove off down Gowan Avenue, passing number 29, Stella was too busy settling the children to think of looking again at the house where Jill Dando lived. Where Jill Dando had just been killed.

Three

Jack and Jean came to London for their honeymoon in 1950. They stayed for a week at a hotel in Paddington, the name of which Jack had long since forgotten. They had their photograph taken in front of the fountains in Trafalgar Square, Jack in a chalk-striped double-breasted suit, Jean in a two-piece outfit, coat and high heels.

Herbert Jack Howard Dando was thirty-two and Winifred Mary Jean was nine years younger. 'You pick 'em young,' people used to say to Jack. 'But Jean was ... well ...' Jack searches for the right phrase. 'She was ... she knew what life was all about.' She worked as a clerk for the Gas Board then, though Jack made her give that up. 'I don't want you working if we get children,' he told her. 'You can't look after children properly if you're working.' So Jean never worked again, though she ran Tupperware parties later, for a while.

Jack had met Jean at dance classes in a church hall in Weston-Super-Mare some time after he was demobbed in 1946. He was new to Weston and dancing seemed like a good way to make friends, meet girls. There was another young woman before Jean, with whom he used to go to the pictures. But she couldn't dance, didn't like dancing and besides, she was a bit domineering, a little too pushy for Jack's taste. Not that Jean fell in with everything he wanted – far from it. She had spirit, and if she didn't like something, she soon let him know.

During the war Jack had served in a workshop platoon as a vehicle electrician with the RASC, the Royal Army Service Corps. He had been through Europe after D-Day and was later in North Africa. He was not, however, an electrician in Civvy Street, as he called it; he was a printer.

Jack's father had recently retired to Weston but had previously worked for many years as a village constable in Somerset. Jack thought of Dando as a Somerset name, and was surprised later to hear that it was French in origin. His paternal grandfather had been a bootmaker, his maternal grandfather ... well, he doesn't have a clue what he did, can only picture him as a very old man with a big beard. Jack was born in 1918 during his father's time in West Coker, a small village on the A30 between Yeovil and Crewkerne, which his father patrolled by bike.

There was not much excitement in being a village policeman in the early part of the last century, but Jack does remember his father once being called out to investigate two suspicious characters who were knocking on doors asking for a drink of water. They were prisoners on the run from Bristol and his father brought them back to the station in handcuffs. Not so much a station, in truth, as an ordinary village house.

Later his father had been on point duty directing traffic, at a crossroads in the Somerset town of Langport which had a stationery and printer's shop on the corner. His father had spoken to the owners, and they had taken on Jack as a printer's apprentice when he left school at fourteen. Jack had never fancied being a policeman, and besides he thought he was too small, but he had imagined himself as a carpenter. Jobs were scarce though, so he yielded to his father's wishes.

Jack had completed his apprenticeship in Dorchester before the war, and afterwards was well qualified to find work almost immediately in the print room of the local weekly newspaper, the *Weston Mercury*, where he remained for the next thirty-eight years, retiring as head compositor in 1984.

Jean had been brought up according to strict Baptist principles. She was a regular at the Milton Baptist Church, where she and Jack were married, and joined the Young Wives Group and later the Women's Evening Fellowship. Jack was not much of a joiner and not much interested in religion. He went to church a few Sundays after their wedding but quickly grew bored. He wasn't a pub-goer – they were rowdy, common places, Jean would've said – but he liked gardening and pootling around on his motorbike, a 350 Matchless which he had bought in partnership with his younger brother, Ken.

Ken Dando had got married the year before his brother and when Ken and his wife, Esme, set up home some distance away, nearer Bristol, Ken and Jack took turns with the motorbike, each keeping it for a month at a time before, as Jack remembered it, he bought Ken out and had the bike to himself.

He recalls going down to Bournemouth once on the bike before his marriage, Jean riding pillion, which was difficult because he had a haversack on his back and there wasn't much room and she had to press tightly against him to hold on. He remembers that very clearly.

Their first home was a one-bedroomed flat in Upper Church Road in Weston. Their son Nigel was born while they were there, in 1952. He was their first child, and for many years it seemed likely that he would be their only child.

Jack's problem with the flat was the man who lived above them, whose lounge was above Jack and Jean's bedroom. He had no carpet on his floor, only lino, never wore slippers and was always walking about, at night, too, sometimes very late at night, right over Jean and Jack's heads. Two or three times Jack spoke to him about it, asked him to put something soft on his feet, but he took no notice.

There were some bungalows being built out at Madam Lane, Worle, on the edge of Weston. Two bedrooms, no stairs, no noisy people overhead – perfect. Except that they were £1,999 and Jack and Jean couldn't afford the deposit.

Jack asked his bosses at the *Mercury* if they would give him a loan. 'How much were you thinking of?' they inquired.

'Well,' said Jack, 'I shall have to buy some furniture, too. I wondered about £500?' His employers agreed, if he would stay with the firm. The deal was struck and Jack paid the *Mercury* back, at £1 a week, and they never charged him a penny in interest.

Once he'd got a mortgage at the town hall, they were all set on their way to Worle. Eventually, the debts were paid and Jack and Jean owned the bungalow outright. The only drawback being that it was semi-detached and fuelled by an anthracite-burning Parkray stove. Each boiler backed on to the boiler of the bungalow next door. The neighbour insisted on riddling his boiler, sweeping out the ashes, stoking it up to keep it going, every night around eleven o'clock or even as late as midnight. The noise, the rattling, would go straight through Jack and Jean's bungalow, invariably waking them up. Or waking Jack up, at any rate.

Jack had a word with them and they were very nice about it, hadn't realised the trouble they were causing and brought their riddling forward to a more respectable hour. But it didn't make much difference. Rattle, scrape and riddle: Jack dreamed of a detached home.

Jack never had a bank account until after Jean died and when he brought home his weekly wage packet, which was cash, he handed it straight over to Jean. He had a weekly allowance, his pocket money, which he made do with because money was always tight in those days. Jean was very good with the money. She had a chart she relied on, putting aside various sums for their household needs and holidays. Later, she even began a fund for Jill's wedding.

Jean's blood group was Rhesus negative, which in those days carried the risk of complications in a second pregnancy, at worst the risk of a foetus not surviving to birth. Esme, Jack's sister-in-law, always thought this potential problem made Jean afraid of having another baby, but if this was true, Jack has either forgotten it or he never realised. As far as he was concerned no more babies were forthcoming after Nigel and, after a while, he just assumed it wasn't going to happen. But they were very pleased, he said, when Jill turned up, of course.

Esme never knew whether Jill had been an accident or whether, in the end, Jean just decided to take a chance. Esme and Jean were close, but you didn't discuss those kinds of things then. Times weren't as they are now.

Jill was born on 9 November 1961, nine years after Nigel – the same age gap as that between their parents. Before long it was apparent that all was not well with this much-loved late baby. According to Jack, there were many trips to clinics and hospitals and many different tests. And what looked like a sign of blooming health – Jill's rosy cheeks – was in fact just the opposite: along with her breathlessness, it was a symptom of the blocked valve and hole in her heart. She was a blue baby. Nigel can still picture her blue finger nails and her red cheeks.

The condition was diagnosed before Jill's second birthday but the corrective operation was not performed until she was three. Heart surgery was in its infancy then, and it seems that Jill was the object of some fascination at the Bristol Royal Infirmary. Jack once saw eight consultants and doctors round her bed and watched them troop off for a confab afterwards.

It was made clear to Jack and Jean that the operation did not guarantee success and that there was a chance Jill might not survive it. Esme recalls the couple's confusion and dread. She remembers them picking her up on the way to the hospital, not knowing where the infirmary was and struggling to find it.

Jack recalls a room with two beds in it was set aside for them to stay over during the crucial forty-eight-hour period after the operation when Jill would either live or die. She was in intensive care, tubes and wires all over her, and a monitor, beeping. Jack would never forget this. The monitor stopped beeping. Jean went white as a sheet and Jack thought, this is it. He shouted out to the nurse, 'Nurse! Nurse! It has stopped beeping!'

She ran over. 'Don't worry, Mr Dando,' she reassured him. 'It's only a wire come loose.'

Jill got through the first couple of days and was kept in bed for another two weeks. Then one day Jack and Jean arrived on the ward and the nurse asked them to wait. She went off and reappeared with Jill holding her hand and when Jill saw her parents, she ran down the corridor to them, looking pink and healthy and lovely.

There were regular check-ups for years but no more problems, and Jill grew increasingly athletic and robust. She became closer and closer to her mother, and Jean drew Jill closer and closer to her. In the end – Jack said it, everyone said it – they were like sisters.

In later years many of Jill's friends and colleagues were only dimly aware that she had a brother. They would think of her as an only child.

Nigel was like his dad – kept his own counsel. It was one of Jean's favourite expressions about him: 'He never gives much away.'

Nigel has fuzzy memories of his early years and of his baby sister. He remembers family holidays, Devon beaches where the sea was blue (unlike Weston, where the sea was grey and brown); learning to drive on the beach at Weston in his father's Ford Perfect; recording pop songs into a tape-recorder with Jill. His sister's outgoing character developed at an early age. Nigel was more comfortable with people he knew. Why that was, he couldn't say. 'Everybody is different,' he says.

He was briefly in the Boys' Brigade at the church, but that wasn't really him. He wasn't a joiner. Jill, on the other hand, joined the amateur dramatics society. That would've been anathema to Nigel. Jill was just so very straight.

Nigel zoomed away from Jill and the family home in his teenage years. He felt stifled by school, the futility of academic study and the petty rules, about hair, for instance. He was for ever being whipped down to the barber's for a short-back-and-sides. Clippers buzzing along the back of his head, prickly spikes instead of hair. There had to be more to life than this.

As soon as he could, which was as soon as he left school, Nigel grew his hair long, bought Led Zeppelin records, got himself a girl-friend – Jack remembered her, all right – who went around barefoot. His mum and dad worried a little, thought he was falling in with the wrong types, hanging out in pubs and snooker halls and the like.

In 1970 Nigel went to the Isle of Wight pop festival where he saw Hendrix play and stayed up all night watching the Who, which blew his head away. Great days, and not days he could share with Jill (who was, after all, only eight at the time).

Nigel met Vanessa while playing darts with friends in a Weston pub. When they began living together Jack was sure Jean would disapprove, but she surprised him by taking it in her stride. Jack thought of himself as more open and easygoing than his wife.

When they eventually married, in 1978, Nigel and Vanessa had a low-key, somewhat unconventional wedding. There were no bridesmaids, and no hymns, because, Nigel said, their friends wouldn't have sung them anyway. Jill was sixteen by then and was very disappointed not to be a bridesmaid. But she didn't tell Vanessa that for ten years.

In another ten years, when Jill was planning her own wedding, she had to take Vanessa aside and ask if she thought Nigel would be prepared to wear a morning suit. Vanessa was sure he wouldn't object, just this once, so as not to let the side down. Jill didn't feel she could ask Nigel this herself, directly. She didn't like to. 'You know what he's like,' she said to Vanessa, meaning he was shy, not one for show. But that was what Jill was like, too. Not very good at being direct. Unless she was really riled.

Nigel couldn't face the thought of any more exams when he left school and, inspired by the thought of the freewheeling lifestyle of the reporters at the paper where his dad worked, fancied a life in journalism.

Jack asked the editor whether there might be an opening for Nigel at the *Mercury*. The editor said there might, if he was any good. Nigel was given an interview, submitted a 500-word essay and was duly taken on. He was sent to journalism college in Cardiff for training and stayed at the *Mercury* for the next three and a half years, qualifying as a senior reporter in 1972 at the age of twenty. It was almost exactly the same path Jill would follow a decade later. She would even be asked to write the same essay, more or less.

Early in 1973, Nigel joined the *Bristol Evening Post* and remained there in various capacities for the next twenty-eight years, until after Jill's death, when he stopped being the *Post*'s chief reporter and joined BBC Radio in Bristol.

When he started in journalism Nigel hoped he might one day work on one of the nationals in London. He hadn't been to London more than once or twice them, and the more he saw of it the less he liked it. It was fine for a brief visit, but he wouldn't want to live there. Nevertheless he applied for a couple of jobs, at the *Telegraph*, and maybe the *Mail* – he isn't sure now – but he lacked the drive. He was quite happy where he was.

Once he had left home Nigel would not see Jill or his parents very often, not more than three or four times a year. There was no umbilical cord pulling him back. He happened to be in Weston one day, though, for a dental appointment, when he saw Jill coming out of the *Mercury* offices where she was then working and he realised that she was not his kid sister any more. She was growing up – a young reporter at the beginning of her career.

Four

On Tuesday 19 January 1999, Jill went to the Criterion in Piccadilly Circus for dinner. It was an important occasion and she wore a new black Escada dress, very expensive, which she had bought especially on a shopping, eating and drinking excursion to Florence a fortnight earlier.

Much as she loved Harrods, Selfridges, Harvey Nichols, Louis Feraud and all those other glorious emporiums of fine clothing and accessories, Jill was not in the habit of going shopping in Italy. She had been a late addition to the trip, invited by her friend and colleague Jane Lush, the two of them, plus Alison Sharman, a director on the *Holiday* programme, and Yasmin Sethna, a travel PR they all knew who had organised it.

Jane Lush had been the editor of *Holiday* for six years, leaving the previous September to become the BBC's head of daytime TV. She had also recently been appointed Jill's 'talent contact' at the

BBC, acting as Jill's point of contact and liaison, the conduit for all the new programmes Jill might present and which might be included in her new contract.

The negotiations for the new contract were not going at all well.

That was the purpose of this dinner: to smooth things over and move the discussions along, for the BBC to outline to Jill the programmes they wanted her to make during the following year. Jane Lush would be there. She saw no conflict between her separate roles as a senior BBC executive and Jill's 'talent contact'. Despite their friendship and close working relationship, Jane was still acting for the BBC. And the BBC's interest was Jill's interest, after all. Jill wanted to be on screen all the time, and the BBC wanted her on screen all the time. No conflict there.

This, however, was not how Jon Roseman, Jill's agent, saw it. He was suspicious of what he thought of as Jane's two hats. He was suspicious of almost everybody, in fact. As a talent agent, his sole aim in life was his clients' continuing success and wellbeing. He was out to get the best deal for Jill and, so far, he was distinctly unimpressed by what was on offer. He was going to the Criterion and was, as always, ready to express himself plainly and without frills. Jill had once, maybe more than once, referred to him as her Rottweiler, and the image rather appealed to him. It rather suited him, too, something of which he was probably secretly quite proud.

The Italian trip had been a great success. They had all bought loads of things, giving the other, older Florentine culture a complete by-pass. At first Jane had not thought of inviting Jill, but when she had mentioned it to her Jill had said it sounded fantastic.

'Well, do you want to come with us?' Jane had asked.

'Can I?' Jill had said. 'Can I really?' Of course she could.

It had begun with a blip when Jill's luggage failed to arrive with the plane. Of all the people whose luggage to lose. Jill had been the main presenter of *Holiday* for all the years that Jane had been editor. There was almost nowhere she hadn't been, and here she was on a brief hop, and the airline had lost her bags. Jill was slightly irritated, as anyone might be, but quickly recovered when the bag was recovered and delivered to her later that evening. In the meantime she borrowed a change of underwear from Alison Sharman, later returning it through the BBC's internal mail.

They had shopped at all the factory outlets for the posh labels such as Gucci and Prada. Especially Prada, which Jane Lush and Alison Sharman loved. Seventh heaven. Unfortunately, they arrived there just as it was about to close for lunch. Jane and Alison had to go back after their own lunch, when it reopened. 'Oh, you two,' said Jill, 'you're obsessed with designer labels.' She had a mild sulk and refused to go in, choosing instead to take a nap in the back of the car, wrapped in her coat, until the other three came out, Jane and Alison with their newly purchased black nylon coats.

They had visited the proper shops, too, which was where Jill had bought her Escada outfit. As well as a dress there was a jacket and a pair of trousers, which she wore on the journey home. Alan was meeting her, and she wanted to look her best. The other three knew she was crazy about him.

She wanted to look her best tonight as well, for the Criterion, and she did. Jane thought she looked really sexy and Jill was obviously feeling good. She was flirtatious with Peter Salmon, the Controller of BBC1, as he was then. But that was early on in the meal, before it turned nasty.

The line-up for dinner this evening was: Jill, Jane Lush, Jon Roseman, Peter Salmon, and Anne Morrison, who was the BBC's head of factual programmes. All there for Jill. And for the BBC, of course.

Jane was close to Jill but still not privy to the main reason Jill seemed so radiant: Alan had proposed to her on Saturday night and she had accepted.

They had gone away overnight to the Bailiffscourt Hotel in Sussex and after dinner on the Saturday evening they had been side by side on the sofa in front of the open fire in their suite and Alan had asked her to marry him. Jill had made him repeat it on bended knee before her. Only then had she said yes.

Alan had, in his own meticulous way, thought it all through beforehand. He didn't buy an engagement ring in advance but, not wanting to drag Jill round the jewellers' shops, he had gone to Asprey's in New Bond Street and established that he could afford to buy one there. He had been assured that he could have a very nice ring made for the kind of money he was talking about.

He had booked an appointment for a private fitting. The last thing he wanted was to stand in an open shop with Jill, examining engagement rings. As Alan had anticipated, when they went together to Asprey's to choose the ring, Jill had asked if he was sure he could afford it. Once reassured, she set about choosing the diamond and the gold band into which it would be set, which was how you bought a ring in this poshest of posh jewellers. It was now being assembled and would be ready for collection at the weekend.

Jill and Alan had decided to keep their engagement to themselves and their families for the time being. They already had a party planned for the end of January. Many of their friends, on being invited to this party, had assumed it was to be an engagement party anyway. It hadn't been originally, but it was now.

So Jane Lush, along with everybody else at the table, was oblivious to this change in Jill's circumstances. This long awaited change.

Jon Roseman listened as Anne Morrison began with a run-through of the programmes the BBC were earmarking for Jill. They had a big hole to fill: not only would Jill no longer be reading the news, she had decided to give up *Holiday* as well. She had been threatening for a couple of years to give up *Holiday*, and had now decided it was time.

All Jon could hear were vague ideas and Carol Vorderman's cast-offs (Carol Vorderman, an increasingly popular presenter at the time, had just been signed up to ITV). There was still *Crimewatch*, a couple of *Panorama*s – Jill wanted to retain her credibility in current affairs – but not a lot else, as far as Jon could tell. Watching Jill knocking back the champagne, he felt she was being swept along by the occasion and going along with these frankly half-baked ideas.

Eventually someone said: 'Well, Jon, what do you think?'

'I'm not sure, I think I want to say something, but I don't know if I should say it.'

'Oh, come on, Jon,' said Peter.

'Yes, come on,' said Jane.

'No,' replied Jon. 'I'm going for a pee.'

He got up and went off to the Gents' where he stood thinking: I'm fifty-one with thirty years in the business, and I've never heard so much crap in my life.

Jon returned to the table. 'Look, I don't want to cause anybody any offence here, but if you really want to know what I think, I think it sucks. You've given us these cast-off programmes. You've had all these weeks to come up with something, not a trial-and-error thing, but something new, anything ...'

Jon could see that Peter Salmon was unhappy about what he'd said. 'What you've come up with is hardly a year's work. It's an insult to Jill.'

Peter Salmon turned to Jill. 'Jill, have you thought about radio?'

Radio? That really did it for Jon. 'Fucking *radio*?'

'Come on, Jon,' reasoned Jane. 'There's nothing wrong with radio.'

'I'm not saying there's anything wrong with radio,' said Jon, 'but we're talking about Jill Dando's television career here.'

'There's nothing wrong with radio,' insisted Jane. 'Michael Parkinson does radio, Chris Evans does radio. Des Lynam does radio—'

'Hang on a minute,' interrupted Jon. 'Michael Parkinson is nearly dead. Des Lynam? Excuse me. And she ain't no Chris Evans.'

Jon thought Peter Salmon was going to pick up a Perrier bottle and hit him with it. He could sense Jill cringing. He knew how much she hated confrontation.

Jane Lush could also see that Peter Salmon was very angry. Jill got up to go to the loo. Jane noticed that she was tipsy, and followed her, wondering if they were both heading there to escape the unbearable atmosphere at the table. Jon stayed where he was, listening to Peter Salmon and Anne Morrison talk about anything but the BBC. He imagined Jill and Jane in the loo, slagging him off.

In the Ladies' Jill said to Jane, 'Oh God, this is awful, so embarrassing, I can't believe Jon's behaving like this. What must Peter think?' Jane agreed that it was too awful for words. 'Please tell Peter I had no idea Jon was going to rant and rave like that,' Jill went on. 'It's not the way I operate.' Jane knew that. Jill never wanted to upset anybody.

Jane was used to Jon's abrasive manner, and she knew how much Jill liked him, which was strange because, as a rule, Jill did not like people who were coarse or vulgar. Jane figured that, as her agent, Jon could say things that Jill would never dare to voice. But this time, she felt, he had overplayed his hand.

'What are we going to say when we go back,' asked Jill. 'I don't want to give a bad impression.' So they didn't go back – or at least not for ages. When they finally returned to the table, someone said, 'We thought you'd escaped through the window.' Jane thought Jill probably would've done if she could.

As Jon remembered it, he took a cab with Jill afterwards and dropped her off on his way home. He said to her that if he sounded out of order, he meant every fucking word. She couldn't afford to be manipulated, because the next two years of her career were really crucial. And he wasn't sure that somebody else's cast-off programmes were really the right way forward. He wanted something from the BBC that showed they really cared about Jill and her career.

He didn't think they did care, or not enough. Much as he adored her, he worried that Jill was indecisive and vulnerable to exploitation. Every time they made a decision together she seemed to want to take a straw poll of the whole of London on whether it was the right thing to do when what he wanted her to do was just take the decision and stick to it. He actually said to her once, 'You know, Jill, your problem is that if the BBC asked you to do a soft-porn film you'd do it, you really would.' When he realised she was dumping *Holiday* he had said to her, 'No more manipulation. We've got to know what we're doing, because the next two or three years are very important to Jill Dando, right? We've got to get it right. So no more Miss Nice Guy.'

But that evening, after dropping Jill off, he was sure she must be very close to firing him. He was right.

The next day Jon called a friend in the upper echelons of the BBC. Jon told him about the dinner. He said that he couldn't believe the crap he'd listened to and that the BBC contingent hadn't got an idea between them.

'Yes, I know,' agreed his friend.

'You're not supposed to say that, you're supposed to say something like, "Yes they have."'

Peter Salmon remembers the dinner as cathartic, a chance to lay the ghost of the *Six O'Clock News*, which had plagued the last months of the previous year, 1998. He had fought hard for Jill during the debate and recalls thinking at some point during the dinner that he had been pretty exposed himself over the *Six*, and why did he have to sit there and take it from these people. These people, of course, being Jon.

On the other hand, he thought, they'd all had a bit to drink (well, maybe not himself so much), and Jon was passionate about Jill, and felt very emotional about the way she had been treated, and he had her best interests at heart. If only he hadn't been quite so emotional. If only he hadn't been quite so loud.

In truth, Peter recognised that the contract the BBC were now offering Jill was not the best contract, not the best portfolio of programmes. He was trying to make the best of a difficult situation and did not want Jill to think that the BBC had so much as blinked. He was disappointed too but he understood that for her it was more personal. For him it was business and he had to get on with running the rest of the channel, but he had tried to remain open and approachable for her, letting her know how he felt, realising that controllers could sometimes seem remote and inscrutable.

He had meant no disrespect when he had mentioned radio. He thought it bizarre that some people – such as Jon, evidently – considered radio to be second-rate or unimportant after television. He simply wanted to know if there were areas of Jill's potential that they had overlooked. That was why he had asked the question that had caused Jon, as Peter put it, to blow up.

He never thought for one minute that Jill was anything other than an important television presenter, but there were plenty of important television presenters who did radio as well. Jeremy Paxman had a career on BBC2's *Newsnight* and Radio 4's *Start the Week*. Sue Lawley hosted *Desert Island Discs* on Radio 4 alongside her television career, and Melvyn Bragg did both, too.

In his memory – and he really wasn't trying to put a rosy glow on it – that Criterion evening had been a great evening. It had cleared the air. He and Anne Morrison had put their case in no uncertain terms, as Jon had done, though perhaps Jon's rant had left him rather exposed. Jill had been fun, as she always was, quite naughty and entertaining and later, when Jon had excused himself again, Jill had apologised for his outburst and they'd all had another drink and laughed and made up and poured out on to the streets of the West End afterwards, Peter aware that he had spent the evening in Jill's company, which was special.

A couple of days later Jane Lush met Desmond Lynam for lunch. Des, the senior presenter of sport at the BBC, was thinking of giving it up after the 2000 Olympics and proposed to Jane over lunch that he and Jill become the 'Richard and Judy' of the BBC, to compete with Richard Madeley and Judy Finnigan, who were then hosting ITV's popular daytime show *This Morning*.

Jill and Des were already due to co-present the BBC's coverage of Millennium Night, though in the event neither would be available. By then, Jill had been dead for eight months and Des Lynam had 'defected' to ITV to continue as a sports presenter.

Jane Lush liked the idea of Des and Jill as Richard and Judy, and filed the thought away. She mentioned it to Jill, who seemed incredibly flattered. Jane knew that Jill was keen to do a daily show and maybe Jill's attitude to day-time television was changing. She had received an offer many months earlier to present a daytime programme airing five days a week, and had told Jon Roseman that if she did it, she would be forgotten after a year.

'Who is going to forget you, Jill?'

'The prime-time audiences,' Jill had said.

'Bollocks,' retorted Jon.

As Jon had told her then, daytime was no longer the 'shithole' it had once been.

Jon had had enough of the BBC and called a contact at ITV network centre. 'Would you guys be interested in Jill?'

'Are you serious?' asked his contact.

'Yes,' said Jon. 'You speak to David Liddiment.'

'You're *really* serious?' Liddiment was ITV's most senior executive, and Jon's contact did not want to be used by Jon as some ploy in his negotiations with the BBC.

Jon assured him that he was not playing games. 'This is not about money, this is about programmes, right?'

'OK,' said the ITV contact.

So Jon and Jill went to a meeting with David Liddiment and a couple of his colleagues at a hotel near the ITN building, where the network is based. Jon knew that Jill was afraid of upsetting the BBC, but surely even she could see that the contract the BBC was offering wasn't the greatest gift in the world.

Jon thought David Liddiment's performance at the meeting

was remarkable. He just seemed to have an instinct about Jill's abilities. He stressed all her attributes, there was nothing negative. Jill asked what programmes he had in mind, he outlined some of them and Jill said that she wasn't sure. Jesus, thought Jon, she is so inculcated in that whole BBC philosophy, she just thinks everything ITV does is low-rent. David Liddiment asked her what she wanted. Jill said she wanted to retain some gravitas. Liddiment told her that every factual programme the network was interested in passed across his desk and that she could sit there next to him and choose anything she wanted and, as far as gravitas was concerned, she could do the news whenever Trevor wasn't doing the news. Sir Trevor McDonald was the main presenter of ITN's *News At Ten*.

News At Ten was ITN, not ITV. 'Can you do that, David?' Jon asked. David reminded him that ITN was a subsidiary of ITV. Jon wondered what one of those BBC types might have said in such circumstances. Ooh-er, probably.

It seemed obvious to Jon that Jill could have done anything she wanted at ITV. He thought the broad prospect was fantastic. No doubt the money would be good, too, when they sat down again to talk details. If they ever sat down again. Everyone shook hands and went away to reflect.

Like most consultants in gynaecology and obstetrics, Alan Farthing did not know much about the business of television and fame. He was, however, learning fast, during these rollercoaster weeks before her death, during the many discussions with Jill about her future; about their future.

Later, amid the hyperbole surrounding her death, it might have seemed as if she was at the peak of her career, lauded by the BBC as an icon, so loved and cherished by the corporation that it would have done anything for her. But that was not how it felt at the time, not to Jill.

If only she had known, Alan thought, how much she was valued, she might have been bolder and stood up for herself more. As it was she was driven, at least in large part, by fear. She was scared of losing everything, of making the wrong decision, of becoming, in Alan's words, yesterday's girl.

He heard all about how mortified she was by Jon's behaviour at the Criterion and he knew she had called Peter Salmon afterwards to make further apologies. There was talk of leaving Jon Roseman, though Jill was not very good at leaving.

She still, in fact, had another agent, her first agent, Kate Moon. She had not been able to leave her when she went across to Jon Roseman, had kept Kate on for some corporate work. If she couldn't leave Kate, she was hardly likely to leave Jon. Perhaps she would have had three agents. She was very loyal.

It had taken her long enough to leave Bob Wheaton, her partner for six years through the first half of the 1990s. 'Bob and I have split,' Jill had announced to Jane Lush one day, when they were in Claridge's, getting ready for a charity do. Jill was having her hair done. 'I know it's a quick decision,' she had said.

Jane Lush had laughed: 'Jill, I can't believe you said that. It's taken about five years for you to break up with Bob.' This was a slight exaggeration, but even so. 'How can you say it's quick?'

Jill had blustered: 'Oh well, you know, it just happened.'

So leaving was difficult, leaving Roseman, leaving the BBC, were not easy steps for her to take. Going to ITV, she reasoned with Alan, might be cutting off her nose to spite her face. And she would hate to give up *Crimewatch*, which she loved as a fixture in the evening schedules, one of those core programmes that shaped BBC1. As she well knew, this was a defining moment, and whatever she did, it had better be right.

That Saturday after the Criterion Alan and Jill went to Asprey's to collect the engagement ring. Jill put it on in the shop. It looked beautiful. Naturally, she wanted to keep it on, to wear it out of the shop. Alan was paranoid about her being spotted. He thought of New Bond Street as a place where paparazzi lurked. He discussed it with Jill and she took off the ring.

They left Asprey's and went next door to the café downstairs at Nicole Farhi, where they immediately bumped into a couple they knew. They sat and had lunch with them and never said a word about the ring or the engagement. Jill must have been bursting to reveal their secret.

She finally put on the ring for the engagement party a week later. She walked in with it on, and it was immediately spotted by eagle-eyed friends and admired and pored over for so long that the announcement Jill and Alan finally made to their guests was somewhat academic.

Everyone knew anyway, or had a pretty good idea. Cliff Richard and his crew even arrived with a gift and an engagement card, which they had all signed. The card featured a photograph of Alan and Jill, dressed to the nines, standing in the kitchen of Cliff's home in the later stages of a long evening during which, they appeared, judging by their faces, to have drunk rather a lot. The gift was a framed enlargement of the photograph. On this night, too, a good deal of alcohol was consumed: 120 bottles of celebratory champagne – a bottle a head – by the end of the evening.

Jill and Alan had arranged for their families to meet before the party at Alan's home in Chiswick. Alan's parents came, along with his brother Mark and his sister Carol and her husband. Jack was there, with Nigel and Vanessa, and Uncle Ken and Auntie Esme.

Ken and Esme's daughter, Judith, was living in France and had told Jill she wouldn't be able to come over for the party. She was working as a ski resort manager and this was the busiest time of the year. Jill had to call her back after the proposal and tell her it was now important that she came, and why. Judith flew in that day and back out the following day and Jill paid half the fare. She really wanted her there. Judith and her new boyfriend Michael went straight to the venue and were waiting there with a glass of champagne when Jill and Alan arrived.

Judith had been asked to be unofficial photographer for the evening and zapped around taking pictures, a bundle of energy as ever. She thought the whole thing was great. Her mother, Esme, was less comfortable. She felt herself becoming distanced from Jill's new life.

Esme had been a surrogate mum to Jill, in many ways, since Jean's death and she still thought Jill was natural, a family girl. But this party life in London – making small talk with a glass of champagne in one hand and a plate of canapés in the other, in a roomful of celebrities and other smart people – was not her scene.

Esme had tried to put Jill off going to London in the first place and now she felt her instincts had been right. Jill was doing too much. Too much publicity. She was overdoing it. People would get fed up with her, just as Esme and Ken would get fed up later seeing that Carol Vorderman on television and in the papers every time they looked.

Judith thought her mother was wrong about this. Perhaps it was a generational issue. Judith could see how far Jill had travelled, had observed it at every step. Jill wasn't being pretentious: these were the circles she moved in, these were the people she knew now. They were very nice people, too, and it was a very nice party, everyone mixing and mingling.

Many of Jill's more recognisable colleagues were there, fellow newsreaders such as Anna Ford, Michael Buerk, Martyn Lewis and Andrew Harvey. Cliff, of course, and Gloria Hunniford. But there were plenty of old friends as well. Jill always kept in touch. She might have moved on, but she didn't leave people behind.

Jon Roseman arrived late and soon heard what he had suspected all along, that it was really the engagement. He immediately knew that Jill Dando's engagement – which, by some miracle, to Alan's relief, had not leaked out in the previous fortnight – required a press release. He needed to speak to Jill and Alan about that right away, before one of the guests picked up a phone and spilled the beans to a tabloid. His colleague, Allasonne Lewis, acted as go-between across the room.

Ally handled Jill's affairs on a day-to-day basis, and was in constant touch with her. Ally loved Jill. She had teased her over the party: 'Oh, Jilly D., I hear wedding bells.'

'No, no, no, no, no,' Jill had said.

Now Ally felt really awful as she tried to persuade Jill and Alan to come and talk to Jon about the announcement. Jill didn't want to do it – not right in the middle of the party. 'I just want to be happy,' Jill said. 'I don't want to have to talk about this, not now. This is my time.' It was as if Ally was bursting her bubble. But Ally knew the next day would be a nightmare, a scrum, if they didn't organise something tonight. It had to be done, it was part of being famous.

In the end the conversation took place, Jon wrote and issued his press release and there were photographs and interviews the next day. Then *Hello!* and *OK!* started calling, and that was to be a whole saga in itself.

Five

Jean Dando did not travel far when she died, the cemetery on Ebdon Road in Worle being just across the road from the last home she shared with Jack, the bungalow (detached, of course) where Jack still lives, up the hill on Cornwallis Avenue.

The family arranged for a headstone, inscribed with white letters on black marble:

JEAN DANDO
1928–1986
You were truly wonderful
now so sadly missed
rest in peace sweetheart

Jill often visited her mother's grave and sat there and talked to her. She did this with some regularity and continuity. 'I've told my mother all about you,' she said to Alan twelve years later. Though Alan noted that on their last two trips to Weston, Jill did not go and see her mother.

When the police began investigating Jill's life after her death, they formed the impression that Jill had been lonely before she met Alan. Not lonely in the sense that she was short of company or friends, or that she stayed at home a lot and had nowhere to go. What the police probably detected, in Jill's diaries, in her letters, in the expressions of yearning, was the absence of her mother. Perhaps Alan would have filled that spiritual void. It was certainly a big space to fill.

Jill used to tell her former partner Bob Wheaton that he wasn't just her lover and her friend, he was her mother, too. She never told Bob that he was her father, though there was probably an element of that going on as well. Another void, there. Everyone who got close to her would hear about Jill's mother and how much she missed her. They wouldn't hear much about Jack.

It was obvious from the start, when I began exploring her life, that Jill's mother had been especially important to her. It took me a while to get the measure of that and it wasn't until I returned to Weston again, after the trial of the man convicted of Jill's murder, that it finally began to make sense.

I asked Jack if he had ever felt excluded by the closeness of his wife and daughter and he said he had. For a long time. Then I met Pete Baylis, who had been in a relationship with Jill when she was in her early twenties and been besotted with her, and was, so far as I could tell, still besotted with her now, as were many of the men I knew about who had been in her orbit. Pete found himself going on dates with Jill and her mother. They used to go to Sands, a nightclub in Weston. He would dance with both of them. One night when Jill left the table to go to the Ladies', and they both watched her walk away, Pete turned to Jean and said: 'I really love that girl.'

'Yes,' said Jean. 'She is a bit special, isn't she?'

They would often sit in the kitchen of their home, Jean and Jill, with Pete. Jack would have been in the living room, out of the way. Jean and Jill would make jokes at Jack's expense. Not cruel or malicious jokes, but exclusive jokes, as if Jack was a bit of a spare part in the house. They used to say that they were going to build a ladder to the attic and that Jack could go and live up there. But it was all just teasing and banter.

I don't think Nigel, Jill's brother, can have been left in any doubt about who was his mother's favourite either and it certainly wasn't him. It wasn't Nigel who got the expensive sewing machine for Christmas or who was drawn into the intimacies of his mother's life.

Jenny Higham, who knew Jill best of all, never heard Jill say a bad word about her mother, which was unnatural, because nobody's perfect. Everyone's mother is irritating or annoying sometimes. Jenny realised that Jean's death had frozen the mother-daughter relationship, preserved it just as it was, embalmed by loss and all the sentiments that went with it.

When Jenny thought about the relationship, having heard about it so often from Jill, she did not think it was entirely healthy, being as close to your mother as Jill had been; to know quite as much about your mother as Jill knew. In fact, she thought in some ways that it was an example of how not to bring up a child. Not good for individuation, as the experts would say; not good for becoming your own person. Not very good for Nigel, either, or Jill, having favourites.

Others would say that Jill missed out on something in her youth, almost had no youth at all, was made old before her time by this sisterly bond with her mother. I think that may well be right, that she was doing things in 1997, in her mid-thirties, that teenagers did years later – having crushes and flings and revelling in the attention she received both as a celebrity and as a woman, or girl, as she surely would have referred to herself, even at the age of thirty-five: girls together, doing girly things, having girly chats, dating 'boys', who were really men.

But it was a bit late by then and there was this yearning, to find the elusive partner-for-all-time, the knight on a white charger, as some would say Jill sought; to settle down with this knight and have children. It was curious that Jenny considered Jill one of the least desperate women she knew in this regard, while others would say Jill was exactly that. Lonely. Missing something in her life. Lacking security. Frankly, desperate. How sad then that she had found Alan, and had the pleasure of the expectation, was right there on the edge of happiness when she was killed.

However much Jean and Jill were alike there were certainly differences between them in the way they lived their lives. Jean refused ever to fly – she said she'd have to be unconscious before you got her on a plane, generally did not like travelling. She never went abroad, not once, in all her fifty-eight years.

Jack remembers a boat trip on the River Dart, during a family holiday in Torquay, when Jean was seasick all the way from Brixham to the estuary and all the way back as well. She only had to look at the water to feel queasy. This was how Esme thought of Jean too. Her sister-in-law was such a delicate traveller that she wouldn't even get into a car unless she herself was driving. That was Jean, in Esme's memory, a steady and reliable person, not adventurous (a quality she shared with Jack – not one to kick over the traces, as Esme would say), dressed without frills who, for all that, always had a twinkle in her eye, and could share a joke with Esme about their two 'boys' – their husbands, the brothers Jack and Ken.

Esme's daughter Judith was quite close to Jill when they were young and would be closer still later. Judith was eighteen months older than Jill but remembered how precocious she seemed in the sense that she spoke and dressed like an adult.

The two families would come together for Christmas and there would be Judith and her siblings in their modern outfits, and there would be Jill in her old-fashioned, fuddy-duddy clothes. She always looked as if she was on her way to church with her mother, in her Sunday best. Always smart, though, even if she was behind the times, like her mother, like Weston.

It was funny how Judith thought of Jill and her parents, the three of them coming over, Jill perfectly polite, Jack, his eyes already going bad, Jean worried about the drive home – not wanting to leave it too late – departing early, returning to their little house in Weston. They were like the country cousins. Not that her own family were rich or thought of themselves as superior in any way, it was just that Judith observed the differences between them.

She remembered family visits the other way, to Weston, Auntie Jean entertaining them by playing the organ. It was not an unwelcoming house but perhaps a little austere. If Judith's mother had people for tea she would open the pink salmon, but over in Weston it would be fish paste sandwiches.

When she was older, Judith could see how her dad and his brother Jack would make good husbands. They would be easy to put up with, as men. You could easily be married to them for fifty years. But she knew too that, back then, people didn't always marry for love. They married for lots of different reasons, for companionship, sometimes, or for fear of ending up a spinster, which was the impression that Judith had of Jean. Judith wasn't even sure that Jean liked men very much. She was very independent.

Both Jenny Higham and Judith would hear from Jill that, like many women of that generation, her mother had married so as not to be left on the shelf. Jill had known this from an early age, having been told by her mother during open moments between them, when parental secrets were being shared. You could be stuck up there on the shelf soon enough after the war, and things were different than now, for sure, but even so, Jean was only twenty-two when she married and obviously younger still when she and Jack had started courting. Hardly shelf material, even by the standards of the time.

So perhaps the disappointment Jean evidently felt was all hers and nothing at all to do with Jack. They had chosen each other, after all; Jean had chosen Jack, she knew the man he was. If she had dashed hopes for the life she might have led or failed aspirations or ambitions, they were unlikely to have been based on false promises from Jack.

Jean wanted everything for Jill and encouraged her and took pleasure in her early successes. Those pleasures must have been vicarious for Jean. Pleasures she had been unable to achieve for herself. She gave Jill her disappointments and took Jill's pleasures in return.

Jill was urged to find fulfilment, not to marry too soon or for the wrong reasons. Perhaps too, with her mother's compliance, she missed out on a better relationship with her father and brother. She certainly seems to have sought out older men often enough in later life. She was quite open about it. She liked older men. She liked older men with status.

Jack and Jean moved from Madam Lane to a three-bedroomed house on Ryecroft Avenue in the centre of Worle, which was the house where Jill grew up. It was not yet built when they bought it and Jack took photographs of its progress to completion.

The next-door house was empty when they moved in but soon a young family came along with a crying baby that kept them all awake at night. Then the young family got a dartboard, which they fixed to an adjoining wall so that Jack could hear the thud of darts on cork. The husband had friends round to play cards and they would sit up into the small hours, whooping and shouting over their hands. Jack had a quiet word with him. He was still thinking about that detached home.

Jill went to school and made steady progress – steady and reliable, nothing exceptional – through Greenwood Junior and Worle School, the local comprehensive. At sixteen she moved on to Broadoak Sixth Form Centre. She was always popular, always had lots of friends. When she became head girl at Broadoak, it was through election by her peers. She was newly emerged then, from gawky adolescence, from being bespectacled and spotty with obtrusive front teeth.

The minister from the Baptist Church, Philip Gathercole, recalls a period, when Jill was about thirteen, during which Jean was less than diligent in her church attendance and he went round to speak to her about it. He told Jean that Jill needed her example and encouragement now that she was of an age when she could make a vital decision to become a Christian. Jean duly turned up the next

Sunday with Jill, and the Sunday after that, and on the third Sunday, Jill went to sit upstairs in the balcony with the other young people from the church community. She remained in this community for most of the rest of her teenage years.

Philip Gathercole's son, Andy, was a young member of the church, too, went to the same school as Jill, but really got to know her in the Young People's Fellowship, which was the church's youth club, for which Jill was later the secretary.

Milton Baptist Church was then a strong church, not especially charismatic, as some Baptist congregations are now, not much given to hand-clapping and arm-waving; a traditional church, representing and reflecting the traditional Christian values of the 200 to 300 Weston people in its fellowship. Jill's maternal grandmother, Mrs Hockey – Lucy Alice Hockey – had been in the same church. Jean was very close to her, and looked after her in old age.

Andy recalls Jill coming up the drive of his home and his younger brother, who could only have been eight or nine at the time, seeing her and saying, 'Yuk, she's got glasses.' She really was a very plain girl, nothing striking about her appearance, not one of those stunning girls with long, blonde hair. They were around too, those stunning girls, but it was Jill who attracted people to her, with her liveliness and her humour, especially her laughter, her giggle – the same giggle as it was twenty-odd years later, when Andy still knew her.

The YPF, as it was always known, was a typical church youth club which met in the hall on Tuesday and Friday evenings. There were talks and discussions on Christian and moral themes and games and fooling around and away weekends and putting on shows, drama, sketches and songs, with Jill always in the thick of what was going on. Very active, very involved, despite her apparent shyness and hesitancy, her diffidence.

As time went on there was a lot of adolescent dating, and Jill probably went out with most of the boys in the club, holding hands and kissing, nothing much more. Maybe some mild petting here and there. Parties with no alcohol, or maybe just a little alcohol – Andy could remember a group of them once discussing whether they should drink at a Saturday-night party and, if they did, whether they should stop at midnight, because that would be the Sabbath, a day of abstinence. There were no drugs, it was a very safe world. No rebellion. They were all quiet kids. Quiet and respectable. When punk came in, in 1976, they would wear bin-liners to parties and pogo like mad when they danced, but it was just pretend-punk, not the real thing. That was the year Jill was baptised by full immersion: nothing very punk about that.

Andy spent the summer of 1997 with Jill – the summer of 'Hotel California', the Eagles song, which became their song then, the soundtrack to their summer romance, which began one evening after service. They sat on the sofa in Jill's lounge, which Andy can still picture – it was part of a striped three-piece suite – they watched television and listened to music and smooched or necked or snogged or whatever the word for it was then. Sometimes a group from the YPF would sit at the Formica-topped kitchen table. Jill's home was always a comfortable place to be. Jean wasn't rushing around plumping the cushions or straightening the mat beneath their feet.

Andy never professed his undying love to Jill, nor she to him. He went away for a couple of weeks and when he came back they ended their relationship. There were no tears or ill feeling, though Andy felt some envy of his older brother later when his brother went out with Jill, because by that time she had given herself a makeover, ditched the glasses for contact lenses, permed her hair and become altogether sexier in her appearance. Andy felt he had missed out there.

He and Jill kept in touch over the years. She came to his wedding and he would have attended hers. They had both been guests at the weddings of other friends from their YPF days. Andy became involved with a Christian charity, the Matthew Project, which helps young people in difficulty through drugs or crime or family trauma, and Jill became its patron. After Jill's death Andy got in touch with another old YPF friend, Roy Jones. In sadness, they teased each other with their memories of Jill, Andy claiming he was the first to snog her, Roy agreeing but saying she said Roy was the best.

Roy had celebrated his fortieth birthday in the spring of 1996 with a reunion of the YPF. To mark the occasion they had produced a joke edition of their old newsletter, *Jungle News*, to which Jill contributed an article recalling her three-week romance with Roy, during which they had held hands in the balcony of the church during the Sunday service. The same balcony where they had all cracked up every week during hymns over the woman with the funny voice in the grown-up congregation below.

The memorable thing about that reunion was that Jill had arrived there, with Bob Wheaton, wearing dark glasses, behind which were the beginnings of what would become two very black eyes.

I heard the story from Bob later. Jill had made a lot of effort to get herself ready for this reunion, had put on a new trouser suit, Louis Feraud probably, and as she went to go down the stairs of Bob's house she caught her heel on the hem of the trousers and fell head first to the bottom, where her face hit the wall, leaving lip-stick traces there and she was very briefly concussed.

Bob, who was sitting reading at the time, waiting for Jill to be ready, went to her and she came out of her daze and said, 'It was because I was being too proud.' She was dressing up to show off to her old friends, and pride had come before a fall. She was very shaken by this incident – not just by the fall, but by the meaning she ascribed to it.

They stopped at a small out-of-town hospital on their way to the reunion but her eyes just got blacker and blacker as the bruising came out and later that week it became a story in the *Sun*. Jill and her shiners. There was a wild rumour doing the rounds at the BBC that Bob must have hit her. He hadn't. He would never hit her. Jenny Higham later saw the wall herself and was amazed that Jill wasn't more seriously hurt. She also knew that Jill would've been straight out of the door if any man had been violent towards her. Still, it was not very nice for Bob that people were willing to think that of him.

In 1978, on the day before her seventeenth birthday, Jill had a set of studio photographs of herself taken. Auntie Esme has those pic-tures now. She thought they may have been a birthday present, from Jean, perhaps. They were an early attempt at glamorous photos, a novice model learning to pose for the camera, big smiles and a lot of hair, slightly awkward posture. Nothing risqué.

Jill must have hoped to use these pictures as a calling card. She must have been keeping an eye out for opportunities, even then. She kept them in an album in which she had placed a torn out strip from the *Sunday Mirror* from 1980 in which readers were offered the chance to become a hostess on the television game show *Mr &*

Mrs. A 'Super *Sunday Mirror*' competition which Jill had apparently entered, using a more recent photograph, a copy of which was also in the album.

Andy Gathercole remembered Jill saying she wanted to be Jan Leeming. That was a clear memory. They were watching television and the news came on, the regional news, read by Jan Leeming, and Jill said, 'That's who I want to be, Jan Leeming.' Jan Leeming was also heading from the region to the centre, where she would become a BBC News presenter.

It doesn't sound as though Jill's ambitions were very focused in those days. She also sometimes expressed interest in becoming an air stewardess. When Nigel and Vanessa were clearing out Jill's room at Jack's home after her death while Jack sat in the living room out of the way – the thought of going into Jill's room was unbearable to him – they found a large number of letters of reply and rejection to jobs which Jill had applied for in her early years. All kinds of jobs in the media, none of which she had got. She must have been very keen and determined and not easily dissuaded. It takes a considerable degree of self-belief to keep plugging away in the face of constant rejection.

When she was completing school at the turn of the decade, taking her A-levels, Jack again spoke to his bosses at the *Mercury*, just as he had done for Nigel. Jill took a test, wrote an essay, attended an interview and was taken on as a probationer, like all junior reporters, attending training in Cardiff before beginning work.

She could have gone to university, and later she sometimes regretted that she hadn't. Particularly when she had all those BBC eggheads to contend with. At the time some contemporaries were surprised she wasn't pursuing a degree, because she seemed very bright to them and it meant getting out of Weston, which was the first ambition for many youngsters, including Jill, her friends thought. Some wondered if she was simply staying close to her mother.

When Jill began working at the *Weston Mercury* she pinned a picture of Cliff Richard up on the wall next to her desk. She really liked Cliff Richard. In the summer of 1979 she had been to a Christian rock festival, Greenbelt, at which Cliff Richard had been the star turn. He was then at number 1 in the charts with 'We Don't Talk Any More', and this was the first time he had performed the song live.

When Jill and Alan came together and were comparing notes on their previous lives, they realised they had both been at that festival. It was when Jenny Higham, who was to bring them together, compared their CD collections that she realised their future potential as a couple – two people with very similar middle-of-the-road tastes in music.

Many local newspapers have changed over the years, become freesheets, carrying more advertising and less news, trying to ape their national tabloid counterparts, racier and less wedded to a civic role. But in the old days, in Jill's day, one of the principal aims was to squeeze in as many local names as possible every week, as many pictures of local residents as possible preferably standing with the mayor. Lists of flower-show competitors, dense reports of council meetings and thorough accounts of proceedings from the magistrates' courts which entirely overlooked any salacious details or buried them in the sixth paragraph. Births, marriages and deaths, and plenty of them.

Jill's family placed a notice in the births, marriages and deaths columns of Jill's own newspaper, to mark her twenty-first birthday, in the edition on Friday 3 November 1982.

DANDO – Jill. Fondest congratulations for your 21st birthday on November 9th. May the keys of health, happiness and success be yours today and always. All our love. – Mum, Dad, Nan, Greg, Vanessa and Nigel.
[Greg was Jill's boyfriend at the time.]

That edition of the newspaper carried an extensive account of the Weston Chrysanthemum Society's ninety-ninth annual show, alongside a picture of the prize-winners with the mayor and mayoress. The mayor was reported to have been left speechless by the beauty of the blooms.

A Worle man had broken his wife's jaw in an argument and been fined £25 by the magistrates. Three weddings were covered, in text and pictures, beneath the headline WEDDING BELLS RING OUT. There was a golden wedding, advance notice of Age Concern's Adopt-a-Granny-for-Christmas campaign, an obituary of the former head of English at Worle School, a report that some local scouts and guides had held their first-ever joint bazaar in a village hall and raised £120.

This was the news, in Weston, in Jill's provincial heyday. You can be sure that she would have recognised or known many of the people featured in the paper that week. And they would have known her. Weston was a small place, a conservative place, rather isolated, homogenous as milk and just as white. Everyone knew everyone, or so it seemed, and they all knew each other's business.

Andrew Ray met Jill at the magistrates' court in the autumn of 1981. She was the reporter and he was the clerk of the court. You couldn't have missed her, he says, if you were a red-blooded male. Those strawberry lips. They went out together for a few months. Like many of Jill's later relationships, the fleeting relationships, it was a rather private and exclusive relationship, just the two of them. He didn't introduce her to his friends and she didn't introduce him to hers. In fact, he had the impression that she didn't have many friends. Lots of acquaintances, but not many close friends.

They went to concerts, to the opera, to jazz nights at local pubs. They stayed in and watched *Brideshead Revisited* on television. They had a good laugh always and Andrew felt he was a bit in love with Jill. Though evidently not so much that it stopped him having another relationship simultaneously which made things rather complicated and made Jill rather cross when she found out.

Andrew felt that Jill was a little mumsy, a shade frumpy for a twenty-year-old. He thought that she was conscious of that, and did not feel very elegant herself. She was also pretty tall, whereas Andrew was not. He remembers going to a ball at the Winter Gardens, mixing with the magistrates and the other worthies of the town. They had great fun and he was proud to be Jill's partner, but he couldn't help feeling self-conscious with Jill up there somewhere in her high heels and him down there in his Hepworth's evening suit, which Jill had helped him choose. Perhaps the timing was wrong. In any event the relationship did not develop and they drifted apart as a couple, but kept in touch all the same.

Jill, always getting involved, very busy, joined the Weston Amateur Dramatic Society and was in her first production that Christmas, playing Angelina in *The Land of the Christmas Stocking*. She took driving lessons with Greg Johnston-Keay and they, too, went out for a while, much to the delight of Greg's mother, Liz. They had their photograph taken together at a friend's twenty-first birthday part in the summer of 1982, sitting at a garden table, their fingers entwined. Liz wrote on the back of this picture, 'The Proposal??'.

But there was no proposal. As Liz would later concede, her son Greg was happy to stay where he was, and Jill was flying high. Liz embraced Jill and treated her as one of her own children. As Jill flew up and up she kept in touch with Liz through visits and letters; many, many letters describing her exciting life and the places she went and the people she encountered, which Liz enjoyed like any mother would.

Both Andrew Ray and Greg Johnston-Keay were of a similar age to Jill, just slightly older. Pete Baylis was quite a bit older, almost twice Jill's age then, touching forty. He was divorced, too, after an early and brief marriage. He was an executive at Westlands, then a big local employer, and had a sporty Audi, a small boat at the marina and a healthy disposable income, which Jill helped him to dispose of. The most expensive girlfriend he ever had, as he would say. Not that he minded. Not at all.

They met at an annual dinner for local hospital radio, voluntary broadcasting in which Jill participated, like many local newspaper reporters. A mate of Pete's who was also involved invited him along. His friend's date for the evening was Jill, but it was Pete who talked to her all night and called his friend the next morning and said, 'I must have her number.' 'Oh,' the friend replied. 'All right, but it'll cost you a curry,' a debt which Pete was happy to honour.

Pete felt that the relationship he had with Jill was her first grown-up relationship. She was quite open about liking the company of older men, and he was sure she enjoyed the status of his job and the life it enabled them to lead. They went away for weekends – she loved driving his car – had expensive meals in restaurants, went out on his boat and generally had a ball.

He was nervous about meeting Jean and Jack, a divorced older man – he was closer in age to Jean than to Jill – entering this religious domain. But Jean took to him straight away, he could tell, and he took to her. It was the twinkle in her eye, just as Esme describes. That sense of fun. Even if much of the fun was directed at poor Jack, who Pete liked equally but could see was an outsider in his own house.

Almost more than anything, Pete liked making Jill laugh. Once she started she just kept going, in rolling waves of hysterics, helpless, on the brink of wetting herself. Completely uncontrollable. Jean could be the same too. One evening the three of them were sitting in the kitchen waiting for the plumber to call. Jean had a line of newly washed underwear strung out to dry and then there was a knock at the door and Jean, in a panic of propriety, whispered urgently: 'Quick, knickers down!' When she and Jill realised what she had said they were practically on the floor with laughter.

Jean never minded when Jill and Pete went away or that Jill went to stay with Pete at his flat most weekends. She encouraged their relationship and enjoyed it. In Pete's experience it was unique, to like your girlfriend and her mother. And it seemed quite natural that they should take Jean out with them sometimes. After all, Jean and Jill were like sisters.

Pete thinks Sands a grotty place now, a dive, but in those days it was pretty good, and had a dinner-dance club with live music where you could have a meal and a dance afterwards. Jean and Jill would both dress up – Jill wasn't one to go casual on a night out somewhere like that. She was quite old fashioned in that way, he says: strait-laced, seeming older than her years. She was also rather gauche, which was the word she used to use to describe herself. Gauche. Pete was never quite sure what it meant. Clumsy, unsophisticated, he supposed. She was very precious to him.

Pete and Jean used to go to all Jill's appearances at the Playhouse in the amateur dramatics. He remembered that she borrowed his leather flying boots for her role in *Johnny Belinda*, in which she played a deaf mute. He recalled how she struggled with a crude bit of sign language, worrying how her mother would react, seeing her perform such a thing.

Jill was a big hit at the Playhouse, popular with her fellow thespians, becoming assistant secretary of the Dramatic Society and admired for her performances as well as her looks. Some of the older members could see that she lacked self-assurance and self-awareness, and thought she never had the slightest idea of the effect she had on men. She seemed buttoned up, and a bit old fashioned but when they put on a production of *Pardon Me, Prime Minister*, a risqué farce (well, it was risqué by Weston standards), Jill did not object, appearing in a modest state of undress. Some of the other women said, 'Oh, God, I'm not taking my clothes off if she's taking hers off.'

That was the totality of Jill's life in those days, as Pete saw it. Her work at the *Mercury*, the amateur dramatics, her mother and going out with him. There didn't seem to be time or room for very much more.

Pete was fighting shy of commitment then. The last thing he wanted after the failure of his marriage. He realised later that he wished he had married Jill, or at least asked her to marry him. 'I really wanted to marry you,' he told her.

'Well, you never did ask me, did you?' she said.

They kept in touch, always, as friends. Pete went to Gowan Avenue many times. He would knock on that door and Jill would answer and smile, 'Hey, Pete! Come on in.' And Pete would sit on her sofa and feel really inhibited for the first ten minutes. 'I can't talk to you,' he'd say. 'You're famous.' He really felt that. Then she'd say, 'Don't be stupid,' and in a few minutes she would be his old mate again.

If they went out to a restaurant in London, people would be coming up to the table asking: 'Excuse me, are you Jill Dando? Can I have your autograph?' Pete would be embarrassed, but Jill would open her bag, in which she kept a stock of pictures of herself for these eventualities, and she would sign a picture and hand it over and everyone would be happy.

Pete never made a big deal out of knowing her but he was very proud of Jill, not born into her success, coming from such an ordinary background – there was nobody more ordinary than Jack – having risen so far. He remembers when the *Weston Mercury* was sending her to Strasbourg for an EU press day – 1985, he recalled – and Jill was terrified because she had never flown before and Pete, who travelled often for work, tried in vain to reassure her. In the end he arranged a business trip to France for the same day so that he could go with her to Heathrow and help calm her nerves at the airport. She flew and loved it.

His worst memory is of the afternoon they went out on the boat and Jill turned to him and started saying she was young free and single. 'Do you know what that means, young, free and single?' she asked Pete.

'Yes, of course.'

'Well, that's what I am,' said Jill.

He already knew that she was friends with John Crockford-Hawley, a local politician, and now she said she wanted to stop going out with Pete and spend more time with John.

Pete was pretty upset about that though he could see why Jill would be interested in John, who was quite different by Weston standards, cultured and intelligent and quite a powerful figure locally. He was one of those characters everyone knew. Pete had seen him strolling around town one summer in a striped blazer and a straw boater. Just the touch of class that would turn Jill's head.

John Crockford-Hawley was in his mid- to late thirties, younger than Pete but still significantly older than Jill. He knew her from council meetings, from a meeting of the transport committee of Woodspring District Council, if he remembered correctly. He found her very personable, and it was always a good idea for local councillors to keep in with the press. He and Jill would meet up sometimes, go out for the occasional meal.

In 1984 he became deputy mayor and knew then, because it was Buggins' turn, that next year he would be 'le grand fromage', as he called it; Weston's big cheese, its mayor for a year.

He did not have a wife and his mother told him she would not serve as his mayoress, as did his sister, and the next available female relative was his sister-in-law. So she became his mayoress but she wasn't always available so John asked Jill if she would fill in sometimes, which she was glad to do. She couldn't wear the chain but she loved the events, the functions, and was great at them.

At some functions they would be expected to have the first waltz. John was hopeless at dancing and detested having to get up and do a circuit, but he and Jill would shuffle round the floor, John hissing in mock earnestness to Jill, 'For God's sake, smile!'

Weston did not have an official mayoral car and relied instead on a retired schoolteacher with a Volvo, on the bonnet of which would be placed a magnetic crest. It was fine around town, policemen saluting as it passed, which made those inside feel rather grand, but on longer journeys, say to the local RAF station, the magnet would lose its grip and the pennant would slide up the bonnet of the car towards the windscreen and they would have to stop and jump out and push it back down towards the radiator.

John's family had come down to Weston from Birmingham when he was a child. Weston had become popular as a holiday resort in the Victorian age, and ever since Midlands families had made a beeline for the town for their fortnight by the sea. Some liked it so much that they retired there, or moved there permanently. It was an isolated place, almost turned in on itself, turned towards the sea and its many miles of shoreline, its seven miles of sandy beaches.

Though he had worked away for a while, John had spent most of his life in Weston, working as a teacher, retiring as head of department at a secondary school. He had always thought he would stay a few years and move on, he says, but there must be something in the ozone, something that creates a sense of lethargy; you blink and twenty-five years have gone by and all your ambitions with them.

He knew that Jill worried about being left behind, being stuck at the *Mercury* for ever. All local papers have those people, who are still there and always there and serve as a reminder to younger reporters of the fate that awaits them in that blink. The *Mercury* was just the same. Jill liked the paternal role those people played for her – she just didn't want to become one of them. On the other hand, she feared the wider world and leaving the security of Weston and her mother; feared she was not good enough to make her way.

One evening John and Jill went to a charity do for the St John

Ambulance Brigade. There were some television people at the party – including the comedian Frankie Howerd, who was given a lift home by John and Jill and offended them both with his vulgar and grubby behaviour – and Jill had also talked to a presenter at HTV who arranged for her to go to Bristol for a screen test for regional television.

She was very nervous and told John afterwards that it hadn't gone very well at all. They had said that she was too girl-next-door with her bouncy hair; too much like Mary Poppins. That seemed to be the end of Jill's television prospects, there and then. She was disappointed but not apparently very distressed.

John said that he and Jill were close, had a close relationship for a relatively short time. She was discovering herself and he was discovering himself. After her death he was quoted in an article in a tabloid newspaper as saying, 'I was the first', as if he was the first man in Jill's life. It was a preposterous article, he says, and bore almost no relation to his conversation with the news agency reporter who interviewed him. It did not do much for his popularity in Weston.

In later years Jill would refer to John as 'the old gay mayor', which suggested that, rightly or wrongly, she had made a judgement about his sexuality. One can imagine that Weston – and especially its local Conservative Party, in which John had once been a leading figure – did not warm to gay men and that speculation about people's sexuality was not without malice.

Jill's relationship with John caused some friction between Jill and her mother which was not resolved at the time of Jean's death and was a source of continuing regret and some guilt to Jill. Jean disapproved of John every bit as much as she approved of Pete Baylis, and tried to encourage Pete to fight for Jill. She once called him at work and told him that faint heart never won fair maiden. Jean and Pete went out for a drink a few times to discuss it. When Jill went away with John and another man, Jean and Pete joked and teased Jill about who had slept with who.

Pete says that Jean warned Jill of the rumours about John and tried to persuade her to stop seeing him. Jill refused. The only time that she ever really defied her mother.

Jack doesn't think that Jean began her Tupperware evenings to earn extra money, more to meet local people, for the social aspect of it. She used to make cakes and coffee and invite women round for the evening or be invited to their homes and, by the end of it, with a bit of luck they would have bought lots of plastic containers that Jean had paid for up front. Jack used to keep out of the way. He'd go up and sit in the bedroom and read.

Eventually Jean ran out of people to invite to her parties, everyone she knew having already bought as much Tupperware as they needed. There was a lot of Tupperware left over and when Jean died Jack found loads of it in the house, which he gave away, all except for one or two boxes which he still uses.

Jean began caring for an elderly widower who lived in the village, whose wife Jean had known. She had done everything for the man and he was helpless, or hopeless, at looking after himself. He would join Jean and Jack for Sunday lunch and Jean would do his shopping, cook his meals and tidy his home.

Jack went and sat with him sometimes, and had a whisky with him, but he was not really Jack's cup of tea. He didn't know a thing about gardening. He used to replant his roses every year in fresh soil and put all the old soil in his garage, which was not the right way of doing it at all. Jack was a keen gardener. The man had also dug a trench in the middle of his lawn in the shape of a cross after his wife had died, and planted flowers in it. He certainly had some funny ideas.

It was no more than a couple of years before the man died, too, leaving Jean as the sole beneficiary of his will, which was quite a surprise. Jean and Jack bought a Honda Accord, fresh out of the showroom, the first new car they had ever owned, power steering, air-conditioning, the lot. They felt quite rich driving around in that car.

They also started looking around for a detached bungalow, and found one for sale in Cornwallis Avenue, which was perfect for Jack – no noisy neighbours – but Jean was ambivalent because, lovely though it was, it was also some way out of the centre and up the hill and you couldn't really walk to the shops. In the end Jean was convinced by the through lounge, which was the kind of room she had always wanted.

It was not long after they moved in that Jean became ill, tired and listless, experiencing swelling in her stomach, getting ever weaker, spending more and more time in bed. They didn't know what was wrong. At first the hospital said it was her spleen, and that she would need to have it removed – or at least this is what she told Jack. But Jack soon realised it was quite serious and decided he would give up work, after thirty-eight years, though he had hoped to put in forty.

He resolved to learn to cook and asked for a pressure cooker as his retirement gift. He had been on at Jean for ages about getting a pressure cooker to make things easier for herself.

Jack did all the shopping and would busy himself in the kitchen, following the instructions Jean called from the bedroom: how much salt to put with the potatoes, how long to cook an oven roast and all that business, as Jack said. Jean was probably teaching him to look after himself, in preparation for her death.

Jean didn't want anyone to know that she was dying of leukaemia – especially not Jill, who was by then looking hard for a new job, looking to leave Weston. Jean didn't want her to stay behind on her account and miss her moment. Roger Collins, the minister at Milton Baptist Church, had the feeling that not even Jack knew. He cannot recall her ever using the word leukaemia, which left him to work out what it was that was killing her.

On Jack's account Jean had gone into the Bristol Royal Infirmary for the operation to have her spleen removed, and he went in to see her one day and she was in tears, telling him they were not going to perform the operation after all because she had leukaemia. So she came home and took lots of tablets and stayed in bed and sometimes would have terrible haemorrhages, unstoppable nosebleeds, and would have to go in to hospital for a few days.

There was a lot of ferrying back and forth between Weston and Bristol, and Jack's eyes had deteriorated so much that he had to give up driving. He and Jean gave their lovely Honda Accord to Jill, she ferried them around whenever she could. Esme and Ken, too, gave lots of support, and often took over the driving, especially later, when Jill had changed jobs and left Weston.

No doctor had ever said this to Jack, but he was sure his years in the printing trade had ruined his eyes. He missed the print room. Could recall the smell of the ink which was thick like treacle and the paper dust when they were unloading the reels. You would know that smell anywhere.

He remembered the busy newsroom and the reporters, even Lola, the mother of Jeffrey Archer, who was famous in Weston for her column, 'Over the Teacups', in which she recorded her domestic life. She was a snooty sort, that Lola, says Jack. But then who was Jack to her, except a lowly compositor?

Jack had loved his work but he was sure it was the cause of his encroaching blindness. An optician had said to him one day, you've got glaucoma. Well, it was a bit late by then.

He would have one operation and still lose the sight in his left eye. He would have a second operation after Jill's death, which was planned beforehand, with the intention that he would be able to walk unaided down the aisle with Jill on his arm, to deliver her to Alan. Nigel was probably going to help him half the way.

When Jack gave up driving he went out and bought a motorbike. Why he thought he could ride a motorbike when he couldn't drive a car, he couldn't say. It was just something he wanted to do, at the age of sixty-seven. It was a Japanese motorbike, though he had forgotten the make. He sold it after six months.

Jill finally got her new job, at BBC Radio Devon in Exeter, in 1985. She held her leaving do at Piranhas nightclub in Weston, having celebrated her twenty-third birthday there some months earlier. She had been at the *Mercury* for nearly five years, which was a long apprenticeship by anyone's standards.

Radio Devon took her on as a programme assistant because there were no reporters' jobs available at the time but she was soon reporting and soon after that she was co-presenting the breakfast programme. Jean used to tape the programmes. Pete Baylis thought she was already famous then. He had no idea what was coming.

Jill became close to Pete again at the time of her mother's death, as friends. Pete visited Jean at home and in hospital. The word leukaemia was off-limits. At first Pete thought it was something passing, the flu or something. 'No Pete,' Jill said. 'It's not like that.'

Pete could recall being at the hospital often before Jean's death, on 7 January 1986. Jean wanted to die and kept saying, 'Let me go. I want to go home.' One of the last things she said to Pete was 'You will look after Jill, won't you?'

'Yeah, I'll always look after her,' he promised.

These moments were often relived by Jill and Pete later, and Jill always ended up in tears. Then Jill died and Pete felt that he had let Jean down by not looking after her daughter, even though, as he well knew, this was ridiculous – Jill was not in his charge. Jill appeared in Pete's dreams after her death, in nice dreams, which made Pete feel better.

Jack remembered that he was able to kiss Jean goodbye and say goodbye to her. Jill would later recount how she called Nigel to tell him that their mother had died and Nigel said, 'All right, okay.' That was the last time they ever discussed it. That was Nigel, keeping his feelings in check.

Six

Here comes Helen Doble, down Wardo Avenue, right into Sidbury Street, left into Gowan Avenue, crossing the road to the south side, to the side where Jill lives, catching sight of her friend Vida Saunders, carrying a baby on her hip, as Vida disappears back into Charlotte de Rosnay's house, number 55. Vida wearing her peaked cap, just as Helen is wearing hers; seeing an elderly black man, wearing a hat, walking westwards on the north side of Gowan Avenue. Helen doesn't know him, but smiles at him in greeting just the same as she crosses an otherwise empty street.

It is just after 11.30 and Helen would have gone out earlier but was delayed by the late arrival of the man from Premier Lofts, with whom she has been discussing the final preparations for the building of the loft conversion into the roof of her first-floor flat.

She has seen all the houses with their armies of builders, the rubbish skips in the road, their conversions and refurbishments and now she will be having her own skip outside from which she will watch the local people, the skip-foragers, as she calls them, those magpies, rummaging beneath the tarpaulin cover, looking for unwanted doors or scraps of timber or old fireplaces or any discarded objects that might be put to use or have value.

Helen observed the life that went on around her as she moved through Fulham. Put her in a café to watch the world go by, that was brilliant. Ask her which houses had building work going on, which parked car belonged to which house, or where the celebrities lived, and she could tell you.

After the loft man had left Helen made a phone call to a friend and left a message for her. This was at about 11.25. It had taken her a few minutes then to collect her things together to go out.

My own interest in the life of Jill Dando emerged out of her death, in the early summer of 1999 when I was assigned to write about the mystery of her death by the *Sunday Times Magazine*.

I remember that I took the assignment with some reluctance, thinking that this mystery was going to be solved any minute and I might put in a lot of work that would be wasted. I did not think there would be much mystery in the life of Jill Dando either. In truth, I didn't think about her that much at all. Not at first. Which is pretty ironic, since now I hardly think about anything else.

Anyway, I happened to be talking to a very old friend on the phone one day and mentioned that I was beginning work on this long article about Jill Dando. 'Oh well,' he said. 'You've got to talk to Helen.' 'Why?' I asked. He seemed surprised. 'Don't you know?'

My friend David Treloar had known Helen Doble back in the mid-1980s and we had all socialised together for a while. During that time Helen had bought the flat in Wardo Avenue, escaping to Fulham from Shepherds Bush which was not then very up and coming. Helen remembered that it was one of a number of local properties being shown to potential buyers by the estate agent Suzy Lamplugh.

David was then working as a copy-writer at Thames Television at the top end of Tottenham Court Road which was where he met Helen, who was an assistant to the producer of *This Is Your Life*. I worked at the bottom end of Tottenham Court Road as a feature writer for the listings magazine *TV Times*. Helen often asked me about the celebrities I had interviewed or written about and talked about the celebrities that were featured on *This Is Your Life*. I knew that she was related to Rolf Harris. I had not seen or spoken to her for many years.

By the time we met she was gripped by what I took to be post-traumatic stress disorder. As anyone might be, who had seen what she had seen. She was explicitly obsessed with the events of that day and everything that had happened since. She saw coincidence at every turn and every turn led back to Jill and then there I was, reappearing in her life, because of Jill. I was another coincidence to her and, I must say, it was quite a coincidence for me, too. I began to be drawn in.

Helen had been interested in showbusiness for as long as she could remember, both as an observer and as a potential participant. She had done some television extra work, on dramas such as *Worzel Gummidge*, while at school and college and always hoped to work in television, music or fashion.

She liked to read about showbusiness people who had become successful, in biographies and newspapers and magazines, because it was intriguing to know how they had got wherever they happened to be.

After working on *This Is Your Life*, Helen had been offered a presenting job of her own on an environmental programme, but she was under contract to another company by then, as a celebrity-booker for a chat show, and she was pregnant too and wasn't able to take the job. Naturally, she had always wondered how that missed chance might have affected her career. Bringing up her daughter alone she had begun doing more of her work from home, becoming a question-setter for quiz shows such as *Blankety Blank* and *Strike It Rich*.

She had a set of questions with her that morning when she left home, which she was returning to the copy shop because the text wasn't properly aligned. The questions were for *My Kind of Music*. She was also carrying her new mobile phone.

As always, Helen wondered if she might see Jill. She had not seen Jill since her engagement to Alan, which Helen had read about some weeks earlier. She had not yet seen the engagement ring. She realised Jill was spending much of her time at Alan's now which must be why she hadn't seen her.

As Helen walked down Gowan Avenue she caught sight of Jill's car ahead, parked outside her house, and hoped that perhaps today she would see her, going into or coming out of her house as sometimes happened.

Helen had been interested, discovering Jill one day in the next street to hers. This was an area that obviously attracted famous people to it. There was John Lydon, once known as Johnny Rotten, who lived nearby. Sue Lawley had formerly lived in Doneraile Street, just across Fulham Palace Road from Gowan. The actor-couple Glynis Barber and Michael Brandon had rented in Gowan for a while, during their heyday in the television drama *Dempsey and Makepeace*. Very little escaped Helen. She used to see Cliff Richard travelling along Fulham Palace Road in his distinctive Range Rover, while he was appearing in *Heathcliff* in Hammersmith.

She thought Gowan Avenue was particularly appealing and she always chose to cut through it if she was going to the Fulham Road. The houses had high ceilings and many attractive features, such as their tiled porches and those narrow balconies with French windows to the front bedrooms. She loved the cherry blossom too. It made a little wonderland in the middle of London and you could rely on the bloom which gave a sense of continuity, of security. Helen would occasionally walk the entire length of Gowan, which was something she would later wish she had done on this morning, because who knew what she might have seen, that others must have missed.

She would often bump into Jill in the street or in the corner shop on Fulham Palace Road. They fell into conversation and Jill told Helen that she liked her home for its privacy, for the hedge that shrouded her front window from view. Jill met Helen's daughter too and would ask after her when she saw Helen and ask Helen how she managed, with a career and a child. Her daughter made an angel Christmas card for Jill and Jill told them it had taken pride of place in her living room. You must come round, Jill had said, but they both had busy schedules and had never yet made the arrangement. Helen had met Jill on the street outside her home with Alan and they shook hands by way of introduction and Helen thought he seemed really great.

Because of her work Helen read many of the celebrity magazines such as *Hello!* and *OK!* as well as magazines that featured celebrities, such as *Vogue* and *Tatler* and *Elle* and *Harpers & Queen*. She would cut out articles that seemed particularly interesting or useful, including articles about Jill. She read once, with some surprise, that Jill did not have a secretary to help her and made a mental note to ask Jill if she might be able to help out, next time she saw her.

As she drew level with number 29, Jill's BMW on one side of her and the house on the other, Helen looked to the doorway in the hope that it might be open, in the hope that she might see Jill. And when she looked, that was when everything changed.

She saw a woman slumped in the corner of the porch, up against the front door. She wondered what the woman was doing in Jill's doorway. She saw a lot of blood. She noted the hair and the engagement ring on her left hand and knew that it was Jill. She could tell that Jill had not simply tripped and hit her head, rather that it was the scene of a crime and that Jill was dead. Her hands were already blue. She assumed from the blood that Jill had been stabbed.

Helen was surprised afterwards that she hadn't screamed. She was conscious of the need to keep it together, to stay calm. She stood on the pavement with the closed gate in front of her. If the gate had been open, she would've gone up the path to Jill, which would've been the wrong thing to do. The closed gate made the path, the space Jill occupied, somehow inviolable and kept Helen where she was. She knew, too, it was a crime scene, which should not be disturbed.

Jill's black shoulder bag was sitting on the path, open, its strap looped over her right arm, a bunch of keys clasped in her right hand. Helen could see Jill's possessions inside the bag and assumed the crime was not robbery. Inside the bag Jill's mobile phone started ringing. It rang for a while and stopped and then started again and this kept happening.

Helen looked around and saw that Gowan Avenue was deserted. It was that quiet time of the Fulham day, after the school runs.

Even so, the emptiness of the street, its stillness, added to her growing sense of unreality.

She unzipped her bag and took out her mobile phone and keyed in the PIN number to unlock it and dialled 999. It was 11.43 am. A plane passed overhead and Helen missed the operator's response, was not sure if the call had connected. The operator must have repeated the words. 'Which service do you require? Police, fire or ambulance?' This time Helen heard. 'Ambulance,' she said.

'Ambulance Service, hello?'

'Hello, ambulance. I'm walking down Gowan Avenue … 29 Gowan Avenue. It looks like there's somebody collapsed.'

'I'm sorry, which area?'

'Fulham, SW6.'

'SW6, Gowan Avenue.'

'And, confidentially, it looks like it's Jill Dando, and she's collapsed in her doorstep. There's a lot of blood.'

'Right, is that outside number 29?'

'Twenty-nine, which is her home.'

'Fine. Is the lady actually conscious at the moment?'

'No, she's not.'

'Can you just approach to check that the lady's breathing for me.'

'She doesn't look as if she's breathing. Can you—'

'Yeah, the ambulance will be coming, but it's very important that you check that the lady's breathing. Then I can tell you what to do over the telephone, if you would like to assist her.'

On the recording of the emergency call, a female voice can be heard in the background, apparently another voice, talking about blood from the victim's nose.

'She's got blood coming from her nose. Her arms are blue.'

'Right, can you just—'

'Please …'

'Sorry, it's very important, I'm sorry to push you, I just need to find out if she needs … if she's breathing. Could you just ask somebody for me, please, or check yourself?'

'How does one check?'

'Right, is the lady's chest going up and down?'

'Oh my God, no. I don't think she's alive, I'm sorry, I don't think …'

Helen sounds distressed.

'OK, don't worry, don't worry. I'm going to get some help there as fast as I can for you.'

'Please.'

'It shouldn't be too long. We'll see you very soon. Bye-bye.'

'Thank you.'

Helen thought, well, I've made the call. Now what? The scene seemed surreal. She felt in need of confirmation that this was really happening, but the street remained empty. Jill's phone was ringing again, and Helen so wished that she could answer it. She wanted Jill's family to know what had happened before all hell broke loose. She wanted Alan to know. She wondered if that was him, trying to get through on the phone. She thought this ought to be kept private.

She remembered Vida at Charlotte's home and ran back along the road to number 55 and banged on the door. Vida appeared with a cup of tea in her hand. Helen wanted to be discreet. She didn't want Charlotte to know what was going on. 'Vida,' she said, 'I need your help. There's a lady who's been attacked, will you come with me?' Vida came out with Helen, still holding her tea.

On the pavement, Helen said, 'Vida, it's Jill Dando, I think she's been stabbed and she's dead. I've called the emergency services, can you come and be with me? Can you come and help?' The two women ran back up the road.

Later, when he listed to the tape-recording of Helen's 999 call, Detective Chief Inspector Hamish Campbell would become convinced that there was a second female voice on the tape and that the call had therefore been made after Helen had collected Vida.

Hamish would himself be arriving in Gowan Avenue in thirty-five minutes, to take charge of the inquiry into Jill's murder, as senior investigating officer. The timing of the call and the timing of Helen's discovery of Jill's body were important because they helped to define what the police called the 'killing time', the time span during which Jill had been killed. The police looked upon this time as the killer's window of opportunity. It could also tell them how far ahead the killer was, in leaving the scene. It was also a way of determining how long Jill had been lying there, alone and unnoticed.

The exact time of her death was unknown but must have been soon after she arrived home, which was approximately 11.30 am. The earliest possible timing being the retraced steps of Geoffrey Upfill-Brown who was leaving his house at 11.26 am, which must have been immediately after the murder.

If Helen had made the 11.43 am call straightaway then Jill had been lying there for around a quarter of an hour, possibly as long as seventeen minutes. If Helen had made the call after fetching Vida then obviously the 'killing time' was some minutes shorter.

Hamish was sure that this was so but Helen was adamant that it was not. She heard the tape as well and said the background voices must have been at the emergency call centre, at the other end of the conversation. Hamish could only conclude that Helen had convinced herself that she was right, although in fact she was mistaken. It would not be unusual for witnesses to do this, especially in traumatic circumstances. Helen was equally certain that Hamish was mistaken. It was, as you may imagine, a difficult thing for her to concede.

When Vida looked over the gate she said, 'She's dead.' 'I know,' Helen replied. 'Where are the emergency services?' Vida said, 'I'll go and see if there's a doctor.' Vida went to the surgery at 21 Gowan Avenue. Helen was alone again, which was the last thing she wanted, looking again at Jill and wishing she could cradle her and, she knew this was weird, she felt at least that she had put a ring of protection around her.

There was no doctor at the surgery, Dr Gossain having left some twenty-five minutes earlier to visit his friend at Lille Road. Vida returned instead with Suzanne Docherty, the practice manager, who looked at Jill and said, 'She's dead.'

'I know,' said Helen. 'Where are the emergency services?'

Helen's phone rang. 11.48 am.

'Hello?'

'Hello, it's the ambulance service. Somebody called us.'

'Yes, yes.'

'Right, the vehicle is on its way from Fulham. It'll be with you very shortly.'

'Thank you.'

'Can you just tell me roughly how old this woman is?'

'Well ...'

'Is she an elderly woman, or...?'

'No, no, no, confidentially, it's Jill Dando, the television presenter.'

'Jill Dando?'

'Yes, she's about thirty-six. Thirty-five, thirty-six.'

'What's happened to her?'

'I was walking along the pavement ... I know her, I saw her car, I looked towards her door and saw this figure slumped in the door.'

'She's in the doorway, right?'

'In the doorway. Blue hands, loads of blood.'

'Right, OK. Can you do me a favour? Do not touch anything, OK?'

'We're not ... we haven't touched her, that's why we didn't want to go near her.'

'Right.'

'Because it looks like somebody obviously stabbed her ...'

'Right, OK.'

'... or something.'

'The police are on their way as well.'

'Thank you.'

'All right then, bye-bye.'

'Bye,' said Helen.

Upstairs in his bedroom next door, Richard Hughes heard voices outside and decided to go down and investigate. He opened his front door. He would remember the ensuing conversation differently from the three women. He recalls being asked by one of the women if that was Jill Dando. Helen, Vida and Suzanne would say they already knew it was Jill Dando and didn't need to ask him.

Helen recounts Richard asking, 'What's going on?' and telling him, 'Your neighbour, Jill, she's been attacked on her doorstep. She's dead.' Richard saying, 'Oh my god, oh my god. I heard her scream, I heard her set the car alarm, I knew she was home. I looked out of the window and saw a man heading to Fulham Palace Road.'

Richard came up and looked over the dividing wall between the two homes and saw Jill. They were all standing there and then a police car appeared, Helen flagging it down, two uniformed officers emerging, taking over and then an ambulance arriving, an air ambulance landing in the grounds of the school on Munster Road, more police officers, Helen and Vida ushered into Richard Hughes' front room, Helen watching out of the window as the street came alive, people appearing on their balconies, coming out of their front doors, talking on mobiles, Helen watching them, imagining they were calling the press, those residents, shaking Helen's faith in human nature, where were they when they could've seen something, some later reappearing in smart jackets, preening for the cameras, showing no dignity when Helen had tried so hard to be dignified, to keep it dignified and private for Jill, dignity, discretion and respect, for her family and for Alan.

Helen heard the emergency crew working on Jill, trying to save her and thought that perhaps she really was still alive and then worried that she could have done something sooner and wished she had gone beyond the gate and given the kiss of life, or at least put Jill in the recovery position, or something – anything. When they saw her being taken to the ambulance her hand had regained its colour, and Vida said, 'My God, there must be hope.'

The police asked a few questions, not many, and then Helen went with Vida back to Charlotte's to have a cup of tea. As they walked away a detective came running up and said, 'Have you any idea how to get hold of the family?' Helen swung round and said, 'Haven't you done that yet? Alan Farthing, gynaecologist, St Mary's.'

When she left Charlotte's, Helen went back to the police cordon and asked a uniformed officer to tell a detective that they should also call Jill's agent. As she walked home along Sidbury Street she felt very alone, so she called her best friend and cried so much she couldn't speak and her friend said she was on her way.

Seven

Jill lived in digs when she first moved to Exeter, with a landlady, Mrs Mather. As Jack recalled, the Baptist minister had helped to make the arrangements, which put Jean's mind at rest about Jill leaving. She lodged there for six months but then wanted some further independence, without living entirely alone. A colleague from the radio station, Gill Capewell, offered her a room as a tenant and Jill moved in with Gill when she returned to Exeter after her mother's death.

Gill was a producer at BBC Radio Devon, ten years older than Jill, defiantly passionate about radio, to the extent that she did not even have a television in her house. After a few weeks Jill said, would you mind if I brought in a television and 'you should've seen the look of horror on Gill's face', but she said, no she didn't mind. The television arrived and from then on Jill would sit watching the six o'clock news in the front room, while Gill sat in the kitchen listening to the six o'clock news on BBC Radio 4.

Gill knew that people sometimes struggled to make the switch from print to broadcast journalism, because it was a different style of writing and required a whole new set of technical skills but Jill seemed to pick it up quickly and her voice just went straight down the microphone – a natural broadcaster's gift. It was apparent to Gill that her tenant and colleague was very determined and ambitious, though she could not imagine her ever climbing on others' backs to get ahead, as some people did in that business. Jill worked hard, set high standards for herself and, above all, hated to get things wrong, was always slightly worried that her work might not be quite good enough.

Even in the aftermath of her mother's death, Jill's joy of life seemed intact to Gill. She was fun to be around, her sense of fun was infectious. It was a sociable, open-plan newsroom and groups of them would often go to the Mill on the Exe on a Friday night, the group invariably including most if not all of the four Jills or Gills who then worked there.

Jill Dando had big hair, a curly perm, and loved shopping for clothes in the local high-street stores. Gill Capewell was not much of a clothes shopper and would sometimes hear Jill arriving home with a rustle of bags, dashing up the stairs to her room. 'What have you got there?' Gill would say.

'Oh, nothing,' Jill would call back from the stairs, as if she felt guilty at the self-indulgence.

She seemed old for her age, quite conservative, old-fashioned. Gill could imagine her saving herself for the right man, the man she would marry, for whom, it appeared to Gill, she was already searching. Jill had a few casual relationships and several more admirers but nothing of apparent significance ever happened.

Though Jill was very upset one night after she had been out for

Mother and baby,
Jean and Jill Dando.

The Dando family:
Jack, Nigel, Jean
and Jill.

Jill's childhood in Weston.

The changing faces – and hairstyles – of Jill Dando.

Jill and her best friend Jenny Higham on holiday in Greece in 1988.

Jill with Jenny's daughter Emma, aged six weeks, in the summer of 1994.

Jill and her cousin
Judith Dando on
holiday in Majorca in
1998.

A 1991 promotional
shot for Jill's first
series, *Safari UK*,
which she co-
presented with
Julian Pettifer.

With News
colleague Nicholas
Witchell (*left*) and
Crimewatch co-host
Nick Ross (*below*).

Jill with Bob
Wheaton and Jenny
Higham and her
husband, Ed Naylor.
Marlow Hotel, New
Year's Day 1993.

Jill and Jan Knott.
They met on a
Holiday trip to
Jordan in 1996.

Jill was always willing to lend her support to the people and causes, past and present, close to her heart. At a missionary supper in Tunbridge Wells with Philip Gathercole, formerly minister at Milton Baptist Church in Weston (*above*), and with Jane Lush and Eamonn Holmes at a charity dinner at Claridge's (*below*).

dinner, her first date with a local television presenter from Plymouth, a man with whom she was quite smitten. They had been to an expensive restaurant in Plymouth and the man was driving her home and she felt queasy and had to ask him to stop the car so that she could step out to be sick at the roadside. She felt foolish and embarrassed and Gill Capewell could see that she was still quite young in some ways, trying hard to be grown up.

Jill and Gill went on holiday together a couple of times, to Albufeira and Menorca. Jill lay on the beach in the sun, reading light fiction such as Jeffrey Archer, while Gill got restless and hot and went exploring.

Back in Exeter, Gill signed up with a dating agency and Jill sometimes answered the phone to her callers to vet them, putting on a Birmingham accent and pretending to be Gill while she interviewed them.

For her twenty-fifth birthday she held a joint party with a Plymouth-based colleague in a hired room at the Happy Eater on Haldon Hill, on the road south from Exeter. She was the victim of a Gorillagram.

During this period, Jill revived her relationship with Andrew Ray, her friend from the Weston Courts. Andrew was aware that Jill's mother had died, just as he had been grappling with a family trauma of his own, a brother who had been diagnosed as schizophrenic, which was a tremendous strain.

Andrew could tell that Jill had changed, emerged from a shadow, almost, becoming more her own person and, most significantly for him, becoming more open and physical and uninhibited.

She would call in to see him at his flat in Bristol and sometimes stay for weekends. Again it seemed rather a private relationship, no one else involved, no going out in groups or foursomes. They spent a lot of time alone in the flat and on one occasion they exchanged locks of hair and Andrew kept Jill's, sealing it in a small wrap of cellophane.

He was really in love with her now and ready, he thought, to make some commitment, although the very fact that he was ready to make a commitment made him vulnerable and nervous. He could see that Jill's career was taking off and didn't know where that might take her. He had been hurt before, in the ending of a long relationship, and didn't want it to happen again. He did however consider marrying Jill, or proposing in the hope that she would wish to marry him. They even discussed children, which they both wanted.

Andrew remembered that they celebrated his twenty-seventh birthday together, just the two of them, in February 1987 and he then went skiing with his cousins. He was sitting on a T-lift on 3 March 1987 – he could specifically recall this because it was the day *The Herald Of Free Enterprise* capsized – being ribbed by his favourite cousin about his love life and telling her that he had met someone and was thinking of getting married, but was worried about it.

He came back from the holiday and went to a dinner party and met another woman and moved in with her almost immediately and ended up marrying her instead, a year later.

Shortly before his marriage, Andrew went to see Jill, who was by now living in London with her cousin Judith. With hindsight he knew exactly what he was doing, which was making a final check to ensure that he was not marrying the wrong woman. He and Jill went for a drink at the Star and Garter pub in Richmond and then Jill drove them across London for a Chinese meal in Islington. Even at the time Andrew thought this was a hell of a long way to go for a Chinese meal.

They talked lightly about their recent relationships and Jill said that Andrew would be surprised at her. 'You wouldn't believe what a tart I've been,' she said, more in play than self-criticism, it seemed to Andrew.

After the meal they drove back across London and Andrew stayed the night at Jill's home, though they slept apart. In the morning they were talking in the garden, by the goldfish pond, and Andrew mentioned then, having carefully avoided it the previous night, that he was about to get married. Jill was cross and pushed him backwards so that he slipped into the goldfish pond and got one leg wet. Andrew left the house immediately, and walked away with one shoe squelching.

Andrew, who had first qualified as a barrister, became a successful criminal solicitor with his own partnership in Bristol. He did not hear from Jill again and did not contact her either. Then, around Christmas 1998, she pulled up alongside him in her car while he was waiting at a junction in Weston. He was in a daydream and didn't notice her at first until she said, 'Are you going to ignore me again, Mr Ray?' They got out and chatted for twenty minutes and Jill said she'd love to meet some 'villains', some of his clients – alleged villains, of course – and find out what made them tick. Maybe she'd write a book one day, when she threw in the towel as a presenter. She suggested he could take her to a prison with him when he went to meet a client. Andrew's response was that taking Jill Dando the *Crimewatch* presenter into a prison was not such a great idea. It would lose him clients, make him seem like a copper's nark.

During their friendship Jill had written a number of letters to Andrew, all of which he destroyed, except one, which amused him because she described leaving Sainsbury's with a bag of potatoes under her arm which she had forgotten to pay for, a most un-Jill-like thing to do. 'Their store detectives can't be up to much, that's all I can say.'

In the same letter, dated 30 October 1986, she told him that she was presenting the breakfast show three days a week for Radio Devon, and reporting and producing the rest of the time. She had decided it was time to see how the land lay at BBC TV in Plymouth, and had just that day been down there for a chat with the manager, which had been one of the most encouraging conversations she'd had for some time. The manager had said that he would be very interested in considering Jill for presentation and reporting work, though there weren't any presenting vacancies just then, and a reporter's job would depend on the readiness of her boss in radio to release her. 'So wheels may be moving at last!'

While she was waiting for BBC TV Plymouth, Jill applied for a job with the regional ITV network, then called Television South-West, TSW. She was taken on by the regional newsroom early in 1987 and, within a few weeks, the job at the BBC came along. After a brief wrestle with her conscience she jumped back from ITV to the BBC, where she first presented the daytime regional bulletins, the opt-outs that then preceded the national news.

Gill Capewell remembered that the BBC Radio Devon newsroom came briefly to a halt on the day that Jill did her first opt-out, while they all watched her performance on their screens. When she had finished the radio newsroom applauded because it looked as if she had been reading bulletins on television all her life; she was inexperienced, obviously, but she looked as though she belonged, as if this was always what she was meant to do.

It had been the same that summer when she had gone for her television audition at Plymouth. No thoughts of Mary Poppins now.

Suzanne Yates, later a good friend of Jill's, was also visiting that day and would shortly begin work there as an RJ, a regional journalist. She watched Jill's audition along with the rest of the staff. Suzanne had once had her own audition and had been very frightened and completely wooden. She was destined for a career off screen.

Jill had so much hair that it practically obscured her eyes, but she stood out so noticeably among the contenders that the staff just said, 'It's her, isn't it? It's her.'

Later, Suzanne was with Jill when she was presenting the regional segment of the 1987 *Children in Need*. She saw that Jill was talking to the camera as if it were a person. As Suzanne well knew, this wasn't as easy as Jill made it look. Jill later told her that as a child she used to read the news to herself in front of a mirror.

One lunchtime they nipped into Boots in Plymouth and a passerby recognised Jill. Jill really liked that. Suzanne thought Jill was just dying to be famous. She reached out for it and was driven by that ambition.

Even though Jill was a genial member of the sociable group of people who worked there, Suzanne felt that she was very slightly aloof; setting herself apart. Suzanne said it was the best time of her career. They had such a laugh in the newsroom that the elves must have written the bulletins.

By a great stroke of good fortune Jill had been at BBC TV Plymouth a few weeks when the main presenter of the evening news programme, *Spotlight*, suddenly left after ten years, and Jill replaced her. This raised her profile both in Plymouth and at TV Centre in London, where the BBC was then engaged in a trawl of regional talent.

Suzanne Yates went for an interview of her own in London early in 1988 and was asked how they were coping down in

Plymouth since the old presenter had left. She said that Plymouth was coping very well, thank you, with its new young presenter Jill Dando.

Pete Baylis, who was still in regular contact with Jill at this time, is the only person who thinks that Jill actually applied for an advertised job in London. Everyone else says that she was simply noticed and admired and plucked out of little-league Plymouth to join the grown-ups in London on *Breakfast News*.

Pete can distinctly remember Jill applying for a job in London. Maybe it was a different job at a different time. Maybe it was to join *Breakfast News*. It only matters in the way that Jill's career would become mythologised. It was as if she did nothing to further herself; as if she only had to sit back and allow others to notice her and propel her onward.

Still, after five years on a local paper, the sudden acceleration of her career was remarkable. Programme assistant, local radio reporter, local radio presenter, regional television newsreader, regional television presenter, *Breakfast News* newsreader, in just over two years.

Jill had left Gill Capewell's home and bought her own modern house in Ivybridge, near Plymouth, a once-pretty village on the southern edges of Dartmoor now being developed as a Plymouth overspill. The cost of the house was £38,000.

Jack remembers it as a lovely spot, a row of houses with a big green at the front, with high trees. He helped Jill to furnish the house, giving her some money to buy furniture, a pine table and four chairs for the kitchen.

When Jill began working in television, Jack had to get a special aerial fitted to his own home so that he could see her broadcasts from way over there in Plymouth. The fitter told him that he needed a high gain aerial, because the signal was blocked by nearby Worlebury Hill; it wouldn't be a perfect picture, Jack was told, but it was good enough. At least he could still see the television: nowadays he relies on the radio and talking books.

Jill had come home most weekends during her mother's illness and still kept in regular contact with Jack. He went down to stay with her at Ivybridge one weekend and they discussed her job offer in London. She was on a seesaw, Jack could tell. She had obviously taken one of her straw polls because she told Jack that some people were telling her to go while others were saying that if she was happy, why change?

Jack thought she ought to take the chance. 'Look Jill,' he said to her, 'it's up to you, but if you stay here in Plymouth there's nowhere else to go. If you go to London, goodness knows where you could end up. It's wide open for you, if you're good enough.'

That was part of Jill's problem. The self-doubt. Was she good enough? Was she ready? She didn't think she had enough experience; she felt she had more to learn before she went to London, although that was where she eventually wanted to be. Gill Capewell said, 'Well, if they want you this badly now, they'll probably want you this much again in the future.'

In March 1988 Gill and Jill went on a skiing holiday in a big group organised by a friend and colleague, Ben Bradshaw, later a BBC correspondent and MP and now a government minister. The coach stopped at Earl's Court to pick up a couple of extra people and one of these was Jenny Higham, who knew almost nobody on the trip apart from Ben, an old schoolfriend. She had just ended a relationship and was at a bit of a loose end, which was why she went skiing.

During the journey, Ben said to Jenny, 'You'll probably be sharing a room with these two,' those two being Jill and Gill.

They had a great time and got to know each other very well. They would lie in bed late at night having intimate conversations about 'love and death and everything'.

Jenny heard all about Jill's mother, and how she felt that she had lost not only her mother but her sister and her best friend. One night when they were talking about this Jill began sobbing and Jenny started to apologise for upsetting her but Gill said, 'no I think you should ask her, you should talk about it because there are so few people she does talk about it to.'

Jill told Jenny that she had turned down the big job offer in London and had decided to stay where she was in Plymouth. After the skiing holiday, Jenny went down to the West Country for a reunion. By then Jill had obviously changed her mind. Now she was again thinking of coming to London, though she seemed almost distressed by the ambivalence she felt towards the move. 'I suppose at least you'll be there as well,' said Jill.

'OUR JILL GETS TOP TELLY JOB', wrote the *Weston Mercury* in May 1988.

Perhaps the greater influence on Jill's decision was the presence in London of her cousin Judith, who proposed that Jill move in with her.

They had met up when Jill came to London for her BBC interview. Judith was working at an advertising agency in Paddington, and gave Jill a guided tour round the office. It was a buzzy and creative place which seemed to enthrall and overawe Jill. To Judith, she seemed the same rural cousin she had always been.

Judith had served in the Falklands with the Army. Captain Dando, based at British Forces headquarters. When she was being transferred back to an MoD role at Earl's Court in London she got hold of a tube map – not a common commodity in the Falklands – and tried to work out where she'd like to live. Fulham seemed ideal, but when she arrived there she quickly realised it was too expensive. Out came the tube map again, and Judith looked at Putney, but that was too expensive as well. She asked the estate agent where she ought to be looking with the money she had to spend and the estate agent said, 'If I were you I'd try Southfields or Tooting.' So Judith went further out to Southfields, where she bought a two-bedroomed flat.

Judith, who was energetic and very organised, now suggested to Jill that they sell their two properties and pool their resources to buy a house together on the Grid, the smarter part of Southfields, where Judith aspired to live. For the first few months, however, Jill lived in the box room of Judith's flat, which was really very cramped with little hanging space. Not that this mattered particularly because Jill had so few clothes, or at least, so few clothes that were suitable.

She arrived from Plymouth with her Dorothy Perkins wardrobe and Judith, who was well established in her new London life and then earning more than Jill, soon found herself more or less dressing Jill for her daily appearances on breakfast television. It was fortunate that they were of a similar build and prone to similar fluctuations in weight. Jill wore a lot of Judith's shirts. Not only did Jill have a very limited wardrobe she didn't have much dress sense, either, or so it seemed to Judith.

When they went up to the Grid one day for tea with a girlfriend of Judith's who had moved there, she told them about some neighbours who were thinking of moving. Judith and Jill went along, knocked on the door and asked, 'Are you selling your house?'

'Maybe,' was the reply. 'It depends how much you are offering. Come back tomorrow.'

When Judith and Jill returned they were told that the asking price was £162,000. It was a four-bedroomed property with a loft conversion and the longest garden in the street, but even so it seemed extortionate. Judith and Jill had agreed on a limit of £140,000 but they both really liked the house. They went into Wimbledon and sat down over a plate of pasta to discuss it. They agreed to put in a once-only offer and to pull out if it was turned down. They offered £158,000, which was accepted. Judith took a 60 per cent share and Jill the other 40 per cent.

Unhappily, especially for Judith, this was nearing the height of the property boom, approaching the bust, and when they sold the house some six years later it was worth only £130,000. It makes Judith sick even now to think about that loss and what the house might have been worth if she had been able to buy out Jill's 40 per cent share to keep it on for herself.

They moved in, and Jill bought all her furniture up from Plymouth. Judith remembers her tasselled lampshades from British Home Stores and that Jill was very keen on the style evoked by *The Country Diary of an Edwardian Lady*, a book which was all the rage at that time.

Jill was up and out before dawn every morning and off to work, and by the time Judith came home in the evening she would be sitting in front of the television in her dressing gown with her feet up. They might share a glass of wine, or Judith might change and go out to the gym. By the time she came home Jill would by laying out her clothes – or Judith's clothes – preparing for the morning. She would watch the news, read the papers and be most obsessive about getting her sleep.

If Judith had friends round for supper and there was music play-ing, however quietly, Jill would be down the stairs in a strop. 'Jude, Jude, I'm trying to sleep. I've got work tomorrow morning.' Judith would be thinking, oh God. Sometimes they'd have real shouting matches to clear the air, just as Judith might with her sisters.

When Jill met Judith's friends they would say to her, 'It must be great working on *Breakfast*, but what time do you have to get up?'

'Oh, it's absolutely dreadful. I have to get up at four o'clock every day, and it's such hard work, and I've got no social life.' Judith would be listening as Jill went on, seething, thinking, she works three hours a day. I come home and she's been sitting there all afternoon with her feet up, eating chocolate.

Lots of chocolate and biscuits were consumed in their house-hold. Jill would eat out of boredom and, of course, for comfort. In those early days, before her own London life really began, Jill would come home and watch the recording she had made of that morning's programme. She would pick at some food and mope, and put on weight and pick at more food.

When she looks back, Judith can see that Jill was unhappy and lonely and missing her mother and almost everything else she had left behind in Plymouth and Weston – her home, her family, her friends. Later, Judith wondered how Jill coped so brilliantly doing so much when she had coped so badly doing so little.

At the time, Judith realised, she was unsympathetic, so busy herself that she wasn't any help to Jill. She couldn't see why Jill was so lonely, couldn't see why she was still missing her mother after two years. Even as her life blossomed Jill still seemed sorry for her-self, and Judith had little patience with self-pity.

To Judith, who had travelled extensively and was always open to new experiences, Jill appeared so conservative. The idea of smoking dope, for example, horrified Jill. Judith could never imagine Jill ever puffing on a joint. She would just about tolerate people smoking cigarettes in the house, but preferred it if they went outside.

Judith did try to involve Jill in her social life. She introduced her to her friends, some of whom Jill briefly dated. They used to go to the Hand in Hand pub on Wimbledon Common, where they mixed with a diverse crowd of people: a policeman, a pilot, builders, plumbers. Some of them were a little wayward, and Judith sensed that Jill was uncomfortable in their company.

There was a night when one of the young men, who was a bit of a wheeler-dealer, though his father was an officer in the Parks Police, was drunk at the wheel of his BMW. When he noticed a police car following him he sped away and went straight across a roundabout and killed two people.

The man went to prison, and even though he had done a terrible thing, Judith had some sympathy for him because she could imagine how he must feel. Jill, on the other hand, was horrified at the idea that someone she knew, not only knew but liked, had killed two people and gone to prison.

There were things Judith didn't tell Jill, or involve her in, because she knew that her own liberal ideas were not shared by Jill, who could be quite the puritan at times. Judith had a dinner party one night for her single friends, five young women and five young men, while Jill was away. It was a brilliant evening. Everyone was wrecked and several stayed the night in couples, one pair in Jill's bed.

Judith changed the sheets the next day, but when she said to Jill, 'I hope you don't mind, but somebody slept in your bed,' Jill angrily replied, 'Well who was it, was it you?' Judith said no but Jill was really miffed that it had happened. Ever afterwards, when

Jill was going to be away, she would say to Judith: 'Now, you can sleep in my bed, but nobody else can.'

Observing the Southfields' house from a distance, Jenny Higham thinks it took Judith a while to recognise that Jill was becoming successful and beginning to be famous, and not just doing some silly part-time job for a few hours every morning. Maybe that was right. Judith said she never imagined Jill progressing much beyond *Breakfast*, always envisaged her being stuck in small-time television. She didn't seem to want to shake the world, and never gave Judith the impression that she was very ambitious. She had not yet flourished, and Judith could never have foreseen how Jill would change. She saw no more than Jill careering around the West Country opening fêtes, making her first personal appearances as a very minor celebrity, accepting every offer that came along and being pleased to do so. She once opened Judith's friend's flower shop in Clapham and was chuffed to receive a bouquet by way of thanks.

Nicholas Witchell recalls Jill, up from Plymouth for the day, sitting in for the afternoon at the *Six O'Clock News*, which he then presented with Sue Lawley, as number two to her number one. Number one opened the programme and read the headlines.

The editor of the *Six O'Clock News* was then Bob Wheaton, a man greatly respected by Nicholas for his skills. He was a craftsman, he understood television news and he had helped to create the current two-handed *Six*, along with senior colleagues Ron Neil and Tony Hall. Like Nicholas, Bob came from a hard-news background, and would be suspicious of the airy-fairy arena of currents affairs. They were, as Nicholas would put it, frightful old hacks and also, perhaps, they were a little caught up in their own importance.

Nicholas had been presenting the *Six* since 1984, when he had been virtually frogmarched into the office and told he was being brought back from Ireland, where he was then at the end of the first year of his first big posting as a correspondent. 'I don't want to do it,' he had said. The then editor had said, 'You are going to do it.' Nicholas always hankered after a return to the life of a correspondent.

That day, there was a charming young woman sitting in the office, though it was not quite clear why she was there. Bob, as Nicholas recalled, was his usual attentive self – he could be charming, too.

Later that year, Sue Lawley gave up newsreading and Nicholas became the main presenter with Anna Ford. Soon it would be Peter Sissons and Anna Ford, Nicholas having been made another offer he couldn't refuse.

Breakfast Time, as it was then called, was regarded as a poor relation of the other news programmes. The opportunity of longer time on air weighed heavily against the smaller audiences and the softer approach. It was an uneasy hybrid of sofas and hard seats, having two presenters and a separate newsreader, known in the jargon of the business as a modular format. Jill had been brought in to read the bulletins, the 'news belts' – as they were called. An opt-out role, in effect, not unlike her early work in Plymouth, except, of course that now the stories were national and international and not parochial.

Bob Wheaton went out for lunch with his boss, Tony Hall, to the Japanese restaurant in the Kensington Hilton. Tony had once been Bob's deputy and was on his way to becoming Head of News. Bob could not take all the credit for reinventing the *Six* but it had put the *Nine* on its mettle and was thought to have been a success.

Tony would tell Bob that he had the magic, and that they wanted him to use it elsewhere. 'It's not all magic,' Bob argued. 'It's hard work and a bit of ability, too.'

Over lunch Tony asked Bob to tell him what was wrong with *Breakfast Time*. That was easy, Bob said: the programme had drifted, despite the presence of talents such as Jeremy Paxman, Sally Magnusson and Kirsty Wark. Tony told Bob he wanted him to go there and work his magic. Bob, who had no immediate desire to work on *Breakfast*, felt trapped and outmanoeuvred, perhaps flattered into it, Bob and his magic.

Breakfast did not have the greatest reputation as a place for career development. On the other hand, it was a place to experiment and bring on talent; work with a bigger team and oversee considerably more air-time. A place where Bob really might work his magic. Bob believed in analysis, news and background. Journalism without analysis was a waste of time; a story with a few facts thrown in, a scattergun technique, had no impact at all. It was, he said, to coin a phrase, a bias against understanding, a famous phrase as Bob well knew, first uttered a decade earlier in an article co-authored by Peter Jay and John Birt, who was now the deputy director-general of the BBC, reshaping the Corporation's approach to news and current affairs according to his soundbite philosophy.

At the *Six* Bob had helped to develop the style of stories backed up by explanatory pieces, maybe three or four different angles on the same event: the analysis. That was his brief for *Breakfast*, to add some beef. Bring on the heavyweights.

He was to swap jobs with Dave Stanford, the editor who had brought Jill to London. Bob was anxious about how this move would be announced, about what it meant and how it might be interpreted. 'What's up with the *Six*?' he had asked Tony Hall.

'Don't you like it?' It was vanity, too: was he up or was he down? He was relieved to hear that Dave Stanford's brief was to leave the *Six* unchanged. He made sure *that* would be part of the announcement.

A little later Bob took Nicholas Witchell out for a curry. He wanted Nicholas to come to *Breakfast*. Nicholas was not keen at first, not at all, and he took some persuading. Tony Hall spoke to him about it as well. Nicholas was outmanoeuvred too.

Bob began at *Breakfast* that December, 1988, and began to consider the possibilities. He had been watching Jill's progress in the newsroom before he moved on from the *Six*, watching her from his desk, seeing her side-on, noting the way she held herself, her back and her neck, the way her shoulders moved, both professional and totally natural, talking to the camera in a natural way.

Some people were like stunned mullets. Bob had worked with all of them, and he knew how hard it was. He certainly wasn't a natural himself, and he had decided early on that he was not suited to an on-screen role. He looked for a triangle, eyes, brain and mouth: the triangle of understanding which, if it was missing in a presenter, left just a glazed expression. All the good presenters had it, and Jill had it, too.

He could see she needed channelling and guidance because she was just a young kid, just arrived, her steel had not yet been tempered by years of experience, as it had with Bob and others, such as Nicholas.

Of course, it helped that Jill had looks, but she could still have been a good presenter even if she had been plainer. Though it was true that she might have been better suited to radio. There were plenty of non-lookers on television – Alastair Burnet, Robin Day for example – but not many of them were women. Well, Kate Adie, perhaps, or Anne Robinson.

Jill was a country girl, she needed grooming, and Bob believed in grooming. That BBC culture of not worrying too much about appearance, especially among the university-educated types, who thought it was too American, Bob didn't agree with that at all. Viewers expected you to be well groomed when you came into their homes. Bob himself was well groomed, always. 'You spend more time on your hair than I do,' Jill would tease him later.

He remembered the old values, an old Yorkshireman in the newsroom, effing this, effing that, 'I'm not effing thinking about what we're effing wearing.' That was how it used to be but it was changing, because appearance did matter.

Bob began to experiment with the formula in advance of the relaunch of *Breakfast*. Early on he sat in the canteen with Jill and told her he had a vision of how the programme would take shape. He knew which people were going to present it, and she was one of them. Jill must've gone off and told Jeremy Paxman, or somebody who was making mischief, because it got back to Ron Neil, and Bob was in trouble for blabbing his mouth off.

Bob told Jill, 'You have to get wise, you're in London now. This is a big bad place, there are people around who will take advantage of you personally, physically, socially and professionally. Yes, it is, or can be, a horrible place. I'm a Zimbabwean, I know about these things.'

In some ways, Bob felt that he and Jill were kindred spirits, Weston being almost as far from London as Harare in cultural terms. They were both outsiders, they had an affinity.

Bob looked for ways of moving Jill up, giving her a more prominent role. Despite his early assurances, she was terrified that she was going to be left out. He tried her in a light arts segment which would have given her fifteen minutes in the back half of the programme. It didn't go well in rehearsals, and after one run-through he saw her disappear into the loo in tears, clearly afraid for her future.

Then Jeremy Paxman was going off to *Newsnight*, Sally Magnusson was pregnant, Kirsty Wark was moving on, opportunities were opening up.

Bob would've been happy with Jeremy but it would've been a very different programme. He was not disciplined in the way that Nicholas Witchell was. Nicholas wrote the material and delivered the goods. Jeremy was a great presenter, a great interviewer, but he didn't like reading the autocue. With him it was blood on the carpet first thing in the morning. 'So you've made a mess of this, Minister,' was a favourite opening line.

Bob was doing a different show now, a two-hour version of the *Six* — rolling news, a precursor of all the digital, cable, satellite rolling news channels to come — and by the time the programme was relaunched in 1989, *Breakfast News* had Nicholas Witchell as number one presenter and Jill Dando as number two.

In his pep talks, Bob had told Jill that she had to play the game, to use people — well, not use them, exactly, but she needed to network. There were always people out there who could help you. Later, he could imagine that his BBC colleagues would be saying that this was exactly what Jill had done with him. He could almost hear the gossip, as gossip there certainly was, 'Well, she knew what she was doing all right, getting hooked up with Bob Wheaton. He can assure her career.'

But that was not how it was. Not at all. Even if he had wanted to, Bob couldn't simply promote someone because he fancied her.

It wasn't unusual for producers to become close to their presenters — especially those producers who were passionate about their programmes, who watched their presenters from behind a screen, watched and admired them and the way they marshalled the material and commanded the programme.

Bob felt that with them all, men and women. These were the people who were doing your bidding. You were helping them, putting your experience into play, relying on their talent, talking to them, lunching with them, being with them, launching new things with them and it might sound terrible to then go off and have an affair with them but it wasn't so surprising, either.

And from day one Bob had looked at Jill and thought, my God, this is the person I've been waiting for. The relationship did not develop for a long time, so in some ways he had been really rather well behaved, just put it to one side and decided, sorry, I'm getting on with the work.

Of course, Bob was fourteen years older than Jill.

Both Jenny Higham and Judith heard all about Bob from Jill long before the relationship began. Judith was told how dishy he was, immaculately turned out, beautifully dressed, clean and crisp and well-coiffed. Jill told her they flirted on the internal mail, good morning and how are you today, and all that kind of thing.

'Nice bloke at work, da-di-da-di-da,' as Jenny put it. She heard about his past, his son, his earlier relationships, the two previous marriages. Jenny knew Jill was keen, that Bob wouldn't have to carry her off kicking and screaming.

Jill called her one day and said that Bob had suggested they go out for a picnic together by the river. Jenny heard about it blow by blow and there was a shall-I-or-shan't-I moment of embarkation, which passed and that was the beginning of Bob and Jill. The beginning of the second significant relationship in Jill's life after her relationship with her mother.

Jenny felt that Jill was ready for a longer partnership at this point – that she was not in it for marriage so much as stability after a long period of playing singles and a number of brief outings with friends and friends of friends and colleagues and friends of colleagues.

For all the loneliness and uncertainty that she continued to feel, it was a sociable world that Jill moved into as she emerged from her shell in Southfields. Jenny went to quite a few parties there, dinner parties, lunch parties and all-out parties with a rich mix of people.

Jenny met Jeremy Paxman in Southfields. He and Jill went out together briefly and sustained a friendship as colleagues over the years, even though Jill publicly credited him with teasing her with the nickname WPC Dando, which, privately, she found hurtful.

Jenny was then a junior doctor, doing research into blood loss during the menstrual cycle. Jill wondered if Jeremy might like to date Jenny. 'Good God, no,' he said. 'I couldn't possibly go out with somebody who handled used tampons all day.'

Jill had spoken to Judith of her time in Plymouth and how she had been out with a number of different boyfriends. Judith formed the impression that she was not entirely proud of this but, at the same time she quite enjoyed it too, had been getting something out of her system. Some repression, perhaps.

In London, too, now and later, Jill had a number of partners. The margins often blurred, the dates overlapping, Judith and Jenny not always knowing which were sexual relationships and which were not. They didn't necessarily ask, and Jill didn't necessarily tell them.

She was not particularly secretive about her love life, but she could be quite compartmentalised about what information she disclosed and to whom she disclosed it.

I did not attempt to compile a definitive list of partners but sought out those relationships that seemed of significance, that might reveal something about Jill and her changing attitudes and values and approach to life. This was sometimes a delicate area.

In 1992 Jill wrote a letter to Liz Johnston-Keay in Weston in which she described, almost in passing, a flirtation with Andrew Morton, the author of the famous books about Diana, Princess of Wales, and other members of the royal family. It dated from the year before she began seeing Bob. 'We had a rather nice three months until quite rightly he decided his family mattered to him,' she wrote. 'I wasn't heartbroken, why should I be or have a right to be?'

A BBC colleague recalled Andrew Morton being a guest on *Breakfast Time* and Jill going out with him afterwards. Jill told the colleague he had asked her out and that she was in two minds about how to proceed.

When I spoke to Andrew and told him what Jill had written in her letter he said she was exaggerating. They had had lunch sometimes, to talk about work, but that was all. He remembered that he had first been interviewed by her while she was still in the provinces and he was on a promotional tour in the West Country for one of his books.

Later, after his first book about Diana had been published, he bumped into Jill one day in the West End, in her car. He got in and she drove around the block while they talked. He subsequently discovered that a fellow journalist had seen him getting into Jill's BMW and got very excited, believing that he had caught Andrew in a liaison with Princess Diana.

Jill told Bob about going away for the weekend with an unnamed television colleague. It was like one of those huntin'-shootin'-fishin' weekends and Jill felt, or was made to feel, uncomfortable, out of her depth, as if she didn't know how to dress or behave. She was insecure and, as Bob says, people could be quite savage in those situations. All that class stuff: where do you come from? What school did you go to?

Maybe a part of Bob identified with that too which was why he remembered it.

One of their *Breakfast* colleagues, Anastasia Cooke was going out with and later married James Baker, son of the former newsreader Richard Baker. James and Anastasia were friendly with Prince Edward, and he and his girlfriend Sophie Rhys-Jones sometimes came to supper. One night Anastasia invited Bob and Jill to join them. She told Jill that there was no strict protocol for the evening, except that they must arrive before the royalty, which was socially correct, and that Jill should curtsey on being introduced, which was just a tease.

When Anastasia looked out of her window, long before the guests were due to arrive, there were Bob and Jill, already sitting waiting in their car. Jill did a little curtsey when she was finally introduced.

Jill loved royalty and was thrilled to meet it socially, though she eventually got a little fed up with Diana and the Duchess of York. At first Diana was 'poor Diana' to Jill, but then compassion fatigue must have set in, and she would refer to the Princess as being rather irritating, with all her problems. And as for that disreputable Duchess, well ... One Christmas, Jill was asked by a newspaper to contribute her New Year wishes. Jill wished that Sarah Ferguson would enter a convent, 'so I wouldn't have to read about her sexual activities any more'.

Any royal encounters she had were often described in her letters to Liz Johnston-Keay. Here was the Duchess of Kent at an awards dinner in 1992, with Jill seated next to her for the meal in her capacity as compère for the evening.

Life has been terrifically exciting of late. You mentioned in your letter the lovely Duchess of Kent. I agree, she is lovely. Bob and I met her a couple of weeks ago ... after initial awkwardness I relaxed and had quite a nice chat with her. She told me about her work with the hospices and how depressed it often makes her: 'So much so that I will often come home and if there's no one in the house or it's dark I'll go to the fridge and have a huge binge to take my mind off it,' she said. 'Then I feel even more depressed because I've eaten so much.' She was also talking about her daughter's forthcoming wedding and how she didn't think all the guests would fit in the marquee which holds 300. Oh, how the other half lives!

A little later she was writing to Liz in anticipation of the supper with Edward and Sophie.

Bob and I have been invited to dine with royalty on Monday evening! Anastasia Cooke is a reporter on *Breakfast News* and used to go out with Prince Edward. She's still very friendly with him and his new girlfriend and has invited us all to dinner at her flat. I don't know what to wear!! Anastasia says it's all very informal but we will be expected to call him Sir! It'll seem strange calling someone who's younger than me 'sir' but I suppose it's better than being dispatched to the Tower for disrespectful behaviour.

Jill used a lot of exclamation marks in her letters. They seem to have reflected the sense of wonder and excitement at the life she was leading. Who would've thought it! Just as anyone raised in ordinary circumstances with ordinary expectations might exclaim when events become extraordinary. It might seem gauche, describing your life in exclamation marks, but the pleasure was pure and true.

Jill often used to call Judith from her mobile phone for chats. Sometimes when she was driving herself, or being driven in the back of one of those comfortable Niven cars hired from Niven & Co., used to ferry the BBC's most important staff and guests to and from their assignments.

One night Jill called Judith on her way from Buckingham Palace from a charity function where she had just met Prince Andrew. Judith had met Prince Andrew too, in the Falklands. There had been some flirting between them. Judith would say that Prince Andrew liked women with blonde hair.

On this night, Jill reported, he had been flirting with her, Jill was being chatted up by Prince Andrew – exclamation marks were in her voice – and she told him about her cousin who had been in the Falklands. Andrew suddenly said, 'Oh, Judith!' Then an upper-crust woman had butted in on the conversation – 'Oh, Andrew, darling, how lovely to see you again. Remember when you stayed at our castle in Scotland?' – and Andrew had said, 'Now, when was that? I'm afraid I can't remember that.' Jill had been so chuffed that Andrew could not remember the posh woman with the castle but had remembered Judith. 'Well, that's it,' said Jill. 'That's two blonde Dandos he's flirted with now.'

Judith asked Jill where she was going. 'I'm on my way to meet Cliff for supper,' she had said.

'Jill, I don't believe it,' said Judith. Judith was just about to have an early night.

Back in 1989, Bob thought of Jill as being at the start of a journey. He helped to guide her, personally and professionally. Not just her lover and her friend but her mother too, in Jill's words.

Bob had been on the Hay Diet since the age of twenty-one and was perennially trim. He started Jill on the diet, too, and helped her to understand a balanced and nutritious pattern of eating: salads, fruit and vegetables, plenty of protein. She did not know how to eat, still less how to cook. She didn't really know how to look after herself at all.

They went out walking together by the river and later sometimes cycling. She started to lose weight and become toned.

Her style of dress was somewhat blowsy and overblown, even brassy. She was grappling for definition on screen. Bob considered, how do we define Jill?

At home they would sit together and look through the pages of a book called *The Kingshill British Designer Collection*, which depicted the current ranges of many fashion designers. They would see a style or a colour and say, 'Well, that would work,' or Bob would point out, 'This is a social one. You couldn't wear those bows on television. You have to look straightforward.' They chose blacks and pinstripes and blues. The television look had to be well groomed, authoritative, not too frivolous, not too fashionable; you could go too far with being fashionable.

They would select outfits from the book and then they would go shopping, to Brent Cross at first, where you could go through tons of clothes on the rails, and later to Harrods. Jill established contact with Louis Feraud. Bob said they made wonderful suits for Jill, lighter pastel colours, simple cuts, classic cuts; not too fussy; good shoulders, not too broad, nicely shaped; cloth that didn't crease. Bob would see nasty comments in the papers about Jill wearing crimplene and bri-nylon, but that just wasn't true. Her clothes were made of the finest cotton or wool that money could buy.

Bob tried to give Jill self-confidence, which he felt she lacked, and a sense of security, which she seemed to lack too. He thought she was prone to be slightly depressive, born not just of the ongoing sadness at her mother's death but also of her rather insular origins which perhaps made it hard for her to face the world on equal terms.

Others would say that, during this time, Jill went through a period in which she felt some embarrassment or shame or awkwardness about her Weston origins. They would say this cautiously, as if it implied a loss of respect for her family. But those kinds of feelings might be familiar to anyone who has moved on, or away, or up the social and professional scale. They might not be feelings of shame so much as conflict, a sense of being pulled one way and the other, caught between two worlds in the process of readjusting and resettling.

Jill wanted to be sophisticated, and there was not much about Weston that was sophisticated. Bob was sophisticated, or so it seemed to Jill. Other BBC colleagues were sophisticated, or seemed so to Jill and no doubt to themselves. They had come from and continued to occupy an entirely different sector of the social landscape where certainty and self-belief were part of the fine furniture. Jill did not have that in her house at home in Weston, and it was not an easy thing to acquire. You could not buy that kind of furniture in self-assembly flat packs.

Perhaps Jill felt or inherited some of the disappointment that her mother had felt; was out there on her mother's behalf, carrying a kind of social disappointment that made her seek out the very world that so intimidated her: royals, pop stars, Oxbridge intellects, celebrity and all.

And in time Jill was not just up there for her mother but for the whole of middle England. For Weston's England; for Liz Johnston-Keay and for *Daily Mail* readers all over the country and for the *Daily Mail* itself, whose values Jill so perfectly embodied and represented. The *Daily Mail* loved Jill, or the image of Jill which she conspired with them to create.

Bob had a big hand in that, understanding, as he did, the nature of television and especially of the BBC. He helped to define Jill, though he would stop short of saying that he created her.

In time, some colleagues would come to think of him as Jill's Svengali. Svengali was a character in a late nineteenth-century romantic novel by George du Maurier. The novel was titled after its tragic heroine, Trilby, who rises from low origins to become a fêted opera singer with the voice of an archangel. The voice deserts her on the death of her mentor, Svengali, a music conductor, portrayed in the book (with anti-semitic abandon) as a malevolent character who has, literally, controlled Trilby by casting a hypnotic spell over her.

The name passed into the language: Svengali is defined in the *Chambers English Dictionary* as 'a person who exerts total mental control over another, usually for evil ends'.

Bob was well aware of the sinister implications of the name and did not think the cap fitted. Yes, he was in the fortunate position of having some influence over Jill, but it was nothing like the older man grooming the young woman, keeping her at bay, controlling, manipulating the strings of his puppet. Theirs was a symbiotic relationship. They were going forward together.

There were a lot of presenters, Bob observed, who you couldn't say anything to because they were so arrogant. Their eyes would glaze over, and they wouldn't listen, they already knew it all and they didn't need any help.

While it was true that he played an important role, Bob did not want to take all the credit. Jill had already made and would continue to make many important decisions for herself. About her hair, for instance, the appearance of which she evolved with her hairdresser, Martyn Maxey.

She had first gone to Maxey while she was still in Plymouth, and he remained her hairdresser for the rest of her life. He was a young stylist at the beginning of his career who went on to open his own salons in Grosvenor Street and at the Harbour Club in Chelsea.

Jill came to him with her curly perm. Maxey proposed to cut it back because flouncy didn't work on television. Flouncy hair caught the light at the edges and looked slightly fuzzy, like a halo. He cut it back just a little at first, and then quite a lot, getting rid of the curls altogether.

Then he introduced highlights. Her natural colour was a mid-brown, a mousey brown. With colour it became a honey blonde, though he changed it often, ever so slightly. He changed the shape, too, always refining, looser and more glamorous later on, as she became more celebrated, never too square and rigid. An easy-care look, because Jill was travelling a lot and needed a style that was easy to look after. She came in every three months or so for colour, which was more often than most, but that was because in her job her appearance was so important.

Jill was a perfect client for Martyn, good for PR, generous at bandying his name about and recommending him to colleagues, such as Anna Ford. Anna is still a client of Martyn's. He saw them together once, in reception, chatting merrily away on the sofa.

Jill was never rude, always on time, or phoned if she was going to be late. She was always in transit, coming from one place, going to another. Martyn thought she seemed a little stressed towards the end, as if the pace was getting to her.

In 1996 Jill was voted female Head of the Year in the National Hairdressers' Federation awards. David Ginola was the male Head of the Year. Jill and Martyn went to the ceremony and Martyn was very proud because the awards carried some kudos, in his business, in the West End salons.

This was not an award Nicholas Witchell was ever likely to win. Tough young Nicholas, as Bob Wheaton described him. Older than his years, having authority beyond his years. Number one to Jill's number two on *Breakfast*. Nicholas wrote his own scripts, prepared and managed his own interviews and really cared about the product. He was the guy at the sharpest of sharp ends, as Bob put it. The rock of the programme.

It was Nicholas who would conduct the big political interviews, while Jill handled the slightly softer ones. You needed the tough journalism because people wanted to tune in to see the best news in the world from the BBC. So they would get Nicholas and then they would get Jill. Jill was attractive so people would see her and think – or so Bob hoped – gee, she's nice, this news doesn't sound half so horrible when she's reading it.

They were, in Bob's mind and creation, a finely balanced pair.

Bob was the editor in the gallery, which was like the pilot on the flight deck of the 747, that was how Bob thought of it, helping to fly his Jumbo, his programme, through the storms to bring it safely to the other side.

On the *Six* Bob always went in 10 per cent over, better to be covered and to drop packages off the schedule than be caught out if the link from Washington went down or any one of the hundred other possible mini crises occurred.

When it went wrong you relied on your presenters to smooth the transition, to disguise the hitch from the viewers so that what they saw was a seamless display of professional competence. Some people thought presenters were little more than ventriloquist's dummies whose only skill was the ability to read an autocue. The newspaper columnist Peter MacKay once wrote something disparaging about presenters in general. Bob rang him up and said, 'Come and see for yourself, come and sit in the gallery and watch it happen,' but the newspaperman wasn't interested.

MacKay would return to his theme later, with renewed barbs, following reports of Bob and Jill's separation, ridiculing Bob as a man so meticulous he ironed his own underpants. That was unfair, a reference to Bob having once said that when you were brought up in the tropics, as he had been, your clothes dried on lines in the sun and bugs settled in them, so if you didn't iron your underwear those bugs might burrow into your skin. So it was nothing to do with being meticulous.

As the editor Bob was meticulous about many things, especially about keeping abreast of the news, which was the core of his professional being, as it should be for anyone in that business, editors and journalists alike. In the BBC especially, where self-importance was part of the culture; pomposity trickled in its veins;

where television, the medium, could sometimes seem to matter more than the message itself.

Bob was a news junkie, 'a boring old news fart', in his own words, which echoed the words of Nicholas Witchell – they were frightful old hacks.

It was a bit of a joke, to Bob, the amount of reading matter that was delivered to his home, which he would get through every day. He wondered how he ever found time to read it. *Time*, *Newsweek*, the *Economist* were the foundation of his reading. Jill would read *Tatler*, or maybe flick through *The Times*, and Bob would urge her, as others did, 'Read the *Economist*, Jill. Just go through it and you'll know exactly what the issues are, what the questions are. The headlines will tell you what the story is and the little boxes contain the key facts. You don't have to read it from cover to cover.' When he had read the *Economist* himself Bob might say, look at this fascinating piece, to Jill, but she probably wouldn't read it. She just wasn't that interested. She had other things in her life.

Bob remembers arriving at work with Jill one morning in August 1991. It was a typical morning, when they would've got up at 2.30, 2.45 am. 'OK, chaps, what's happening?' he would've said to the newsroom as he walked in.

'There's a coup breaking in the Soviet Union.'

'Oh, right,' said Bob, 'give me another one.'

'No, seriously, it's a breaking story.'

Nicholas was away, up in Scotland, out of reach. Bob thought he was off hunting the Loch Ness monster, a subject on which he had written a book. He lived not far from work and normally, if anything was happening, he would've come in, even on his day off. Bob didn't think he ever slept.

So on the morning Gorbachev was overthrown, it was down to Jill to anchor the programme. Of course, she didn't know too much about Soviet political affairs and had never had to handle such a big story before. Some might have said – indeed, some of her critics did say – that it was risky, having someone who wasn't that committed to news in the anchor position, but Bob was trying to build Jill up gradually, to extend her experience. And anyway, this morning there was no choice.

It was one of those mornings, said Bob, where the story more or less wrote itself, as often happens with big events. The pictures come up, the facts unfold and the questions automatically occur. Jill would have stayed on open talkback, as any sensible presenter always did, listening through her ear piece, in contact with the gallery, listening to all the instructions and being fed cues and questions.

Bob was in the background, suggesting the angles, what came next. You wouldn't do that with Paxman; you wouldn't dare, and didn't need to, because he was so experienced.

Jill was no fool. She was trained as a journalist and could think and react quickly. She just needed a bit of help and that morning, Bob thought she did a damned good job. It was a seam-less display.

There were other mornings, though, that were not so happy; mornings when Jill would feel undermined and be distressed after-wards. Sometimes hurt by abrasions from Nicholas, who had his moments of pomposity. 'Oh Bobby, what shall I do?' Running on jet lag from the early starts, up since three, live for two hours, and feeling that she had failed or was not approved of.

Bob thinks that tiredness sometimes magnified the difficulties she felt she faced. 'Is this worth it?' she would ask. 'Can I do this?'

Bob would be critical with her, as he was critical with anyone else. He couldn't spoil her – she had to be told. When she tried too hard in interviews he would say to her, 'Just ask why?' When she was upset because Nicholas had rewritten the scripts, Bob would urge her, 'Just learn from Nick. Watch what he does, go to lunch with him, talk to him, see how he operates.' He knew that some producers were nervous, the sniffy, superior ones: is she going to mess up my story? He knew too that she won many of them over.

In the autumn of 1990, Bob and Jill arrived back at Southfields after an evening out to find the *Sun* on their doorstep. Or at least, this was how Judith remembered it. Drama at Heythorpe Street. 'It was a bit like that movie *Notting Hill*.'

She recalled Bob and Jill coming in, Jill saying, 'Don't go outside, there's press out there.' Then the doorbell rang and Bob went to answer it. 'I'll deal with this.'

A few nights later, Jill asked Judith: 'Have you seen our rubbish?' The bin bags were split open, their contents strewn all over the garden. 'Someone's been rifling our rubbish,' said Jill. An early example of the paranoia which would beset her later in her dealings with the press. She was sure it was the press. Judith thought it was a fox. She was sure she could see bite marks on the bags. Even so, it registered with her that Jill was becoming a bit of a celebrity.

'GOOD LAWLEY! BEEB BOSS IS AT IT AGAIN'. There was not much to the article under the headline but it took up a lot of space. In the centre was a passport-sized photo of Bob, looking particularly Svengali-like with a moustache and a fixed smile. Either side of him were much larger photographs of Sue Lawley (pictures every inch as unflattering as Bob's) and Jill, with a halo of frizzy hair, looking quite demure.

The tabloids had taken an interest in Bob's life before, in 1987, during his relationship with Sue Lawley. As he well knew, the prospect that he was 'at it again' with Jill was meat and drink to them.

As Bob remembered it, he and Jill had been doorstepped on their way to work, flashbulbs popping as they stepped out at an ungodly hour of the morning. There was no quote from him in the article, just a few clichés ostensibly uttered by Jill, clichés which sounded more like the words of the *Sun* than of Jill, who they described as 'the bubbling beauty'.

Still, Jill had obviously spoken to them, if not in the actual words they reported. Bob remembered how poised and generous she had been in the moment of surprise, calmly responding to their presence. That was why the press loved her, said Bob. Because she was a nice person, an open person, warm and generous, even with the press. That was why everyone loved her. Besides, they had nothing to hide.

Many of their colleagues on *Breakfast* were unaware of their relationship and somewhat surprised when news of it appeared in the *Sun*. Nicholas Witchell remembers Jill and Bob turning up for work after the article, which must have been awkward for them, simply carrying on as if nothing had happened.

Nicholas was aware of the change in her, the loss of weight, the gradual process of sophistication. She was no longer the girl up from Plymouth. She was charming and easy to get along with and a very gifted presenter. It was obvious that she had great potential, and he thought Bob was right to encourage her. It would be a cliché, in Nicholas' book, to say she was natural, but that was what it was all about, just being your natural self. There were no tricks. Nicholas would read elsewhere about the tricks of presentation, but he did not know of any. Nobody had ever told him about them.

Women presenters, by and large, received more attention from the editors and producers with regard to their appearance – for instance, Bob never gave Nicholas any cosmetic tips, though Nicholas was aware of his role in grooming Jill.

What came through with Jill was her sincere and straightforward personality. She sometimes seemed a little nervous or ill at ease, especially early on, but even this may have worked in her favour as an endearing quality, and if politicians sometimes appeared to be giving her the run around in interviews, it could reflect badly on them rather than on Jill.

It was a momentous period in modern history when Nicholas and Jill presented *Breakfast* which saw the collapse of communism, the Berlin Wall coming down, Gorbachev overthrown, the release of Nelson Mandela, the Gulf War, even an earthquake in San Francisco.

This was a time to be absorbed in and obsessed with the news, as Nicholas was. He involved himself in the programme and wrote or rewrote many of the scripts, often working on them at his terminal while they were broadcasting. He realised that Jill was not so interested in the news and did not spend as much time reading the newspapers. She might tinker with the scripts, but in the main she left that to him.

Nicholas thinks that she felt the lack of hard-news experience; of never having been a reporter or a correspondent for national news. You could ask if it really matters, once you are behind a desk as a presenter, but it gives you a certain confidence when you are talking on air to correspondents dotted around the world.

Some of the programme's staff felt that Jill struggled with her lack of knowledge during the Gulf War and concerns were raised that this was affecting the programme at such an important time.

As a result Jill was switched to weekends for a while. Bob doesn't remember this and doesn't think it happened quite as others recall. Nobody ever made such representations to him. What he does remember is Jill going to Italy to cover the elections, opening the programme from there and handling the headlines, the links to background sequences and interviews with correspondents and Italian politicians. It was a hard job for someone who didn't read the *Economist*, someone nobody thought was a particularly serious news person, but she did it well, with the support of an experienced team.

Bob knew however that you would never send Jill to cover a war, though that was not necessarily a bad thing, because once you sent glamour to war, you glamorised war itself, which could never be right.

Jill was desperate to be taken seriously as a woman with journalistic credentials. But she had other ambitions, too. She wanted to be on the *Holiday* programme and on *Crimewatch*. She wanted to be embedded in the BBC schedules, in those fixed points of popular culture. Bob could see that she wanted to be, and indeed was becoming, a star.

Eight

I was nearing the end of research for my magazine article about Jill's death when I finally met Alan Farthing. He had not wanted to be interviewed but said he would participate if the police thought it might help the investigation, by maintaining or reviving the public interest, which could bring forward new information. The police agreed that it might, so Alan agreed to be interviewed.

We met in Fulham, at the home of a friend of Alan's, Abel Hadden, who was experienced in public relations and gave welcome support to Alan after Jill's death. Abel and his wife Belinda had known Jill and she too had been a guest at their home.

It might seem odd that Alan needed a public relations adviser, but the media interest had been intense and Abel, who understood how the press thought and behaved, was a useful ally. Alan had acquired a minor public profile through his relationship with Jill and, suddenly, a much greater profile when she died. It was not something he had sought and he was very anxious to behave with dignity, to say the right thing and to protect and preserve the memory of the woman he would have married.

Abel had sat through most of the very few interviews Alan had given. One interviewer, from the *Daily Mail*, had asked Alan if he ever wore any of Jill's clothes.

I felt pretty crass myself, at one point during that first meeting, when I asked Alan if the mystery of Jill's death, the lack of an explanation, was all-consuming. No, he said, not knowing why made it very much more difficult to handle and would continue to make it more difficult, but the overwhelming tragedy of Jill not being there, not sitting on the couch next to him right now was far greater than any fixation with not knowing why.

He was sitting to one side of a two-seater sofa and as he spoke he glanced to his left, to the empty space next to him. I hadn't even noticed that space but now it seemed to fill the room for me as it plainly already filled the room for Alan.

It was, as you might imagine, a difficult interview and I was glad when it was over. Alan was contained, his emotions kept firmly at bay, perhaps seeping through just a little in observations, such as that one. He thought carefully about everything he said and I felt that he was trying hard to keep a distance from publicity, as if he could send the words out there, on their own, while he stayed out of sight, in privacy.

We spent many hours together later and he was rarely very different, until after the trial. He mentioned many times how it was not good form for medical consultants to become publicly known. Any publicity was bad publicity, he said, more than once. This mantra and his determination to uphold it had created some comedy in the months before Jill died.

A day or two after the interview I was driving north along the Fulham Palace Road. I passed Charing Cross Hospital on the right, as I must have done a thousand times. I thought of Alan, at about quarter past one in the afternoon on the day of Jill's death, sitting in the rear seat on an unmarked police car in the car park at the back of the hospital, hidden there from the press who had gathered at the front of the hospital and at the side entrance to Accident and Emergency. I could picture him, just as he had described it, turning his mobile phone on, turning it off again straight away in case it rang. He was waiting to identify a body that was almost certainly Jill's. Part of him hoped that it was not Jill. But to hope that was to wish that someone else had been murdered and someone close to them would be bereaved, as he might very well be already. Which ever way his thoughts turned he found himself thinking the unthinkable.

Of all the images that present themselves in the event and the aftermath of Jill's death, this was the one that stayed with me and is still there. I still pass the hospital frequently, passing the entrance that Alan had been driven through. I see him there every time, hazily, as he half-remembered it, not quite sure of the make of car he was sitting in, nor even of how many others were in the car with him. Was it two or three officers? He thought it was two, no three, no ... well, he was distracted.

I wrote the magazine article and it was published. Usually, with those articles, which have required intense research over a couple of months, or more in this case, the last thing you want to do is more research. You might keep in touch with the people you met and got to know and care about. See how it all turns out, whatever it is. But, please, no more research.

On this occasion, I felt differently; I didn't want to disengage and I'm not sure I could've done even if I had. I wanted to get to know Jill and I wanted to know who had killed her and why. I could not shake off that single recurring thought of Alan and what he was about to see. The last moment when he was still vaguely comforted by that disturbing hope that it could be somebody else, sitting there with a switched-off mobile phone in his hand.

Alan would never tell me, though I asked him more than once, what his last words were to Jill, that morning of 26 April 1999, as he went out of the door of his home in Chiswick to get in his car to drive to work. Nor would he say what Jill's last words had been to him.

He had been up with the alarm at 6.45. Jill had woken too and offered to make him breakfast and he had said not to bother because she had the opportunity of a lie-in that morning. He went to the bathroom and while he was in the shower Jill got up and made his breakfast anyway.

Alan went out at about 7.30, to attend an 8 am meeting at St Mary's, a regular Monday morning meeting of his department. He and Jill said lots of nice things to each other, was all Alan would say, and then he left and they did not speak again.

As Alan left Jill went back to bed, having set the alarm for 8.30. Alan's mother called at 8.01 and they spoke for a few minutes.

Jill was planning to cook that evening. She was going to be a lady who lunches, she had said. She had admin. to attend to, a fax cartridge to buy and she would call in at Gowan Avenue before going to meet her friend and former colleague Anastasia Baker.

Jill and Anastasia were due to meet at the Lanesborough Hotel on Hyde Park Corner at 12.30 to attend a Tomasz Starzewski fashion show, in aid of The Haven Trust, a breast cancer charity. Jill had been invited some weeks earlier and had paid for the tickets by cheque, well in advance.

Alan's meeting was attended by the senior registrar who, by coincidence, had been at the British Legion poppy ball that Alan had also been to on Saturday night with Jill, in her capacity as co-host.

The registrar told Alan how fantastic Jill had been on Saturday. Alan was more concerned about the operation he was to conduct with a colleague immediately afterwards, which he discussed with the registrar because it was an unusual scenario, involving a patient who was having a baby and also seriously ill.

Alan had talked to Jill in general terms about this and she had found the plight of the patient distressing. It was distressing to Alan, too, even though cancer was his speciality and he was bound to encounter a case like this from time to time.

The operation took place in the main theatre suite, beginning at about 9 am, and took an hour. Alan spent half an hour or so afterwards with the patient's relatives, then changed and walked across to his regular Monday cancer clinic, which had already begun when he arrived at about 10.30.

Jenny Higham was working at the same hospital and was due to be operating all that morning. Laparoscopies, a hysterectomy, fibroids – just the standard gynae routine of surgery, Jenny participating and supervising the juniors.

Normally Jenny and Jill would speak every two or three days and, if she had been away, Jill would call Jenny when she returned. They did not speak so often at weekends now, as this was Jill's time with Alan so they often made contact on Mondays.

Before she went to theatre, at about 9.50, Jenny went into a side room and called Jill. She tried her first in Fulham but the phone went to voicemail so she called Chiswick. Jill was still there. They chatted for a while, just catching up with what each had been doing.

Jenny was annoyed with herself afterwards for having neglected to thank Jill for the birthday present she had given her daughter Victoria. Jill was a godmother to three-year-old Victoria. She had sent the gift via Alan, but he had forgotten to pass it on until Friday, the day after Victoria's birthday. Jenny knew how particular Jill was about remembering the children's birthdays, and she didn't want to let Alan down by letting on that he had been late with the present. Instead it had slipped her mind altogether. She remembered as soon as she put the phone down. Damn. She was upset later that Jill had not been thanked for that present.

Jenny and her family had been away that weekend and Victoria had opened her present on the train, a present from Jilly Non-Bear – as Jill was known to Jenny's children (as distinct from Jilly Bear, an elaborate teddy Jill had bought for Jenny's other daughter, Emma, when she was born). The present was a soft toy, a dog that made contented noises when it was touched.

During the call Jill told Jenny she was going to the fashion thing at the Lanesborough. She had asked Jenny a while before if she wanted to go, and Jenny had said that she couldn't. Now Jill asked her if she was sure. 'You definitely can't go?' Jill asked her. There were some things for which Jenny could make alternative arrangements but Mondays were difficult.

'No,' she said. 'I'd love to, but I really can't.'

Jill said, 'Well, actually I've asked Anastasia now but I'm sure you could still come along.'

They discussed their plans for the next few days, having already made a date to meet on Wednesday week. As Jenny was talking an assistant entered the room. Jill sensed the change in her voice. 'You're not on your own any more, are you?'

'No,' said Jenny. 'Quite correct.'

'Oh well,' said Jill. 'I might as well go, then. Bye.'

'OK. Thanks very much,' Jenny replied trying to sound like it was a professional call. 'Goodbye.'

Jill spoke to another friend for a few minutes just after ten o'clock. While she was on the landline, her agent, Allasonne Lewis, was ringing her mobile. When she had finished her call, Jill retrieved Ally's message from the mobile. Ally had said she would call back. They spoke all the time.

Jill must have left Alan's at about this time to drive to Fulham. She stopped at the BP garage on the A4 just before the Hammersmith flyover and bought petrol and milk. She made a call to the box office of the Prince Edward Theatre making inquiries about tickets for the show *Mamma Mia!*, which would be a gift for Alan for his birthday in June. The call from her mobile was made at 10.21 and lasted for ninety seconds. The box office was not yet open at that time. Perhaps she was listening to recorded information. She was recorded on CCTV camera at the garage service till at 10.22.

At 10.30 she was speaking to Ally, who asked if she had received the faxes from the previous week and was told that Jill's fax machine was out of ink, that she was on her way to buy a new cartridge. Two minutes forty-one seconds, the length of that call. Jill was driving down the side of the flyover to Hammersmith Broadway. She called the theatre box office again but it must have been engaged because the call only lasted two seconds. She called Directory Inquiries – twenty-four seconds.

Her car is now picked up by the first of Hammersmith & Fulham Council's many CCTV cameras on the Broadway as it turns left into King Street at 10.36.23, then turning left off King Street, to park in Bridge Avenue at 10.36.58 on Camera 3.

Two police officers would spend over 500 hours looking at all the CCTV footage, plotting Jill's movements across west London.

She reappears on Camera 3 at 10.39.58, walking east past the shops on the south side of King Street. There she is again, at 10.41.49, on the opposite side of the road, heading west. She crosses back to the south side, retracing her steps eastwards, at 10.43.46. Ninety-nine seconds later she is outside Marks & Spencer, and three minutes after that she is further down the road, entering Rymans. Ally has called again, the call going to voicemail.

Jill leaves Rymans after four minutes, having bought a ream of A4 copy paper. She crosses to the north side and walks east towards the indoor shopping centre, King's Mall. She enters Dixons, whose camera records her presence but has an inaccurate time code. She can be seen clearly now, in her black boots, trousers, a red jacket over a round-necked top, her Burberry rain-coat. She has her black bag over her right shoulder and is carrying her copy paper in a Rymans bag in her left hand. She inquires about fax cartridges but Dixons don't have what she needs, and she leaves after 40 seconds. She walks through the mall, perhaps look-ing for another shop that might sell fax cartridges, then exits the mall and crosses the road back to her car. At 11.01 she calls the theatre box office again and speaks to a member of staff who arranges to call her back.

At 11.04.43 Jill is on Camera 2, driving west on King Street, away from the shops, following the one-way system that loops round and out of Hammersmith and back towards Fulham. At

11.10.02 she heads south on the Broadway, turning left into Queen Caroline Street just past the Apollo. She could have driven straight home down Fulham Palace Road, but the traffic always moves slowly here and there is a bottleneck where two lanes are reduced to one near a busy bus stop and a pedestrian crossing.

Queen Caroline Street, meanwhile, takes her on a well-known short cut: past Riverside Studios, left, then right, then left again through side streets parallel with Fulham Palace Road. She was recorded on CCTV for the last time, by the council's Camera 7, 11.10.41, making the last left from Winslow Road into Manbre Road.

One or two of Jill's friends who saw these images later on television, watched her going home to be killed, would shout at the screen: 'Turn round! Don't go back! Don't go back!'

At 11.13 a woman driving north on Fulham Palace Road noticed Jill stuck in the southbound traffic and recognised her. Jill caught her eye and smiled. The woman immediately called a friend on her mobile to tell her who she had seen. A minute later Jill was telephoned by a woman from a production company with whom she was soon due to begin work on a series of programmes for BBC1 about royal weddings. They spoke for 119 seconds.

At about 11.20, a passerby saw Jill reversing her car, apparently looking for a parking space, in Dancer Road, which runs south from Fulham Road. She evidently parked on Munster Road instead and walked to Cope's, the fishmonger on Fulham Road. While she was waiting to be served she received the return call from the Prince Edward Theatre box office. The call lasted two minutes and twenty-four seconds and was her final telephone conversation. She left Cope's with two fillets of Dover sole in a plastic bag for supper that evening.

She was seen walking to her car in Munster Road at about 11.30 by a man who was on his way to Europa Foods to buy some milk and that was the last time she was seen before her death. A call to her mobile at 11.31 was unanswered and went to voicemail. It could not have taken much more than a minute to drive north on Munster Road left into Gowan Avenue and to park in that conveniently available space right outside her home, just south of Devil's Alley on Fulham Fields.

Alan's cancer clinic, which he shared with a team of six colleagues, was designed to take into account the unpredictability of the patients' needs and to ensure that everyone was seen. The consultations ranged from five-minute routine follow-ups to ninety-minute examinations of patients experiencing a recurrence of their cancer. You never knew how it might go, so you never over-booked. Alan thought he must have seen eight or ten patients that morning.

That day, as on most working days, he was focusing on his patients and his mind was not wandering to thoughts of Jill or the wedding or their house-buying or anything else. He would almost like to be able to say that ESP existed and that at around half past eleven that morning something might have happened to make him think twice and realise the significance of that moment. But it didn't.

It must have been about 12.30, when Alan had finished with his last patient and was about to sit down with his colleagues for a review of the morning's clinic, that his pager went. The message was: 'RING ROSEMAN URGENT.' Alan went back into his room and called Jon Roseman. 'Is Jill with you?' he asked.

'No,' said Alan. 'Why should she be?'

Roseman said he'd heard rumours, someone from the press had called and said that Jill had been attacked and hurt outside her house. He had been calling her mobile but couldn't get through.

Alan said that he thought it unlikely there was a problem, since no one had contacted him. It was well known, after all, that Jill had a partner and it wouldn't have been very hard to track him down. Jon said, 'Well, the rumour is that she has been stabbed or shot or something.' Alan said again that this seemed highly unlikely but that he would check it out and call Jon back. Jon said that he had tried to speak to the police at Fulham, but all calls were being diverted to Kensington.

Alan called Directory Inquiries to obtain the number of Fulham Police Station, then called that number and was put through to the front desk at Kensington Police Station. Alan gave his name and said he'd received a call to say that his fiancée had been involved in an incident.

'Who is your fiancée?'

'My fiancée is Jill Dando.'

The officer tried to call Fulham and came back on line to tell him that Fulham calls had been diverted to Kensington. Alan asked what the significance of that might be, and the officer said that he didn't know but would try to find out. He took Alan's name and number and said he would get someone to call him back. By now Alan sensed that something was wrong and guessed that the officer knew something because he was not being dismissive. He felt in limbo, though there wasn't long for that feeling to develop.

Almost immediately, Alan's pager went again. 'RING SISTER IN CASUALTY' and a phone number. Alan dialled the number and the sister told him that there were two police officers asking for him. They wanted to know where he was so that they could come over to speak to him. Casualty was on the other side of the road in a different building and Alan didn't want to have to wait for them to arrive. Those minutes would have seemed very long, he was sure. 'No,' he said. 'Tell them to wait, I'm on my way.'

His colleagues were just settling down for their post-clinic review. Not wanting to make an announcement, Alan called one of them from the room, explained what was happening and told him that he was going over to Casualty. Then Alan ran, down two flights of stairs, out into the side road, taking the short cut through the old part of the hospital, out the other side, across the road and into the new ten-storey building, running up the stairs to Casualty which was on the first floor. As he ran he became more and more certain that something had happened to Jill. Perhaps she had been knocked down, or attacked, or mugged. It was obviously serious, because she wasn't answering her phone, because other people were taking it seriously, but she would recover. He didn't think, dead.

As he arrived in the Casualty Department he saw the officers, recognising one of them as a senior detective, Richard Quinn, who Jill knew personally, as a friend of cousin Judith. They had been skiing with him and his wife, Vicky. Richard and Vicky had been at Jill and Alan's engagement party. On hearing the reports about Jill on his police radio, Richard had called in to say that he knew Alan, and knew where he worked. Hamish Campbell, anxious to confirm that it was Jill who had been killed, had asked him to take Alan to Charing Cross Hospital to identify the body.

Alan greeted Richard and his colleague and they shook hands. Alan offered to find a room where they could talk, but Richard said, 'No, just come over here,' and they went to stand in the corridor. Richard told Alan that a woman matching Jill's description had been attacked outside Jill's house and had been taken to Charing Cross Hospital, where she had died from her injuries. They did not know for certain that it was Jill, and it might not be Jill. They needed Alan to go to Charing Cross.

One of Alan's colleagues from the cancer clinic arrived, having followed Alan across to Casualty. 'What's happening?' she asked. Alan put his hands to his face. He repeated what the police officer had told him and added: 'She's dead.' Richard reminded him:

'We don't know that it's Jill.'

Alan felt that his world was spinning. He was seeing other people's reactions but had no sense of his own reactions.

'Let's go,' he said to Richard Quinn. They went outside where there was a police car waiting and they put on the blue light and the driver went, as Alan says, like a madman. Alan sat in the back. He cannot remember how many officers were with him. Perhaps it was the two plus a driver. Richard called in to say that he had collected Alan and they were on their way.

Hammersmith Broadway was gridlocked, as usual, and they were caught in the bottleneck on Fulham Palace Road, just a few hundred yards north of the hospital which was actually on Fulham Palace Road and nowhere near Charing Cross.

As they drove Richard explained to Alan how he had heard what was happening and radioed in. He said that the area round Jill's home had been sealed off and that the press knew something was going on and they were knee-deep outside the hospital's Accident and Emergency Department.

Alan's mobile phone was switched off. He thought he should speak to someone – to Nigel, perhaps, Jill's brother, or Jack, her father. He switched on his phone and then thought, what if it rings? What if a reporter rings? He turned it off again. His pager alerted

him to a message from Nigel so he switched the phone back on and
called him. He told him he was in the back of a police car on his
way to the hospital, possibly to identify Jill's body. Nigel said he had
seen on the news that Jill was dead (that was *Sky News*, who had
reported Jill's death without any official verification). 'It's not confirmed,' said Alan, 'because I have to go and confirm it. It might
not be Jill.'

The driver switched off the blue light and turned left to go
along the side of the hospital, driving unnoticed past A&E, to the
rear of the hospital, in through the gates to the car park. The
entrance to the building was locked, so while one officer remained
in the car with Alan, the others went off in search of someone to
open it.

Alan was clinically aware that he was in the early stages of grief,
one of the first reactions being disbelief, which was what he now
felt. Once the concept, dead, had been introduced he could no
longer tell himself that Jill would recover from whatever it was that
had happened to her. The only thought he could cling to was that
it was not Jill. He hoped it was not Jill, but that was to wish that
someone else was dead in her place, which was not an easy thing to
wish for.

All his professional training and experience had taught him that
in a crisis the first thing to do was stop and think. There was nothing that ten seconds of thought could harm, better to spend ten
seconds thinking and then do the right thing rather than act randomly. OK, he thought. Whatever you do, do the right thing.
Let's think about this.

It was very quiet, sitting there in the grounds of the hospital.
There was no one else around at all, Alan noticed. Not like outside
A&E. He and the police officer did not speak.

Alan decided to call Jon Roseman, who was in tears because he had seen the *Sky News* report. 'Look, I'm sitting here waiting to go in,' Alan said. 'We don't know yet; don't believe what you see.' But by now he felt that he was resisting the inevitable.

After several minutes a porter appeared on the other side of the entrance and unlocked the door and the officers then walked with Alan down a corridor. He felt that everyone seemed to be expecting him, as if people were waiting, lining the corridor, to point him in the right direction as he walked. It felt like a very purposeful walk.

Richard Quinn showed Alan into a room off the corridor and Alan saw Jill, who looked very pale, almost as if she was resting. Alan wondered why she had a towel wrapped around her head. He took hold of her right hand and noticed the nail varnish she had been wearing the night before. He was formally asked if this was Jill and he replied that it was.

An A&E consultant appeared and briefly explained to Alan the process of resuscitation they had followed and why, in the end, they had stopped trying. Alan asked him what had happened to Jill and the consultant said that he didn't know but there was a report that she had been stabbed.

Alan was not in the room for very long, the police telling him he could not stay there. Richard Quinn asked him where he wanted to go and Alan said he had no idea. Richard asked if he wanted to go home or to friends, or back to work to collect his things ... or anywhere at all?

'You tell me where I'm going,' said Alan, who was aware that he was in no position to make any kind of decision.

As he walked away he realised that he still didn't know what had happened to Jill, how she had been attacked. He realised he had not seen her left arm, and the hand on which she would have been

wearing her engagement ring, which was probably the most valuable thing she would have been wearing. He wondered again about
a mugging, and thought perhaps she could have been disfigured in
some way. He asked about her left arm. An officer called another
officer, who went to check and the message of reassurance came
back that her left arm was all right.

Richard Quinn took Alan back to his office in Notting Hill.
Alan was grateful to be there, to be with somebody who could take
charge so he could temporarily abdicate responsibility. He received
a message from his best friend, Mark (who was to have been his
best man). Mark had heard the news and was on his way to be with
Alan. Alan paged Jenny, and she called back, having already heard.
She was on her way too.

When he thinks about it now, Alan is not sure he ever had to tell
anyone directly that Jill had actually died. Everyone he spoke to
already knew. This by-product of Jill's celebrity set him apart from
the usual circumstances of the bereaved. There was no room for
escape or denial or pretence, which was probably a good thing.

After about an hour, Richard told Alan that Jill had been shot in
the head and Alan was shocked by this revelation. It explained the
towel around her head. He had assumed it must have been a mugging or a burglary that had gone wrong and that she had ended up
being killed. He didn't think anyone normally set out to kill
anyone. 'That's an assassination,' he said to Richard. Somebody had
deliberately killed Jill. He couldn't imagine why anyone would
want to do that, and right from that moment and ever afterwards,
it just did not make any sense.

In the middle of Jenny's run of routine surgeries there had been an
emergency, a pregnant woman who was rushed into theatre with

torrential internal bleeding. Jenny had performed a laparotomy, and as she was finishing a colleague came up behind her and said, 'Shall I do that for you?' Surgery was interesting but the most boring bits were opening and closing and Jenny was tempted but said, 'No, no, it's fine, I'll finish off,' so her friend waited and took Jenny straight out afterwards and said, 'I've got some terrible news for you.' Jenny cannot remember exactly what she said, only that Jill had been injured or stabbed or shot but she had definitely said 'She's dead,' and Jenny had said, 'No, she can't be dead, she can't be, she must be injured.'

'No,' said her friend. 'It's true. She's dead.'

Alan's consultant colleague, Peter Mason, who was Jenny's colleague too, was also waiting and said he would look after her. Jenny was shaking so much she could not get dressed by herself and had to be helped. Peter took her bag and walked her to his car. Jenny was in a dream world. She wanted to be with Jill, to touch her, and kept saying that she had to see her but when she spoke to the police, they advised her not to go to the hospital, so she joined Alan at Richard Quinn's office and they hugged and cried and briefly began the process of making statements.

As Jenny sat with the officer who took her statement, she kept asking, 'Are you sure? Is this real? Are we really sitting here?' The officer said he was sorry, but it was real, and they were sitting there. Jenny still could not believe it. 'I was only speaking to her two or three hours ago,' she said.

They left later to go to Peter's home and as they walked to the car two street cleaners were passing and Alan overheard them, one asking the other if he knew that Jill Dando had been killed and the other one not being quite sure who she was and the first one saying, 'That woman who does *Crimewatch*.' Alan said to Mark, 'News travels fast.'

Alan spent many of the ensuing hours on the phone, talking to friends and family, updating them on what was happening. It was a helpful coping mechanism. He also watched the news and the BBC tribute programme that went out that night. He stayed the night at Mark's house – his own home being staked out by the press. He had a drink, but not too much; he was given some sedatives but didn't take them.

He considered that, if he had ever had reason to think how he might feel at such a loss, he would have imagined feeling vengeful towards the perpetrator, whoever it was. He was surprised to find that he didn't have those feelings. The sense of loss was much bigger. That and the wondering who and why. He and Jenny would spend hours going over and over their knowledge of Jill's life and still not come to any conclusion.

Alan began a full statement the next morning and briefly met Hamish Campbell. He was still at the police station when an officer said they'd heard that a newspaper was planning to publish a story saying that Alan was being held against his will by the police. Alan learned a new word: 'flyer'. The paper had said this to the police, put the idea into flight, to see what reaction it might provoke. The story did not run, but it made Alan wonder what other people were thinking and what else the press might print. He realised that he was an obvious suspect, at least in the minds of press and public – but the police were soon satisfied that he had nothing to do with Jill's death.

From the police station he and Jenny were taken to the mortuary to see Jill. Unfortunately, she was now behind a glass panel and they were not allowed to be next to her or touch her, despite

Jenny's pleas. Already, after only twenty-four hours, Jill looked different, which seemed to Alan to be the difference between an expression which was lifelike and an expression that was not lifelike.

Jenny's wish was finally granted some weeks later, shortly before Jill's funeral, when she and Alan and cousin Judith and Auntie Esme saw Jill's body in an open coffin in the basement chapel of rest at the undertaker's on the main road in Weston.

In some ways it was too late for Jenny, as the Jill she touched did not much resemble her living self by then. The coffin had a little compartment, like a secret drawer, in which mementos could be placed. Everyone seemed prepared for this except Jenny. Judith had a photograph of her daughter Emilie and a note; Alan added Jill's make-up bag and his own note. Jenny borrowed some paper from the undertaker, which was rather naff paper so that Jenny felt obliged to write an apology to Jill for the naffness of the paper on which she was writing her note.

On the day after Jill's death, Alan finally acceded to the many requests for an interview. He was trying to behave in a way that Jill would be proud of, trying to do justice to her. He didn't feel he could do that in a press conference, so he agreed to do one interview with the BBC which would then be pooled, that is shared openly among the media. The interview was to be recorded in a room at Kensington police station the following afternoon.

About ten minutes before the interview was due to start, the BBC called to say that there had been a change of plan. Anna Ford was now coming down to do it, and would Alan mind waiting a little longer? Alan didn't mind who conducted the interview, but he did mind waiting. The next message announced that she had just arrived. Was that all right? Yes, that was all right.

The interview seemed to have been upgraded in its importance, now, and Alan was anxious to know what he would be asked, to prepare himself so that he wouldn't break down, which he felt would be letting Jill down.

He had met Anna Ford before, and knew her as an acquaintance and colleague of Jill's. She had been at their engagement party, and shared Jill's hairdresser. When Anna came into the room Alan stood up and they kissed, which seemed like the normal thing to do but Alan did not realise this was being filmed and was surprised to see it featured in some broadcasts of the interview.

You did not often see interviewers kissing or being kissed by their interviewees. The BBC certainly seemed to be struggling to find the proper perspective on Jill's death.

When he left the station an hour and a half later, Alan could already listen to himself being interviewed by Anna on the radio in the car. He found that very strange, and was doubly glad then that he had not broken down.

Nine

At the beginning of the 1990s, Judith Dando had a change of lifestyle and gave up being an account executive in advertising, leaving London to travel as a backpacker and to follow the ski seasons, to live and work in the ski resort of Serre Chevalier in the French Alps. Jill visited her there often, though she did not much appreciate the steady flow of assorted ski-bums and friends that Judith invited to stay at Heythorpe Street in her absence.

Judith said it was an alternative way of life that she lived in France, among the ski-bums. When Jill and Bob came out they did not bunk down with Judith in the cheap and cheerful budget hotel, as Jill might have done on her own, but stayed in the nice hotel opposite.

At the end of their stay, the hotel would not accept credit card payment and Bob had to go round town looking for somewhere to withdraw some cash, complaining about the Mickey Mouse hotel.

For Judith, who recognised how brilliant Bob was for Jill in the way he supported and nurtured her and helped her to grow in confidence, this was the flipside of the relationship, that everything had to be just so, which could be restrictive and confining. It was indicative of how their relationship would evolve. In future when Jill came out to see Judith, she came alone.

Judith thinks that Jill might have married Bob at one stage, early on, though he declared that he did not want to have any more children and, perhaps, Jill was never sure that she loved him enough. Though Jenny Higham had been ready to dislike Bob before she met him, she was pleasantly surprised to find this well-preserved, youthful, middle-aged man who was both charming and charismatic. She could see his appeal to Jill as a tutor and interesting partner.

Bob enjoyed being the fount of knowledge, knowing things and, actually, he did know many things, especially about current affairs, the background to the news, and even though he revelled in this role it was stimulating rather than nauseating – you really could learn a lot from him. As they sat there over Sunday lunches Bob had cooked with al dente vegetables, Jenny understood how such wisdom could be translated into many areas such as clothes, food, wine, socialising, good restaurants. It would seem the obvious thing to do and not openly manipulative.

Jenny had felt a little guilt when she met and then married her husband within a few months of Jill coming to London, as if she was deserting her single friend. Jill would tell Jenny she had envied her this happiness and at least now the balance was redressed to some extent.

Jenny sensed, too, that Bob made an effort with her and her husband; that, in his eyes, some of Jill's friends were probably more suitable than others. It was certainly true that other people who knew Jill felt, in the words of one, ruthlessly weeded out.

You could speak to a hundred people about Bob and canvas a hundred different opinions, many of which would be quite forthright. There were those who recognised that he took care of Jill. There were also colleagues and friends who felt bitterness on Jill's behalf at the way he sometimes seemed to belittle her at work or socially. Others understood the way he was with Jill, partly because he was the same with them as well. Anastasia Baker remembers being one of Bob's 'blobs' as she called it, on the *Breakfast* team. She was also a young presenter, with the same insecurities as Jill, in the midst of 'all those pointy-heads on news', the same fear of being found out, found wanting, at any moment.

Bob had guided and groomed her too, and she had responded to his visionary enthusiasm, been galvanised by his drive to improve and create the best. People would say about the BBC that it thrived on the insecurities it created in its staff, which kept them begging and hopeful; that no one ever told you anything until they told you you were fired; all those short-term contracts, and you never knew when they might end, that unless you were married to the BBC, totally committed, you were deemed to show lack of commitment and to be unworthy of the corporate blessing of employment.

It was not like that with Bob, who showed commitment and interest towards you and always had time for you. If he liked you. Or, some would say, if you were an attractive young woman. Even Anastasia had to admit that Bob might have been exhausting to live with, because there never seemed to be any let-up in his mission to improve.

Anastasia always thought Jill was much better as a presenter and much cleverer than she realised.

Another colleague, Sally Magnusson, recognised from the start that Jill had poise, was unflappable, and could bring an authority and a bearing to the news which perhaps belied her experience in journalism. Sally was often pregnant in those years, building a large family, and she was grateful to Bob for his loyalty in giving her work but always felt boring and motherly beside Jill, who in turn seemed to crave the stability of family and children that she saw in Sally.

Yet for all her insecurities there must have been a part of Jill that held the kernel of self-belief; a part of her that believed she had the necessary journalistic credentials and could retain that credibility while she worked in other arenas. Sally saw that, just as Jill appeared to have a vision of a better relationship beyond Bob, she also had a vision of a bigger career.

Jill did have lunch with Nicholas Witchell once, as Bob had encouraged her to do. Nicholas cannot remember the details of that lunch except that by the end of it he was quite taken aback by the extent and reach of Jill's ambitions. Of course, in that environment, they all thought of themselves as being ambitious, but even so, he said, he was quite overawed by her determination.

In a sense she was heading into uncharted territory, trying to combine news and entertainment programmes, news and celebrity, which was not an easy thing to do, which no one else had ever really achieved or even tried to achieve.

She made her first series, *Safari UK*, in 1991, co-presenting with Julian Pettifer, which got them both on the cover of *Radio Times* in tropical dress.

Jenny remembers these as outdoorsy type programmes which was hilarious when you knew Jill as somebody who could not walk fifty yards down the street unless it was to hail a cab, who never strayed ten yards from the beach on holiday, who would have been the last person to suggest a stroll after Sunday lunch. Suddenly there she was in hiking boots, on clifftops, looking at seagulls.

When Jenny cleared out Jill's wardrobe after her death, she went through the acres of clothes, worth many, many thousands of pounds, which Jill had acquired and kept and arranged through her three bedrooms at Gowan Avenue. The middle bedroom for summer clothes and *Holiday* outfits, a complete wall of wardrobes in the main bedroom with clothes by every conceivable designer, plus skiwear and sweaters, everything squeezed in on the rails, along with seventy or eighty pairs of boots and shoes. Here Jenny came across the *Safari UK* clothes, still just about as fresh as the day they left the shop, worn only once.

Bob had been called once by the *Holiday* office, early on at *Breakfast News*, inquiring about Jill's availability and readiness to be a presenter on *Holiday*. He had told them that Jill was not available, and not yet ready. He meant it, too, though he was being a bit selfish as well, wanting to hang on to her himself.

Since then *Holiday* had tried to modernise its image, shaken off some of the old faces, installed a new editor, Jane Lush, and a new main presenter, Anneka Rice. Anneka Rice was not the main presenter for very long, and there was a brief search for a replacement.

Jane Lush remembers sitting in Mark Thompson's office watching a tape of *Safari UK*. Mark was then the head of the department that made *Holiday*. The department seemed to change its name every ten minutes but was at that time called Features.

Jill had heard that Anneka Rice was on the way out and told Bob that she was going to write and put herself forward for the job. She wrote to Mark Thompson. She knew where she was going.

She also discussed the programme with Eamonn Holmes, who had been working on it as a reporter and co-presenter. It was a big break for him, going from daytime to evening television, albeit, at first, a short-term and not richly paid assignment. Three hundred quid a week, or something like that.

Eamonn had been on the sports desk at *Breakfast* with Bob Wilson, another good friend of Jill's. Eamonn and Jill had a joky, flirtatious friendship which never developed into a relationship. Like her he was a 'blow-in', someone who had not come up through the BBC ranks as a graduate entrant. He had watched Jill on *Breakfast*, agog at her appearance of supreme confidence when he knew she was being fed questions on the screen in front of her, perhaps by Bob. After some on-air interviews she would pick up the phone and ask Bob how he thought things had gone. Eamonn was very fond of Jill, but he felt even then that she knew she had been promoted beyond her limitations, beyond the comfort zone.

Eamonn had his limitations, too, demonstrated on *Breakfast* by his attempts to pronounce the surname of the tennis player Goran Ivanisevic. How it looked and how it sounded, to Eamonn, were worlds apart. He would break into a sweat just waiting for it to appear on the autocue, knowing how po-faced they were up there in the gallery and eventually, when he thought he had it beat, written phonetically so that he could see how it was meant to sound — then Jill, sitting next to him, kicked off her shoe beneath the desk and began rubbing her foot up and down his thigh as he read the tennis bulletin.

When the presenting job at *Holiday* came up Eamonn knew that his name had been mentioned and rather hoped it might be his. Jill used to talk to him about *Holiday* and told him she thought he'd be perfect for it. Eamonn felt chuffed and bolstered by her support.

Perhaps it would be his after all. Then he heard that she had got the job and had written to ask for it some time earlier. He was quite huffy with her for about a year after that. She was obviously an accomplished networker and knew far better than him how to play the field.

It would happen again later, in a lesser way, but still he felt betrayed after he had joined GMTV. They were pally, she would call him up every so often and they would have dinner, and bump into each other at events. There was a vacancy at GMTV when Anthea Turner left and the executives went hunting for a replacement, and dined Jill, right there at GMTV, and she never even mentioned it to Eamonn, which annoyed him. She was right not to take it, though, that job would've been completely wrong for her – far too down-market, Eamonn thought. Jill was not a tabloid beast.

All Jane Lush could remember about the particular aspect of the intrigue with Eamonn over Jill's appointment to *Holiday* was Eamonn saying that Jill was the only person he would be prepared to work with as the main presenter. She thought that was odd at the time, given that Eamonn's agent was of the opinion that he ought to leave if he wasn't going to get the job himself.

Jane met Jill for tea at the Kensington Hilton to discuss the programme, for Jane to vet Jill, as Jill would later describe it. There was some liaison with Bob as to how Jill would juggle her obligations to *Breakfast* and *Holiday*. There were then fourteen *Holiday* programmes a year, which would soon rise to twenty and be further extended to thirty by Jill's commitments to spin-off series such as *Summer Holiday*.

In that first year she went to Florida, Cannes, the Canary Islands, Australia, EuroDisney, St Lucia, Bournemouth, South Africa, India, skiing in Italy riding elephants in Nepal, France,

Pontin's, Cyprus ... and after that she would go everywhere and become increasingly tired and increasingly keen to leave. It might sound like a great life, travelling the world business class for free, but it was an unsettling routine that played havoc with your existence and required considerable emotional resilience.

Bob bought Jill a Mulberry travel bag to mark the beginning of her *Holiday* adventures. He took a photograph of her, with the bag, in an elegant trouser suit – Louis Feraud, probably – as she was about to depart from his flat in Cookham in Berkshire. Bob knew the superstition that if you buy somebody a bag they will leave you, so he asked Jill to pay for it.

Jill made the cover of *Radio Times* for the second time for the start of her first series of *Holiday*. There were many more covers to come.

Nicholas Witchell has never yet been on the cover of *Radio Times*, not that he is complaining. I only know that because I asked him and I only mention it because the comparison tells you something about Jill and the BBC, about gender differences, about the marketability of 'pretty English girls' with blonde hair, and about the fact that Jill was really flying now.

Like most successful television series, *Holiday* adhered to a strict formula. There were always four or five films per programme, a holiday in the UK, one in Europe and one long-haul. Among these, one would be a beach holiday, another an activity holiday; one would be on a budget, another expensive and aspirational – *Holiday* was peddling dreams as well as holidays.

The individual films were formulaic too: the food shot, the night shot, the beach shot, the scenic 'pretties' and some patter from the reporter/presenter which might be Jill, Eamonn, Gloria, Frank, Nicky, Fiona, John, Sankha, Sheryl, Des, Carol, Monty,

Gaby, Paul, Zoe, Toyah or any one of the many other guest reporters and presenters who passed through.

As the main presenter Jill had additional work at all her locations filming the links, and she often did back-to-back trips, going from one place straight to the next, which she preferred because they saved time, though they were also especially gruelling.

She always carried a reporter's spiral-bound notebook which she used to make notes and write the links, when they weren't being written for her. She was a good traveller, with her big can of hair-spray and her make-up bag. She did her own make-up, changed behind the bushes or in the van and was not especially precious, or not too often, at least. She was not generally too particular about how she was filmed, though she drew the line at being seen in a bikini, never wanted to look foolish and was – depending on which director or cameraman you spoke to – variously hung up about her big feet, her thighs or her bottom.

Presenters could feel very vulnerable in front of a camera and some of them could be very fussy indeed. Anneka Rice always wanted to be filmed from the left, for instance, which you could imagine was a challenge for the cameraman.

When Martin Hawkins went away with Jill for the first time he asked her, over coffee at Heathrow, 'Just so that I know, do you have a good side that you prefer?'

'No,' she joked back. 'Just my backside, probably.'

Then, at the end of the next day, the first filming day, she came up to him and said, 'I've been thinking about what you said at the airport and I don't know. Do you think I have a good side?'

Martin said, 'Oh, every side's a good side, Jill,' which it was, to Martin.

For all that *Holiday* played hell with your home life, it could be quite an intense experience for the travelling crew, who were all in it together, through long working days and the relaxation when it was over. Crews worked together over and over again and became close, shared extraordinary things that other people might never see or do, shared daft things sometimes, such as Abba or Wham! singalongs in a hotel room, and intimacies in late-night talk over the wine. Presenters who joined in and were easy and fun to be with could inspire some devotion, as was the case with Jill and Martin, among others.

Jill went to Venezuela one year with another favoured cameraman, Jonathan Keeping. They were tracking monkeys from an isolated ranch about an hour's flight from Caracas. After the meal one evening a group of them went out to the middle of the grass airstrip and lay down together, heads close like a starburst. They lay there for a long time, looking at the sky and telling jokey stories and crawling around in a circle like crabs. It was just a moment that quickly passed. Nothing special to anyone except those who were there and would always remember it.

Jane Lush, the editor, was loyal and encouraging to her staff and gave people opportunities they might not have found so readily elsewhere, young women who began as production assistants and ended up as directors or producers.

Fenia Vardanis was one of those and she got to know Jill very well, their closeness completed when Fenia's mother died and Jill responded because she had been there herself and understood how it felt.

Jill would tell Fenia how she and Bob would sit and watch the *Holiday* tapes, and Bob would be hypercritical, or so it seemed to Jill, and Fenia felt that he was breaking down her confidence. She thought of Jill as a bird trapped in a cage.

Bob was trying to preserve Jill's news credibility, her authority, which was quite difficult when you were being seen weekly on television in beachwear. During the research for this book a friend of mine who used to work for the BBC told me he would be so incensed by the idea of a newsreader standing on the sand in a diaphanous sarong that he would sometimes phone the BBC when he saw Jill on *Holiday* and register a complaint in the duty log.

The *Holiday* teams became used to Jill behaving differently when Bob was around, as he occasionally was on those trips. There was a scene once between the director Alison Sharman and Jill, when Bob was with her, not long after they had arrived at one of the finest hotels in Italy, the Grand Hotel Palazzo della Fonte in the town of Fiuggi, south-east of Rome. Alison thought Jill was being the journalist, which wasn't really what *Holiday* was about. They had only just arrived and to Alison it was one of the most beautiful hotels she had ever seen. Jill knocked on her door. 'There aren't any coat-hangers in my room.' she said.

'Oh, right,' said Alison. 'Have you called the front desk?'

'Yes,' said Jill. 'I've rung twice and I still haven't got any coat-hangers.'

'Well, have some of mine,' suggested Alison. 'I've got loads of coat-hangers. I haven't got enough clothes to hang on my bloody coat-hangers.'

'I don't want your coat-hangers,' said Jill. 'I want them to bring me my coat-hangers.'

Alison could see the hotel was really busy. She was really busy too, and the hotel was extra busy on her behalf. She had a Ferrari booked, a grand piano to move in the ballroom, a sequence to shoot with Jill wafting past those props in an elegant gown. 'Look,' she said, 'the hotel's busy.'

'That shouldn't matter,' argued Jill.

She had a point, of course. If you were a paying guest in a hotel like that you'd expect some coat-hangers. Jill was used by now to the way things ought to be, and she needed everything to be right to get on with her work. 'You don't know what I've had them doing,' said Alison.

'Anyway,' said Jill. 'I want to do a piece to camera about the coat-hangers. About not having any.'

As Alison well knew they were not working for *Watchdog* and tried to choose places where people could come and be happy, if they could afford it; they were selling dreams, and this hotel was about as dreamy as they came.

'Jill,' said Alison, 'if you do a piece to camera about coat-hangers, you're going to sound like a spoilt child. Do you really think that all the people who can't afford to come here want to watch us whingeing on about coat-hangers?'

They were sulky with each other through the rest of the trip and on the last filming day they had another blow-up about Alison's wish to film Jill on a bicycle ride from the hotel.

They drove to an attractive location to film the sequence but Jill said it was cheating and she wouldn't do it because you couldn't actually cycle to this place from the hotel. Alison said, 'Well, don't bloody do it then, I'll do it myself.' And she got on the bike and pedalled around for the shot.

She thought about it later and went to Jill and said, 'Look, I'm sorry, I was a bit PMT,' and Jill immediately said, 'So was I, I was premenstrual.' So they each blamed their periods and everything was fine. Though Alison suspected it was something to do with Bob as well.

Generally, Alison loved going away with Jill because she loved to party, have something to eat, drink too much (albeit she had a low threshold of consumption for turning tipsy), smoke a few of someone else's cigarettes and get raucous.

That was what Alison loved about Jill because there were lots of women like her who wouldn't be able to do that. Women who were so particular about themselves and their appearance, as Jill seemed to be to Alison. Jill made Alison feel grubby in her company sometimes because she was so immaculately turned out, even though Alison wasn't grubby at all. Bob could also have that effect on people.

Alison saw how Jill hated to get things wrong, had an early taste of that on the Gower Peninsula in Wales, filming in fields of strawberries on a gloriously sunny day, Jill holding a punnet of strawberries in her hand and getting cross because, unusually for her, she couldn't get her piece to camera right and suddenly her foot went, a little stamp, which showed she was getting in a paddy and then she said, 'Oh damn!', and those strawberries flew into the air and scattered like seeds and she walked off. Alison wasn't sure what to do but Martin Hawkins, the cameraman, said, 'Just leave her, she'll be fine.' He was much more experienced at dealing with the talent than Alison was then. He knew the right thing to do and left Jill to come back and do the take.

On the last day of that trip they met a family on holiday and the woman said to Jill, 'I can't believe how much you look like Princess Diana,' and that remark made her day.

In the autumn of 1994, Jill went with Fenia and Martin to Jordan, travelling on Concorde for a back-to-back trip, going on to Israel. They first stayed at a newly developed hotel in Taybet Zaman, newly added to the itinerary of a travel company that organised luxury holidays incorporating Concorde flights. The

Holiday crew were accompanied by Jan Knott, a director of the travel firm, who was there to see that everything ran smoothly.

He was staying one step ahead of the crew, making sure the tour was prepared for their arrival, but they met up again next in Amman, where they all had dinner and a fair bit to drink. Jan had seen Jill on television and felt good just being around her. Jill lit up a cigarette and Jan, emboldened by alcohol and Jill's warmth, said, 'You don't smoke, do you? Do you know, the most beautiful woman in the world is ugly with a cigarette in her mouth.' Jill put the cigarette out straight away, which surprised Jan.

'I'm only an occasional smoker,' she said.

The last part of the Jordan trip involved an adventure in the desert, a ride on an old train once taken by Lawrence of Arabia, whose memory was evoked by the staging of a barbecue in a Bedouin tent and a pianist in white tails playing the theme from the film on a grand piano. It was intended to inspire romance and when the pianist began to play 'As Time Goes By', Jan asked Jill to dance, which she did.

That night, back at their hotel, they had a gala dinner to mark the end of the tour. Jill was going on to Israel in the morning. Jan was feeling queasy but didn't want to miss the dinner. He was ready for an early night after the meal but some of his staff were trying to get him to dance with Jill again. When the band played the Elvis song 'It's Now or Never', he asked her and they danced and Jan was not about to go to bed after that, so they stayed up a while and eventually left together to go to their rooms.

In the lift they were cornered by an elderly couple who had been pestering Jill the whole trip and Jan was wishing they would go away and – he could barely believe this was happening – when the couple left them by their rooms, he and Jill kissed and Jill said, 'Do you want to come in for coffee or something?'

When she spoke Jan realised she'd had too much to drink, like him. He was really feeling rough and elated all at once, and said, truthfully, 'I'd love to, but I'm afraid I'm going to be sick,' and Jill said, 'Yes, I think I am, too,' Jill went into her room and Jan went into his. If there had been a cat in that room he would've kicked it.

He wrote Jill a note, something corny about their dance in the desert, and hung it on her door in a bag with a couple of the presentation glasses given to every tour guest. Next morning, feeling even worse than the night before, he heard rustling at his door and when he looked it was a note from Jill on hotel headed paper.

23.9.94

Dear Jan,

What a way to end a trip to one of the most beautiful places on earth! I'm very sorry my final words were so incoherent – I promise you I don't make a habit of this!

I hope you didn't think my invitation last night was a little forward – it was just that I didn't want to end such a magical trip 'on the doorstep'. It warranted a chat and a final nightcap but in retrospect, the doorstep was probably best!

If you were serious about meeting again I should like that very much indeed. I don't know your personal situation but my current relationship is on the wane. However, contact may be awkward as I'm living with him in Maidenhead while I find a new home of my own!

I would love to see you again – you're special.

Jill x

PS I've just seen your lovely gift. Thank you so much.

She had added the phone number of Bob's new house in Maidenhead, with the word 'tricky!' in brackets next to it.

Jill and Judith had finally sold the house in Southfields. Bob had wanted to leave his flat in Cookham and had eventually bought an attractive lodge across the road from the Thames in Maidenhead. He and Jill had decided not to buy the house jointly, but she had given him £35,000 towards the price, which seemed quite natural at the time, though it would cause some trouble later. Jill was looking for a home of her own in west or south-west London, not too far from television centre.

It might have been true that her relationship with Bob was on the wane, but it still had two years to run.

Jan was a gentle man in his mid-forties, fond of wearing bow ties and not in a current relationship. He lived in a converted railway station near Canterbury and was a keen supporter of Brighton FC.

Jill sent him a note on a fax from Israel, a note with some photographs when she got home and a postcard from Mauritius — 'another week, another paradise' — all in the space of eleven days.

They arranged to meet for lunch and Jan went to pick her up from Maidenhead which made him feel a little uneasy. He met her again for lunch and again. He took her for lunch on the Orient Express at Christmas which was great but his PA told him he'd got to do more than just meet her for lunch.

Jan's company was organising a Concorde trip to Vienna for the New Year's Eve Ball and he invited Jill to go with him and she agreed to come. His PA was going too, and it even got to the stage of the PA wanting to know what dress Jill was going to wear so they wouldn't clash.

In the end Jill didn't go. She said she couldn't leave Bob because he was changing jobs, moving to become involved in the new channel BBC World, and he needed her support.

Jill moved into Gowan Avenue early in the New Year. Some friends had told her to go and live in an apartment block with a doorman and proper security, but she wanted a house, a front door of her own, a bay tree by the porch.

Jan visited Jill in Fulham a few times and once stayed a couple of days, which was the longest time they ever spent together. He found it hard to read Jill or the situation. He found it hard to declare his own feelings too. He fantasised sometimes about a future, thought about Jill coming to live with him, then told himself to stop being ridiculous, getting ahead of himself. Maybe it would never have worked — she hated sport, which Jan loved. She once told him she loathed and despised cricket.

He took her to his local pub, the Mermaid, and many people from the pub came along to the ceremonial opening of his new offices, performed by Jill Dando. The landlady of the Mermaid told the landlord that if he mentioned Jill's legs once more she was going home and he was coming with her.

Jill went back to Jan's home with him afterwards and he gave her a pair of earrings as a thank you. He knew that now was the time he should say something, express his feelings, tell her he was falling in love with her. He had been in these situations before and flunked them, and he couldn't bring himself to say anything now, either. He was afraid of hearing the wrong answer, afraid of rejection.

The best he could manage was to describe some thoughts in a letter which prompted a return letter from Jill, on BBC headed paper, which she said she was writing during the long hours between bulletins. She thanked him for his beautifully written note which had conveyed his feelings so clearly:

I'm finding it difficult to commit myself to a relationship –
with you or anyone else at the moment. I don't believe my
long-term future is with Bob but something is preventing me
from bringing it to an end and beginning a journey with you.
Call it fear (of the repercussions), familiarity with my current
situation or sheer lack of guts.

I also know that I'm about to embark on another year of
travelling which is confusing my mind still further. As you
know, I find work so absorbing and have been selfish enough
to put it before everything over the past three years, that I
wonder just how great my inclination is for a relationship.

Basically, I suppose I'm saying that I need a little time and
space to analyse and reassess my life and priorities. At the
moment, I can't feel relaxed when we meet for fear of being
'found out'. That isn't fair to you and you don't deserve to be
treated as 'a bit on the side'. However I do hope you realise
that isn't how I see you.

Let me tell you in more detail why I don't find it easy to
walk away from Bob. Firstly, you can't break away from five
years together without having some doubts about whether
you're doing the right thing. After five years perhaps it's natural not to feel excited by that person any more but to feel
satisfied in the understanding that you know each other inside
out.

He knows the business I'm in and I understand his work
which means we both have a support mechanism at all times.
I have no doubt that I could count on your support at all
times just as hopefully I [crossed out – 'you' inserted] could
count on yours [crossed out – 'mine' inserted, the word
'sorry!' in brackets above the corrections]. I suppose I've

just got used to a relationship in which television is an all-consuming passion. Goodness knows, I'm aware that it has the potential to make a couple very boring!

Darling, I really don't know when I'm going to reach the point of this letter or, indeed, if there is one. Can you cope with a neurotic, demanding (for that is what I am) workaholic travelling woman? If you can, I ask you for a little more of your patience to allow me to work things out. If not, then we should consider limiting our friendship. I believe I've taken enough of your time already so I will quite understand if you think the time has come to enjoy life again!

Jan, I do care very much for you … yet I do feel I'm doing all of the taking and none of the giving. I honestly don't know if I'm capable of DEEP love as I don't believe I've ever found it. You're the sort of person who deserves nothing less than that and I'm not sure if I can deliver …

Consider my words carefully, darling. Take care. With my love, Jill.

Bob was unaware of Jill's relationship with Jan, but he wasn't entirely surprised when he learned of it later. They were in the process of disengaging from one another, and Jill suspected that he was involved in another relationship, too. He says he always knew that Jill would not stay for ever. He recalls a conversation on a plane, early on, with John Humphrys, another of those stalwart BBC news presenters of whom Jill was not particularly fond and by whom she perhaps felt intimidated.

They were flying home from an assignment in Washington and Bob was talking about Jill, saying, 'She is absolutely wonderful, but I am much older than she is and I really wonder whether I should just let her go and let her meet some younger man who has still got a life ahead of him, they can grow together, have babies. I've been there. I've done it.'

'Well,' said John, as Bob remembers, 'if you really mean that, you'll invent a story about an affair. I would just let her go that way.'

That might have been an honourable deceit but Bob was in love with Jill and it was not so easy to give her up. He would be fifty in 1996, and in some ways he had programmed her to move on, helped her to find confidence and success and now she could have whatever she wanted, including younger and more glamorous people.

Jill would sometimes ask him: 'What are we going to do? Are we going to get married?'

'Well,' Bob would say, 'what would you like? We can have it all. We can have the big house and the car and the nannies and the babies. We can both have careers.' Bob never thought Jill was very convinced that he was committed to going through a marriage, having babies, doing the whole thing again.

If Bob was afraid to let go, that was true for Jill, too. 'Bobby, I'm scared,' she would say to him. 'I can't do it without you. I depend on you so heavily.'

When Bob told me this, it reminded him of some of the songs that were important to him and Jill, such as 'The Wind Beneath My Wings', sung by Bette Midler and others. He said this was how Jill thought of him, watching over her, wherever she was, even after their relationship ended,

Her lover, her friend, her mother.

Jill would talk about this endlessly with Jenny, cousin Judith and many others – a straw poll of London, as Jon Roseman might have said. She was afraid she would never meet anyone else, that men might be put off by her celebrity or, worse, attracted to her because of it. How could she know or be sure? She was afraid of being left on her own. Whatever confidence she had acquired did not seem to have very solid foundations.

Some people thought Bob was possessive with Jill and undermined her to keep her in his control. But that was how their relationship developed, it was their fit, with Jill as the eager young protégée and Bob the fastidious tutor. Perhaps this became harder to sustain as the balance of power shifted. Jill's career was in the ascendant and Bob's had already peaked.

On a rare trip to Weston together, Bob and Jill went out with her family for lunch, and Auntie Esme thought Jill was on pins, ever watchful of Bob, apparently seeking his approval or anxious not to incur his disapproval. There was an awful moment when Jill got up from the table and slipped on some food that was spilt and the look that passed between Jill and Bob – the awkwardness between them – made Esme sure that their continuing relationship was unhealthy for Jill.

Both Esme and Judith wrote to Jill and implored her not to stay with Bob. Jill told Jan Knott about this in a letter. 'It's nice to have people who care, isn't it?' she wrote.

Jill had agreed to accompany Jan, as his guest, to a public function that the Queen and the Duke of Edinburgh were due to attend. Jill cried off not long before, in a letter. She had work obligations, she said, and she was also a coward. This presumably meant she was afraid of coming out, being seen with him in public.

Jill suggested it might be best if she and Jan kept their distance for a while – 'until all this horrible business is over?' But then she wrote again a few days later and said she'd love to meet him for lunch – 'would you be interested?'

That letter had a PS: 'I forgot to tell you – I've bought a new car. Don't laugh, but it's a BMW convertible. I call it my tart cart.'

On 4 April 1994 Jill wrote a letter to Liz Johnston-Keay:

> By the way, you can have a lie-in from Tuesday onwards as that will be my last day on *Breakfast News*! The new life begins! I'm due to do some *Six O'Clock News*es from 21 April on an ad hoc basis when I'm not filming for *Holiday*. I'm really going to miss the programme and the people I work with – but I won't miss the hours! It'll be interesting to see how my lifestyle fits in with Bob's from now on!

Jill had written this to Liz from the drawing room of Champney's health farm, where she was spending the weekend with two friends, make-up artists from *Breakfast*.

Eventually, Jill would be assigned to make sixty appearances on the *Six O'Clock News* each year and these would be written into the contract, her all-in-one BBC contract which covered every programme she presented; such a contract was rare if not quite unique, in that all but the highly prized 'talent' had individual agreements for each separate series or piece of work.

Jill was seeking out those key and consistent programmes, those fixtures in the BBC1 schedules. She was becoming a fixture herself, sought out in turn by the BBC who seemed to view her talent as universally applicable. A professional chameleon, as she would occasionally call herself.

She had spoken often of her interest in *Crimewatch*. She had mentioned it to the programme's co-presenter, Nick Ross, among others, and had cited it sometimes in press interviews as an example of a show she'd like to work on.

Helen Phelps, who already worked on the programme, can remember seeing one of those interviews and showing it to Nick's co-presenter at the time, Sue Cook. 'Look, Sue, here's your replacement.' Sue Cook was getting ready to leave, had other things she wanted to do, and sometimes gave the impression that she was uncomfortable with the ethos of the programme as a police service for locking up villains.

Nick Ross said it was the television equivalent of the wanted poster. He and Sue Cook had presented the programme from the beginning, in 1984, when the concept had been imported from Germany. They had been equal partners, and if Nick had occasionally shown a willingness to write the whole script himself, then Sue had resisted that and always fought quietly to maintain her role.

Crimewatch was broadcast live once a month, and when Jill joined, in the autumn of 1995, she was fitting it in among her other mounting obligations, notably to *Holiday*. Production secretaries for the two programmes were for ever negotiating their competing demands on Jill's time, and began a joint computer diary for her, with much tugging and pulling in both directions.

Jill's schedule allowed Nick Ross to step in and become the overall scriptwriter for *Crimewatch*, so that, almost from the beginning, the equality Sue had established on the programme was lost to Jill. The co-presenters were no longer equal partners.

Seetha Kumar, who became editor of *Crimewatch* around the time Jill started, remembers her being quite miffed, early on, that the script had already been written. But once the new arrangement had been explained – Nick's additional fee for the extra work and so on – Jill was fine about it. She was told she could change anything she was unhappy with, though in practice she rarely did.

She was generally charming, in the office and on screen, where her 'natural' warmth enabled Seetha to reposition the programme, focusing more on victim empathy through interviews with relatives of victims, or victims themselves, which Jill could conduct with ease and sensitivity. In this way the programme became as much about ordinary people wanting answers – people with whom the public could identify – as it was a police service.

That aspect of the programme that might titillate or excite, or appeal to the prurience of viewers, was always underplayed, and never much discussed.

Crimewatch was otherwise carefully structured in format and production schedule, which involved a monthly process of case selection, filming reconstructions of the crimes and final briefings by the presenters of all the crimes to be featured for the staff and the various police officers who had gathered to represent their own cases and man the telephone lines.

Because she was so often away, and even though the production team tried to keep her informed, Jill could sometimes seem a little unprepared when she came in on the day and hesitant in the briefings, unlike Nick who, having written the script, would know the cases in all their detail.

She was also occasionally uneasy in her on-air live interviews with police officers, though this would be barely noticeable to the audience, disguised by her talent and experience. This was particularly true in the early days when Seetha thought she seemed almost in awe of the police officers and betrayed a lack of awareness of police procedures. There were other times, though, when she would 'hold something back for the live', give a little bit extra during the broadcast, and create an electricity which everyone involved would feel.

The police officers, especially the more senior ones, who were mostly, invariably, male, adored her, and in the basement afterwards at the post-broadcast party, the hospitality – or hostility, as it was colloquially known – they would flirt and compete for her attention and queue up for an autograph – 'Something personal, please from Jill to Mike,' 'Oh, and just one for my mate' – so much so that it became a bit of a nuisance, and officers had to be told that she was unavailable for personal autographs. Instead they had to make do with one of a batch of photographs that Jill would hurriedly sign in advance, fifty at a time, for visiting officers and viewers' requests. The male officers had the young women from the production team to attend to as well, the 'BBC girls' who would be at the parties, sometimes until two or two-thirty in the morning, usually resisting invitations to carry on back at the bar of the officers' hotel. Some officers, naturally, not all of them. Especially those on their first *Crimewatch*, who could get a little overexcited about being on television and away from home.

Jill, too, enjoyed the company of those young women, such as the production secretary, Zoe Taylor, who was always on the phone to her in some distant *Holiday* location, Zoe in the office at White City and Jill somewhere exotic, in a shop, perhaps buying sunglasses, so that the ensuing conversation about which sunglasses she should choose, round or oblong, would seem quite surreal to Zoe.

There was Fran Shisler and Ashley Lovell from the production team, standing together in hospitality and Jill coming up to them and saying, 'Look at you two, you look so ...' Ashley and Fran could not remember the word she used, perhaps it was 'young' or 'smart' or 'stylish' but they remembered it was as though she envied them their youth and style, always complimenting them on one thing or another so that Fran would go home and tell her mum, 'Oh my God, Jill said she loved my suit!' To Fran that was a big deal.

Ashley once had a long conversation with Jill about the under-eye cream which Jill used to ease away her dark rings, positively recommending that cream to Ashley, who didn't have the heart to tell Jill that she didn't share that particular cosmetic problem. Jill wanted to be one of the girls.

There was no doubt that *Crimewatch* was touched by Jill's glamour and celebrity. The programme blossoming in her presence, building on its earlier expansion into an entire unit with an increasing number of programmes in spin-off series such as *Trial of Guilt* and *Crimewatch File*. At the same time, some of the senior members of the team felt disappointment that she never really seemed to connect to the programme, because she was rarely in the office and, by and large, just came in on the day to do her job. This was not a universal view, by any means, but there were those who felt it. She never formed the bond with *Crimewatch* staff that she formed with the crews on *Holiday*, and never became close to Nick Ross, though she was adept at managing his occasional moments of chauvinism or careless patronising. Nick was held in great affection by the staff, just like Jill, was clever and articulate, but he had his tantrums and a tendency towards the pompous.

If, as he sometimes did, Nick criticised a link of Jill's, on the floor during rehearsals, some staff would squirm while Jill would affect not to notice. She would defer to him on occasions, just as she did to the police officers. She was not naturally combative which no doubt suited Nick.

Nick could recall that conversation, a couple of years before she joined, in which Jill said she would be interested in coming to *Crimewatch* if Sue was ever to leave. He did not know then why she was so keen and never thought to ask, until it was too late and she was no longer around to ask.

Jill was passionate about the programme, but what lay behind that passion Nick couldn't say. He doesn't think she was in it to put horrible people in prison where they belonged; he is not even sure how far she had thought through the whole philosophy of crime and victimisation. It seemed instinctive with her: the empathy for the victims, the occasional tears after a poignant or distressing interview.

Her talent was instinctive, too, or so it appeared to Nick. Being on television is all about the art of doing nothing, being yourself, just talking to people in their living rooms, or bedrooms, or wherever they happen to be watching. It was quite an intimate thing, and Jill did it to perfection every time. If her interviews with officers were not always inspired, or even up to scratch, it didn't matter: she got the information out there just the same.

Nick knew that she wasn't always happy in news and certainly knew how badly she had felt let down and betrayed, later. He had worked there himself and knew how up themselves those people were, what a macho environment it was. They might have looked down on Jill for the broader range of her work along the spectrum of 'entertainment' but he had a whole theory about news as entertainment, because of course news had to entertain too, otherwise no one would ever watch it.

Still, there were times when the conjunction of *Holiday* and *Crimewatch* made some of the *Crimewatch* staff uneasy. Jill being seen, dressed beautifully but skimpily for the beach on *Holiday* in mid-evening and then almost immediately afterwards in a *Crimewatch* featuring rape or other violent sexual offences. It did seem a little inappropriate.

Nick is not unaware of the irony that he would become far closer to Jill after her death than he had ever been in life, speaking publicly about her, and almost for her, in the aftermath of her murder, taking a leading part in the charitable fund set up in her name, and attending many days of the trial, sitting alongside Alan Farthing in the reserved seats. He was there, he said, out of interest and compulsion and to represent the BBC, for Jill, along with the dozen or so other producers and assistant producers and journalists and correspondents who were also there on the press benches to report or, in the case of some of the *Crimewatch* team, to make the night-of-the-verdict documentary about Jill's murder.

Among them were Nicholas Witchell, who had been pulled from his duties as royal correspondent and assigned to cover the trial (and who was even sent on a refresher course to revitalise his shorthand note-taking) and Helen Phelps, who was working on the *Crimewatch* documentary. In a further irony, both of them had fallen out with Jill in the months before she died. That was not an easy thing to do – fall out with Jill.

Helen Phelps had been producing one of those *Crimewatch* spin-offs, *Crimewatch Solved*, a pre-recorded programme which Jill was due to present. There had been an administrative oversight, and Jill had not received her script until the morning of the recording. She walked in halfway through the usual lunchtime briefing, just as the food was being served, and stood there looking like thunder.

Helen had noticed this and said to Seetha, 'Do you think Jill's all right?' Seetha had said she didn't know. Helen had gone over to speak to Jill and Jill had completely ignored her — just as if Helen wasn't there. Helen could see that Jill was in a foul temper. When Seetha spoke to Jill it became apparent that she had not been told that the briefing began at one o'clock. Helen was certain she had been informed by the morning fax. Jill's performance in the recording was fantastic and no one would ever have guessed she was in a strop.

Even so, you were not supposed to upset the talent, and Helen felt badly about it. She was producing for the first time and had made a mistake. Jill prided herself on her professionalism, on her good time-keeping, on never forgetting a thing, whether it was a friend's birthday or a work appointment. She relied on others to do the same in their dealings with her; she needed them to be professional, too. Helen went to Jill afterwards to apologise and said, 'Look, I want to apologise, most sincerely.' But she added, 'I'm absolutely positive I sent that fax.'

'OK,' said Jill, 'you did, you did.' Though it was obvious from her tone that she didn't think Helen had sent the fax at all. Helen wished that Jill would say what she felt, but she didn't, and they never really spoke again except to say hello.

It helped Helen that she was not alone on *Crimewatch* in getting into difficulties with Jill. There was at least one other colleague, whose partner worked for a tabloid newspaper, who had been given a hard time by Jill on the grounds of her partner's chosen profession and because Jill suspected she may have leaked some personal information about her.

In truth, the *Crimewatch* team never knew very much personal information about Jill. It was not shared and she could give the appearance of being quite cool or remote.

Helen Phelps vividly remembered sitting in the corner of a studio once, during the recording of something in which she was not particularly involved and Jill coming over to join her and going into this long and impassioned monologue about meeting Alan Farthing, and falling for him, head over heels. Jill was so heartfelt in what she said that it put goose bumps on Helen's skin, the excitement of the romance, the expression of it, just coming like that out of the blue, it seemed amazing, though Helen wondered too what she had done to deserve this disclosure. It was as if she was just there and Jill was just passing through. Just passing through *Crimewatch*.

Most people on the programme agreed that Jill had been transformed by her relationship with Alan. The way she dressed and carried herself, sexier and more confident, the shine of happiness in her eyes, it had affected every inch of her, and permeated her performances on screen, making her more relaxed and assured.

Jill must have been aware that she was not fully engaged with *Crimewatch*. She had simply been too busy to be fully committed, *Crimewatch* only one part of an overflowing schedule of travelling and filming. When she was giving up *Holiday* she spoke to Seetha about the new freedom she would have and Seetha said, 'That's great, because now you can come in more often.' Jill said, 'I want to be involved,' so Seetha initiated regular sessions, fuelled by Prêt à Manger sandwiches and orange juice, in which Jill would be briefed and familiarised with the new material. Unfortunately, these meetings began only three months before her death.

Crimewatch was not the only series which developed spin-off programmes and created a mini empire. It was the same over at *Holiday* where, among other things, they came up with the idea of

Fasten Your Seatbelt, in which presenters were cast in new and unfamiliar roles in the travel industry and expected to act them out on screen.

The prototype was the programme in which Jill became an air hostess for Britannia Airways on a flight from Manchester to Florida. It had once been the peak of Jill's childhood ambitions to become an air hostess.

The programme was directed by Fenia Vardanis, who remembers meeting Jill just before filming was due to start in the air stewardess training rooms near East Midlands Airport. Jill had flown back from a *Holiday* trip the day before and hosted an awards ceremony that evening. The talent was tired before they'd even started. Jill had two days to cram into what was normally five weeks of training. She would only be able to fly as an air stewardess if she passed the qualifying exam.

At the end of the first day's filming, while the crew were packing away their cameras, Jill sat down with Fenia and was in tears as she said she was unhappy with the programme, her head was spinning with all the information. 'I just don't know if I'm going to be able to do this, Fen. You could seriously not have a film.' Fenia guessed that she was afraid of failing, feeling vulnerable, being tested on camera and in front of her colleagues on the crew.

That night the crew went out for dinner and Jill stayed in her room, revising for the air stewardess exams the next day. She sat the exam and scored 98 per cent. Fenia was annoyed with herself for not filming the moment that Jill was told she had passed, when she reacted as if she had just been awarded a First from Cambridge. She was completely thrilled.

Fenia worried that the actual flight, during which Jill would be working properly as an air stewardess, uniform, hat and all, would make dull television. The passengers were to be told to treat Jill as they would any other member of the cabin staff. Jill fetching and carrying cups of water was not likely to be gripping drama.

In fact, from Fenia's point of view, it went like a dream and Jill did everything wrong. She was out of synch in the safety demo, couldn't open the milk cartons in the galley, couldn't manoeuvre the trolley, tried to pour drinks without first opening the can, couldn't stack the food trays in the racks. 'I don't know how they do this job,' she said at one point. 'You'd think stacking trays was easy.'

It was claustrophobic on the plane and even though Fenia tried to keep out of the way, Jill was being followed everywhere by Jonathan Keeping, the cameraman, and the sound recordist. The passengers were watching her every move too. As she progressed down the aisle with the duty-free, Fenia could see that she was becoming very uncomfortable. She liked to be in control and she was way out of control by now.

Jonathan Keeping could see that too. He had worked with Jill dozens of times; a trust existed between them as it should between a cameraman and the person he is filming. She was getting all the calculations wrong for the duty-free, couldn't use the little calculator properly and was getting in a bit of a state.

There was a moment when Jill looked at Jonathan, she didn't say anything but her eyes said she'd had enough. It was a fleeting moment of tension and divided loyalty in which he knew he really ought to stop filming to protect Jill, but carried on because that was his job and because Jill's difficulties were the essence of drama and would make great television. There was no ill feeling between them afterwards, but Jonathan felt he had betrayed Jill, broken the bond of trust.

He was right though – it did make great television, and the programme was very popular when it was screened late in 1996. Jill was voted BBC Personality of the Year in the TRIC (Television and Radio Industry Club) awards the following March. She generously told Fenia that she felt that film had played a significant part in the award. And the experience did not deter her from making another *Fasten Your Seatbelt* some time later again directed by Fenia. In this one, Jill worked at Disneyland in Florida as a character performer and rollerblading street cleaner, 'Dando in Orlando' as it was known.

Jill was featured on the cover of *Radio Times* for the third time in the week that the first *Fasten Your Seatbelt* was screened. Everyone involved had expected her to be portrayed as an air stewardess. Instead she was wearing a black leather jacket over a low-cut white top, black tights and a short black leather skirt. She was posing in such a way that the foreground seemed full of revealed thigh. 'Just Dando. Fasten Your Seatbelt! High-flying Jill as you've never seen her before', read the *Radio Times* cover lines.

John Birt, who was by now director-general of the BBC, asked one of his department heads what a *Six O'Clock News* reader was doing dressed like that on the cover of the BBC's house magazine. He was very disapproving and this must have got back to Jill.

The picture had been Jill's idea. It had been one of a series taken during a session with the celebrity photographer Sven Arnstein, who was Jill's favourite. Jill had chosen the clothes herself and it was apparent to Sven that she was keen to express the sexual side of herself in the photographs. Sven thought portrait photography was quite a sexual business anyway, and always encouraged his subjects to explore their sexuality as long as they were comfortable about it.

It was not a *Radio Times* picture session – it was just a session for Jill. Sven charged no fee to Jill but retained the rights to any fee that might accrue from placing the pictures with magazines. Jill saw the pictures afterwards and was very pleased with them. She loved them, in fact. Sven went ahead and took them to *Radio Times*.

Jill called Sven shortly after they had appeared and asked him to withdraw the pictures from circulation. It would be best, she said, if they were not used again. Sven called the images in from the picture desks and filed them away.

Earlier, in her days as a researcher, Fenia Vardanis had helped to arrange Jill's *Holiday* film at the Vienna Opera Ball. Discussing it in the office, they had agreed that Jill needed a dance partner for the film and Fenia had said to Jane Lush, 'I've got a mad idea. What if I try to get Cliff Richard and surprise her with Cliffy?'

'No chance,' Jane had said. 'You'll never get him.'

Fenia had taken this as a personal challenge. They all knew how much Jill idolised Cliff.

Fenia spoke to Cliff's people and told them what she hoped to achieve. She didn't think it wise to mention that Jill was crazy about Cliff, but said she was very fond of him, a great fan and what an excellent film it would be. How long would you need him for? Fenia faxed over the details, and after some further toing and froing, Cliff was in the bag. Fenia went into Jane's office and said, 'I've got news for you.'

'What?'

'I've got him.'

They celebrated like schoolgirls.

A plot was hatched in which Jill was told many creative lies. She was informed that her dance partner for the evening would be the

Austrian Prince Ludwig Van somebody or other, who was forty-two, spoke six languages and was quite a catch. Jill was taken to Tomasz Starzewski and kitted out with a beautiful dark green velvet ballgown.

In Vienna, on the night of the ball, Jill was upstairs in her room having a bath when Cliff Richard arrived at the hotel with his personal assistant, Roger Bruce. They were briefed on where to go and what to do at the ball. Fenia went off to help Jill get ready and connect the seemingly endless row of hooks and eyes on her gown. Jill said she smelt a rat and Fenia protested her innocence. 'I smell a rat,' persisted Jill. 'There's something going on you're not telling me.'

'I promise you there isn't,' said Fenia.

Cliff was intrigued by the whole thing and both he and Roger were enjoying the subterfuge. Cliff had seen Jill on television and liked her a lot. In fact, they had met some time before, introduced at a Christian media group function when Jill had asked for his autograph 'for a friend' but really for herself and felt silly afterwards, imagining he must have known that the autograph was for her all along, though, actually, Cliff had no memory of that meeting at all.

Earlier that day he had been contributing to a new album by Hank Marvin, which was being produced at the home of the Shadows drummer, Brian Bennett. When he was leaving, Cliff had been asked by Brian where he was going next. 'You'll never believe it,' he had said, 'but I'm going to Austria to meet Jill Dando.' Brian had been suitably impressed.

Cliff and Roger both dressed in white tie and tails for the ball and, once inside, had half an hour or so to wait before the surprise was sprung. Roger took over to ensure that Cliff wouldn't be seen.

They passed the time star-spotting. 'Oh look, isn't that Maximilian Schell? I'm sure that's Mickey Rooney.' Bo Derek and Linda Evans were there, too.

At the crucial moment Jill was doing a piece to camera, saying she was about to meet her dance partner. That was Cliff's cue, as he stood waiting behind the balustrade, behind the camera. He popped his head up just before the cue and saw Jill and ducked away again before she could see him and then he stepped forward from her left and walked towards her through the throng. He saw her scanning the crowd for her prince and do a double-take, and then do that little thing he saw her do many times afterwards, a little tizzy shake of the hands, 'I don't believe it, I don't believe it. Cliff, it's you.'

Cliff saw that there was no attempt to be cool, she was just herself, caught up in the thrill of the surprise. He took to her straight away and they danced on and on while the *Holiday* crew waited patiently for Jill to return to work.

Traditionally, the ball continues through the night and the guests go straight on to breakfast. Cliff and Jill went back to their hotel rooms for a sleep, but dressed again in their finery for breakfast so that *Holiday* could pretend they had danced all night.

Roger remembers how much Cliff and Jill giggled together over breakfast and he could see that Cliff was content, even though he was not much of an early riser.

As the breakfast was filmed in a private room, there was a sudden gust of wind, a freak gale and an almighty crash as a plant pot was toppled from a ledge at the window. Roger remembers being surprised that it didn't smash. But it stayed in his mind because there had been no wind at all a moment before and it seemed odd.

As he and Cliff flew back to London there was no doubt that a new friendship had been forged. Cliff said that he 'fell in like' with Jill and recognised the chemistry between them. There was romanticism in Jill but never anything romantic between him and Jill.

He drew her into his group of friends, his 'little gang', which included Roger and his partner, Alan, Robin Williams, who worked as a cabin services director for British Airways and who also became close to Jill, Gloria Hunniford and her husband, Stephen Way, and Cliff's manager, Bill, and his girlfriend, Pia. Later the group accepted and enjoyed the company of Alan Farthing, just as they enjoyed Jill's pleasure in her love of Alan. As it happened, Alan was a Cliff fan, too.

There were elaborate parties and charity balls and tennis tournaments – Jill took up tennis after she met Cliff – dressy dinners that turned raucous and quiet suppers, and among them all some occasions that became famous in their group.

These occasions were memoralised in the hours after Jill's funeral in Weston at which Cliff had given a reading, a very quiet reading, his voice feeling to him no more than a croak. Gloria Hunniford remembers the incongruity of the funeral, with people outside actually calling out asking for autographs and wanting to just to scream at them to go away. It was an almost unbearable day.

They had travelled down in convoy and planned to return to Cliff's home for fish and chips, but they got caught in traffic on the way back to Surrey and in the end decided to pull off the motorway into a village where there was a pub-restaurant one of them knew.

They sat down and ordered some wine. They were very subdued but otherwise it was just as it might have been when Jill was with them, the group gathered together around a table. It was

Gloria who said, 'Well, come on now, we're going to go round and each tell our favourite story about Jill.'

Cliff recounted the tale of the Vienna Ball. Gloria described the ending of one of their dinner parties, at Robin Williams's home, when Jill was returning to Chiswick to meet Alan (perhaps he was coming off duty) in the early hours of the morning, and they had all gone out on to the drive to see her off. Gloria had strung everyone out across the road, blocking Jill's exit, and led them in a rendition of 'So Long, Farewell', the 'goodnight' song from *The Sound of Music*. Who knows what Robin's neighbours had made of that? Then Jill had driven off and they had only just returned to the dinner table when the doorbell rang and it was Jill, who had forgotten her phone or something, which rather deflated the spectacular exit they had given her.

Roger told the story of his party-piece drag-act alter-ego, Gladys Truckbucket, who had made an appearance during a night at the theatre, when Jill, Alan, Cliff and Robin had gone to see *Chicago* at the Adelphi Theatre and went down to the Royal Room in the interval for a glass of champagne. Roger was lying in wait in the loo, as Gladys the cleaner, with Marigold gloves, a wig, a pink frock and a lavatory brush and burst into the room, greeting Jill Dandini and Alan Halfpenny. Gladys had been invented as a voice on the phone in hotel rooms to deter persistent fans of Cliff.

The story was also told of the incident that had occurred earlier in the evening during the 'Sound of Music' dinner at Robin Williams's home, while Robin had been in the kitchen. His friend Malcolm had been swinging back on his dining chair and had lost his balance and crashed into the fireplace, decapitating three of Robin's army of miniature terracotta warriors.

Everyone had been in hysterics, Jill crying with laughter, Gloria looking, as Roger put it, as if her bra might explode. When somebody pointed out that the figures were probably very valuable and that Robin might be upset, it only increased the hysteria. Robin had indeed seemed briefly put out when he came through to see what all the fuss was about, though in fact they were inexpensive stone figures and he soon recovered.

At some point during the story telling, surreally, somebody in the pub, obviously unaware of who they were or why they were there, had gone to the piano and begun playing 'Roll Out the Barrel', which was so inappropriate it was funny and together with the stories pushed them all from one extreme to the other so that they all began laughing and there was a little release from the sadness.

Cliff would say that like many people in showbusiness he had lots of acquaintances and very few showbusiness friends, apart from Gloria and Bobby Davro, and then Jill.

Roger Bruce, who has known Cliff for many years, thought that Cliff and Jill shared a number of similarities. He suspected that people thought Jill was too good to be true, and he well knew that this was how people thought of Cliff. Is he really as nice as he seems? Roger was always being asked this. 'To be honest, he is nicer,' he would say.

Like others, Roger wondered if something romantic might develop between Jill and Cliff. Jill wondered that, too. Wondered and hoped that it might happen. Everyone who knew her well knew that she was truly besotted with Cliff. It was, said Sally Magnusson, like a holiday romance.

On 28 October 1996 Jill had lunch with Jeffrey Archer at Le Caprice, Jeffrey's favourite London restaurant. Jeffrey thought of

Jill as one of his 'Caprice girls'. A Caprice girl was sensible and intelligent and you lunched her for good conversation and not for anything else. Jeffrey adored the company of women. Most men, he knew, would rather have lunch with other men, but not him. Women were stimulating and fun and perfect companions for lunch, and Jill was the classic example.

They had first met some years earlier when she had interviewed him for regional television during his campaign for one of Margaret's elections in the West Country. Jill had told him she came from Weston, which set them giggling together straight away, and Jeffrey had immediately fancied her. Jill's father, of course, had typeset Jeffrey's mother's column in the *Mercury*. Jeffrey's snooty mother, Lola, as Jack remembered her, and her column 'Over the Teacups' which was often about her son Tuppence – Jeffrey.

He was never in any doubt, because it was the same for him too, that Jill knew exactly where she came from. They both knew they were bloody lucky because only one or two ever get through that net. Luck, yes, and a little ambition.

Jeffrey was a former deputy chairman of the Conservative Party, Lord Archer of Weston-Super-Mare, a Tory grandee, of sorts, before his recent comeuppance.

Even though Jeffrey fancied Jill he had always thought of women as falling into six or seven categories and Jill, he felt certain, fell into that category in which there was a sort of purity, a girl with whom there could be no relationship unless you really were in love with her. He could have been wrong, but he was sure he wasn't.

Instead he liked to flirt with her, outrageously if he could get away with it, because he always liked to let someone know if he thought they were beautiful, as Jill was. She was clever, too, and knew exactly what he was doing, and could be just as flirty and wicked in return.

She was never in his Group A list of friends and he was never in her Group A list but they would often meet at functions, especially at the many charity functions Jeffrey attended, and he would occasionally invite her to be a 'Caprice girl' for lunch.

He knew she had been with Bob Wheaton for many years and used to wonder why they had never married. Though in this modern age he supposed it was a marriage of sorts. Jeffrey knew women with children who were never going to get married so he ought not to have been too surprised. Still, he always sensed some sadness there with Jill which he did not feel able to explore, much as he would have liked to. That sadness only made her seem sexier and more alluring.

At Le Caprice, Jill would talk about her career and where it was going. She talked about wanting to write, as Jeffrey found many people did when they talked to him. He wondered if she was finding her work too frivolous and looking for more grown-up challenges. So many of the intelligent people he knew went through that phase in the middle of their lives. Jeffrey told her that she should write her autobiography. She said it was too soon, but she was thinking about it for later.

As they left the restaurant that lunchtime there was a paparazzo nearby and Jill was sure a photograph was taken of her and Jeffrey together, which worried her. She would have to tell Bob about meeting Jeffrey, just in case it appeared in the papers.

Jill went on to the BBC, where she had some voiceover recording to do for *Holiday* that afternoon. She had not been in the studio long when Michael Aspel appeared with a red book under his arm.

That was the pick-up, as they call it on the programme. 'Jill Dando, This Is Your Life.'

The programme was recorded that evening and broadcast a week later, the day before Jill's thirty-fifth birthday.

Bob had worked closely with the researchers who had prepared the programme. Along with the predictable roster of celebrity guests, they had involved Jill's immediate family and people who had played a part in her early life – the surgeon who carried out her childhood heart operation, a primary school teacher, colleagues from the beginnings of her career – while somehow managing to miss out on many of Jill's closest friends and workmates. She rang round some of them afterwards to apologise. She felt that the programme was not really about her but a version of her, filtered in part through Bob's eyes.

She was flattered, of course, and, as Jenny Higham said, it was a kind of validation of Jill and how much she'd achieved. It was reinforcing and good for her confidence.

Still, Jill was irritated, when she went off to change for the recording, to find that Bob had already laid out two choices of outfit for her to wear, a number one choice and a number two choice. He was just being methodical, thinking of everything, but Jill complained about it later to friends, even though she went ahead and wore the number one choice.

Ally, her agent, was with Jill on the way to the studio in Teddington. Ally had worked with the programme too, getting very cloak-and-dagger with Bob, worrying that Jill was going to think they were having an affair.

Jill didn't look very happy before she went in and Ally said, 'Are you all right?'

Jill said, 'Yes, but I'm only thirty-four.'

'Yes, I know,' said Ally, 'but you can have it done again.'

'Can I?'

'Yes,' said Ally. 'It's not the end of your life.'

Ally sensed that the lack of security with Bob was not helping. Jill said that she and Bob were not 'really together-together'.

After the show and the post-show hospitality, Jill and Bob went home and had an argument, or at least a rather tense conversation. The way Jill described it later, some people were left with the impression that she and Bob had a blazing row, apparently about *This Is Your Life*. That was certainly how she presented it the following morning when she went to meet her family for coffee at the hotel where they had been billeted overnight. Judith, who was in the last term of pregnancy with her first child, had flown in from the Alps, and Auntie Esme and Uncle Ken were there, too. Esme recalled that Jill was upset because of the trouble with Bob the night before, when she had told him he had ruined her special day.

In fact, the disagreement had been, on the face of it, about Jeffrey Archer. Bob said Jill had seemed perfectly happy when they got home and they'd had another glass of champagne, probably both had a bit too much to drink. A stressful time for both of them. Then Jill had told Bob about meeting Jeffrey – or at least, about having had lunch with a successful, married millionaire.

Bob said he wasn't jealous about it – millionaires could take who they like out for lunch – but ought not to do it without their wives knowing. Did his wife know? Jill said she thought not. 'Think about it,' said Bob, inventing a headline. 'JILL DANDO GETS ACCUSED OF BREAKING UP MILLIONAIRE'S MARRIAGE.' Not a particularly good idea.

Evidently Jill was not pleased to receive this advice from Bob and became cross with him. They had argued a while, and then, as Bob recalls, she had said, 'Oh God, why must we have an argument on the day my life and career are being fêted?'

Bob had known that Jill would take pleasure in being the subject of *This Is Your Life*, but he also realised she would be resistant to being seen to be too proud of her life, chancing fate, as she had earlier in the year, falling down the stairs on the way to the Weston reunion. It was tempting providence, *This Is Your Life* when you were only thirty-four; it could seem like a bad omen.

As it happened, Jill was due to meet Jan Knott for lunch on the day after the *This Is Your Life* recording. She phoned him that morning to cancel, telling him about the programme and explaining that she had old friends and relatives to see in London.

Jill did not arrange to be with Bob on her birthday that year, for the first time in their relationship. Bob had always tried to preserve fixed points in the year for the two of them to share. But that was gone now. The fun and the pleasures they had enjoyed together, the Carribbean holidays, their kindnesses to each other, the shared excitement of their professional lives, all in the past.

Their last holiday together, their final trip to Barbados where they had been several times, had been earlier in October, following Bob's fiftieth birthday, for which Jill had arranged dinner for twelve at the Ritz and presented Bob with an Omega watch. It was typical of her, he said, that she could've purchased the watch for two thirds of the price passing through duty-free but had gone ahead and bought it in London, regardless of the cost.

For all that Bob insists he was not jealous, Jill's friends sensed his increasing anxiety as the end of their relationship approached. Jill took to making silly subterfuges when she was meeting a man for lunch, however innocuous the occasion might be. She would pretend she was meeting a woman friend and make sure that the woman knew to cover for her if necessary.

Jenny Higham knew that Jill was embarrassed by this and realised how ridiculous it was, even as she persisted because, apparently, it was easier than leaving Bob. You couldn't necessarily blame Bob's possessiveness for this. It somehow suited Jill, too. They were clinging on to each other.

Jenny had found it irritating, early on in the relationship with Bob, lunching with Jill, because you could guarantee that her mobile would go and Jill would be tense about having to answer it and there would be Bob, Jill saying, 'Yes, I'm here with Jenny. We're just having lunch, yes.' Jenny had no idea whether Bob really was checking up but she felt like saying, 'Get lost, Bob, we're in the middle of lunch.' Towards the end, Jenny noted, Jill didn't even bother answering the phone or would simply switch it off.

Jenny was round at Gowan Avenue one day and noticed some cards and embossed invitations on Jill's mantelpiece. There must have been seven of them. 'The prime minister requests the pleasure of your company …' 'The director-general of the BBC invites you …' Jenny went along the shelf reading them all, the most fantastic, glamorous display, and they all read Jill Dando, or Jill Dando and partner, or Jill Dando plus guest, and maybe one 'Jill Dando and Bob Wheaton'. Jenny said, 'Hey, girl, you're really going somewhere now. Look at all these. Who would've thought five years ago you'd have had all this?' They laughed about it, but the cards told another story too. It was no longer Jill going places because of Bob. Bob was the plus one.

Cousin Judith told Jill, 'You've got to be brave and leave.' Jill knew she had to be brave but she had no confidence that she would ever meet another long-term partner.

In late November Jill flew to South Africa to make a safari film for *Holiday*. She met Simon Bassil, who was working as a ranger on the game reserve. She fell for Simon and made shorthand notes about him in her diary. It was like the woman's equivalent of a schoolgirl crush. Simon was still in his twenties, tall and handsome, every inch the game ranger, though in fact he had a career in computer technology. He travelled to England within a matter of weeks, by which time Jill had already recovered from her crush and was determined to keep him at arm's length while continuing to see him. 'He hasn't come over for me,' she told Ally Lewis, 'and if he has, he's mistaken.' He was the catalyst, though, for the ending with Bob.

Jill and Bob went to a reception at 10 Downing Street at the end of the first week of December. It was the week that Jill's *Radio Times* cover came out: 'Fasten Your Seatbelt. High-flying Jill as you've never seen her before.'

They chatted briefly to John Major. Major's premiership was on its uppers. They mingled and, as Bob recalled it, Jill was the star of the occasion, as always.

After the reception they walked across London, across Trafalgar Square and Piccadilly Circus, then headed north along Regent Street to the Langham Hilton, opposite Broadcasting House. They sat down with glasses of champagne and agreed to call it a day. They talked it through, all very civilised, and then they went their separate ways.

Jill and Bob remained in contact by phone and it was apparent to her friends that Jill retained great affection for Bob and continued to rely on him for advice in her career. Bob says she once told him she thought about him every day. She invited him to join her, as a special thank you for everything he'd done, when she received her Television Personality of the Year award.

They did not meet again until a year later, when they bumped into each other while shopping in Selfridges. Bob had begun a new and enduring relationship within three months of their separation. He had left the BBC and was working as a media consultant. Jill had just come back from Australia with Alan.

Jill noticed Bob's sports coat and felt its cloth between her fingers. 'That's very nice,' she said. 'Armani, isn't it?'

'Yes, ' said Bob.

'I've just bought Alan one like that,' said Jill. That was to be one of their last meetings. Bob felt it had settled something; meeting as old friends like that.

Bob took his son to Jamaica after Christmas of 1996, and Jill took her father for a Boxing Day trip on Concorde, which was his Christmas gift, arranged for Jill by Jan Knott.

Poor Jan was soon being ribbed in his local pub, the Mermaid, when reports of Jill's new lover appeared in the tabloids. 'What's she doing with Crocodile Dundee, then?' Jan had no idea.

Jill took Simon with her to see Judith in the French Alps for the New Year. Judith and her new baby, Emilie. Jill bought Simon some clothes and skiwear – there was seven feet of snow that New Year's Eve. They celebrated in a hotel bar, along with Auntie Esme and Uncle Ken.

Esme remembers how tall Simon was and how much he ate, which was a lot. But he was very nice and she liked him (though not as much as she liked Alan, later, of course).

Ken isn't sure, but he has a vague memory that Simon might have dodged buying a round of drinks. That is the kind of thing he noticed, just as he remembers being stood at a bar once with Bob, squirming as Bob lectured the barman on how to mix his drink.

It was strange for Judith seeing Jill with somebody else, just as it must have been strange for Jill seeing Judith with her lovely baby, who Jill adored. Simon was very easy to get along with but, awful though it might sound, seemed out of his league with Jill, his importance to her being that he had served the purpose of the ending with Bob.

They all had a party that evening, B52 cocktails, the lot, and Jill decorated Emilie's baby seat with streamers and put a note on it that read: 'Born to party, 1996.' Emilie slept through the whole evening. When it was time to leave there had been so much fresh snow that they could hardly get the car back up the hill, and Judith's partner had to drive them in shifts. On the last run the car gave up altogether and Jill and Simon had to help Ken up the hill, slipping and sliding, arriving back drenched and in fits of laughter. Judith thought it was great to see Jill so relaxed and not having to mind her Ps and Qs, as she did with Bob.

Welcome to 1997. Jill reborn to party She had twenty-eight months to live.

Ten

Bob was one of the few people who knew about Jill's car accident in the early months of 1997. Neither he nor any of the others who heard about it could remember exactly when it had taken place, and nobody had a clear idea of exactly what had happened. No other vehicle had been involved so there was no record of it anywhere, except in the memories of those she told.

Jill had fallen asleep momentarily or got lost in a daydream at the wheel of her BMW while driving along the motorway. It was probably the M4 but may have been the M5. Some said she was returning to London from the West Country. Others thought she was on her way to Weston. They all agreed that she was over-tired, probably just back from a *Holiday* trip, perhaps jet-lagged. She didn't tell her family, and when she told Pete Baylis she made him promise not to mention it to her father. She had not told Jane

Lush, the editor of *Holiday*, though she talked about it with colleagues on her next assignment.

Jenny was the first person she had called after it happened, calling her on the hands-free from the hard shoulder of the motorway. She was in a kind of hysteria, half-sobbing, half-laughing. 'Oh my God, you'll never guess what just happened to me.'

She had skidded out of control and spun round on the motorway, circling in complete turns across the lanes to the verge, where she had ended up facing in the wrong direction, the emergency rollbars flipping up with the velocity of the spin. There had been lorries just behind her and somehow they had missed her. She was OK, but she had thought she was going to die. She had felt close to death and wanted to let Jenny know that she was alive.

In describing the incident to Fenia Vardanis, she spoke of it as a near-death experience, a spiritual experience in which she had called out to, or thought of, God and felt sure that God saved her.

Both Pete and Bob remembered her saying how terrible it had been, how frightening. Pete knew what a dreadful driver she was at the best of times, let alone when she was gripped by jet lag. Bob thought of the accident again after her death. He always felt that, after her childhood illness, Jill believed she was living on borrowed time.

It seemed to Bob that this explained why she was so vividly alive and sparkling, goodness running through her to the core. That was what most people remembered about her, the overwhelming impression she always left behind, her radiance, her kindness, her warmth, her goodness, her generosity. None of it for show or for self-advancement, just natural and genuine and true. It made those who entered her orbit feel good too.

The cameraman Jonathan Keeping remembered Jill describing

the car accident to him while they were on location. It was apparent to him that she did not feel she had survived by luck but because someone was watching over her.

The car accident may well have reinforced Jill's determination to give up *Holiday*, though it does not appear to have reinvigorated her faith. Or if it did, she kept that to herself.

Jill's relationship with her faith was complex and undoubtedly bound up with her mother and the loss of her mother. The strictures by which she had lived in her youth seemed to have been cast aside. She never attended church regularly again after she left Weston and sometimes came under pressure from her early religious mentors, the ministers from the Baptist Church at Milton, to return to the fold. There was some disappointment that she did not maintain her attendance. She took counsel from them, especially when she was making plans for her wedding, but she continued to move away from the Church and from any public identification with her religion. She would not have married in Weston, nor in a Baptist church.

Alan had had a similar upbringing. His father was a Baptist lay preacher and Alan had been involved in the church and its youth group. He would say that his lapse of faith had been greater than Jill's, that her Christianity continued to be important to her but in a private way, her own faith, worked out for herself.

She had been through an evangelical phase back in Weston, but that was way behind her now. She no longer wanted to be seen to be selling religion, to give interviews that drew attention to her beliefs and might serve to turn her, literally, into some kind of figurehead. She was, however, always willing and ready to play that role for the good causes of her mentors, and would always turn out to support these. For certain charities, in particular

Weston Hospice Care, her old Baptist friend Andy Gathercole's Matthew Project, the British Airways' children's charity, Dreamflight, and the British Heart Foundation, she became a figurehead.

Charities need public figures to draw attention to their causes. Jill would rarely turn anything down, would buy the tickets to the charity functions, casually – and discreetly – pay double the price on the ticket, which was probably expensive enough to begin with, to boost funds. Privately, beyond the celebrity merry-go-round of charitable events, Jill devoted considerable time and effort to the causes that she most cared about, that meant something to her, because of her own past.

The Weston Hospice, by way of example, relied on Jill's name as patron for fund-raising and visible support. However far she had moved away from Weston, Jill continued to remain close at heart to the hospice, albeit mostly at a distance and in tandem with her commitments to the other charities.

In the way of small towns, such as Weston, Andy Page, the hospice fund-raising manager, had known Jill since childhood. She had been two years ahead of him in bible class, in the same class as his sister. Jill always asked after her when they spoke, asked after Andy's wife, Helen, especially when Helen became pregnant. She seemed excited about it and sent them a lovely card when Laura was born. Just small things, really, but they meant a lot to him. That was so Jill, said Andy. And it was. That was Jill, who remembered the details, people's names, the events in their lives, always took an interest, always responded.

Jill's name had helped to raise nearly £100,000 to open an in-patient care unit at the hospice. She was there for the opening and returned for the dedication ceremony which was conducted by the Bishop of Bath and Wells. Andy remembered how pleased the

Bishop was, to have met and shaken hands with that famous Jill Dando from the television.

One of the patients, a young man in his late twenties with two children and a rare, terminal cancer, had been fund-raising for the hospice himself and hit a low-point in his illness so Andy faxed Jill his name and number and a brief explanation and she called him direct – as you might a friend who was in need of a fillip – and they chatted a while and even though he still died, just a couple of months before Jill, the memory of that conversation, the fact that she had take the trouble to call, Jill Dando calling him, was a cherished memory.

She called in at the hospice one Saturday, in the summer of 1998. Telephoned Andy on the Friday, said she was going to be in Weston and would like to visit, stressed that it should be informal and not a press-call, arrived that Saturday afternoon and spent ages, the longest time, just talking to all the patients, just the same with them as she might have been with anyone else, natural and at ease, and even though her celebrity was a big deal to the people there, she made them feel comfortable.

Andy remembered the buzz in the place during and after that visit, the impact it had on patients and staff. And remembered how she would be inquiring later about the people she had met, always by name of course, even though the inquiry was always likely to prompt the receipt of some sad news, hospices being shadowed by death.

They could be sentimental places too, so that the people there would be moved later, by Jill's death, to express those profound feelings of loss and describe, as many people did, in emotive language, the near spiritual quality of her glowing presence in life; the pleasure of being touched by that presence, however briefly.

In the jargon of the modern charity, which was the language of Andy Page's job, there was a lot of connectivity with Jill. She gave good value – she was like royalty – in terms of income-generation and even though the hospice quickly decided on the day not to do anything that might appear to exploit her death, her association with it continued to be of considerable, if not even greater benefit.

So that, even in death, Jill continued to do good.

She was and remained an essentially conservative person, Conservative too, though how far to the right I couldn't say (Alan and Jenny and others were oddly reluctant to discuss her politics. If I was to guess at the reason why, it would be that they may have thought her a little naive in her politics and prone to be reactionary, but that's pure guesswork).

As Alan saw it, Jill believed in God and an underlying purpose to life; believed in respecting and upholding what you might call the core values of decency: kindness to others, politeness, sensitivity. She had less time for the inhibiting rules and regulations of organised religion and even less still for rudeness, self-importance, excessive bad language, discourtesy (all of which could be found in one or two of her BBC newsreader colleagues) – and late taxis.

There were, of course, contradictions in Jill's outlook. While people evolve, the tenets of a faith can remain unchanged, stuck in the past. Jill had moved on. There was an element of her that was pleasingly hedonistic. And even while she continued to present the occasional edition of *Songs of Praise* for the BBC she could become irritated with the way the Church seemed to use her, as she did when Jenny Higham showed her a Christian leaflet espousing churchy values in quotes attributed to Jill.

'I find it really irritating', she said, 'when they use quotes and interviews from years ago and make it look like I just said it yesterday.'

Curiously, Cliff Richard told me that he and Jill hardly ever discussed Christianity. They brushed against it occasionally but never faced each other eye to eye for a discussion. He thought perhaps that conversation had been unnecessary, that they both knew where they stood and what they stood for.

Cliff's PA, Roger, said that Jill had once asked him if you had to be a Christian to work for, or be close to, Cliff and Roger said, no, that wasn't part of it. No one would have known what his beliefs were when he joined Cliff. No one asked him. 'As it happens,' he told her, 'I am a Christian, but probably one of the most unconventional Christians you will ever meet.'

Roger remembered Jill saying how much she admired Cliff and all that he represented, admired him for not being afraid to be counted as a Christian.

Of course, Jill would have wanted Cliff to know that. Her admiration for him was the least of it.

Eleven

In the months that followed, the senior officers would sit in Hamish Campbell's office at Kensington and have agonising conversations about suspects. Names would be put forward and explored and considered and reconsidered, endlessly. They would go over and over the details, especially the whys. Why this and that person could and, always, could not have been responsible.

They became surreal, those discussions, as if Jill Dando wasn't actually dead and no one had killed her because no one seemed to fit. They had to remind themselves. She had been murdered, and somebody had done it. There must be somebody out there who would answer to the whys.

As Hamish came to think of the investigation, it was shrouded in darkness, the officers were in darkness. He would joke with them sometimes, well, half-joking, they might see light at the end, but watch out: it could be a train coming straight towards them, about to hit them head-on.

Some days, on days of shining optimism, they would feel they were so close, just a day away, only a day away from the answer. It all seemed too complicated. You would get that feeling with other murders, that if you could just point the torch here or there the solution would reveal itself. This case seemed determined to resist the revelation. That was the darkness, as Hamish would say, the darkness of Dando. Or part of it. For Hamish, the darkness of Dando was a multi-layered concept.

That morning, as he arrived in Gowan Avenue at about 12.20, Hamish thought they would catch the person responsible straight-away. In that opening drama of confused information he was wrongly told that the murder had occurred within the previous half-hour. This meant that the killer was only a few steps ahead of them and, as he imagined, was bound to be caught.

The ambulance that took Jill to Charing Cross Hospital had only just left. At about the time that she should have been meeting Anastasia Baker at the Lanesborough Hotel for the charity fashion show, Jill was arriving instead at the hospital, dead in all but formality.

The ambulance had passed Hamish going north on Munster Road as he travelled south to turn left into Gowan Avenue. If he could replay those early minutes, put himself there and in charge immedi-ately, he would have said, 'Leave her where she is, don't touch anything, preserve the scene intact.' The scene was everything, it told the whole story, or as much of it as could be known. But of course, the ambulance crews had acted on their best instincts, trying to save her, though in reality she had died instantly and was beyond help.

To make their vain attempt at resuscitation, the ambulance crews had moved Jill from the position in which she had come to rest, almost sitting, slumped and twisted awkwardly in the porch with her back to the front door, and laid her out on her path. There was no way now of being absolutely sure of the exact position in which she had been found.

The investigating officers would recreate the doorway and the porch later, at a police photographic studio, and attempt to establish the correct position using a policewoman as a model and gathering the first witnesses at the scene, Helen Doble and others, to describe what they recalled. They would end up with a sequence of photographs, one for each witness, each one showing the policewoman – the body – in a different position. There was no consensus, and that important piece of information was lost for ever.

It was Hamish's mantra throughout the investigation: go back, go back. Go back to the victim and to the crime scene, what do they tell us? Why is she dead and who killed her? He was not certain at first that it even was Jill Dando. He couldn't believe she had been killed and wanted to be sure beyond doubt. What a blunder that would be, announcing her death and then to discover that the victim was someone visiting Jill. He wanted to wait for Alan's identification of the body before allowing a formal announcement.

When he arrived at number 29, the case falling to him in a routine way as duty senior officer of the Serious Crime Group at Kensington, Hamish really was thinking there would be an instant arrest.

He was told that officers had stopped somebody. That's interesting, he thought, and asked who it was. 'Well, he's been eliminated,' came the reply. 'Who has he been eliminated by?' 'He had been eliminated by the neighbour from across the road, Mr Upfill-Brown.'

Hamish was not satisfied with that. These were his usual rules:

assume nothing, believe nobody, check everything twice. 'Go round and find him now,' he said. It could be him and besides, if the perpetrator wasn't caught quickly, that face would be lost. So they went back to the suspect, but he was a much younger man, too young, and was properly eliminated. Oh God, thought Hamish.

He knew by 12.30 or so that the murder had in fact occurred an hour earlier, at about 11.30. So already the suspect was an hour, soon to be ninety minutes ahead of them. He could be in Guildford by now. Or anywhere. Out of range already, slipping away.

Hamish stood for a long time just looking at the front of number 29, stood very still, being calm, studying the crime scene for what seemed like hours. He retained a mental picture of every murder scene he had visited and could remember the thought process that went on. Thoughts about the scene and how the investigation should proceed. It was not a unique event, being here now, but it was already different and distinctive.

Out of those pictures in his head he could envisage the killings themselves, could go back and almost see the crimes being committed in his imagination. He thought it was the same for many investigating officers. Just here, right now, someone just shot you. That was unbelievable. He hated the mystery of an unsolved case and would be troubled by it, wanting to know how and why. He would be troubled by the mystery of this particular scene.

In his much-favoured bell chart analogy, the bell chart of life, there was everyone and everything that was normal or the norm grouped together in the middle and along the outer edges, there was the out-of-the-ordinary and the odd, there was the murder of Jill Dando, unseen in the middle of the day, a celebrity assassinated on the doorstep of her own home. The uniqueness of that would become increasingly apparent.

The scene disclosed that Jill had been shot, a single shot, the bullet that had passed through her head and the cartridge expelled from the gun lying there separately, the shell on the doormat in the porch, the bullet on the tiles of the porch floor. There was the slight splintering, low down on the architraving of the front door where the bullet had struck.

As the postmortem would soon reveal, the bullet had entered Jill's head just above and behind her left ear and exited just above and in front of her right ear. The gun had been pressed hard against her head so that the muzzle had left an imprint on her skin. This 'hard contact' had created a vacuum which had muffled the explosion of the firing, and acted as an effective silencer.

Putting the splinter mark and the entry and exit wounds together it was possible to work out that the bullet had travelled almost horizontally, which meant that Jill's head had also been low down when she was shot, practically on or just above the raised step of the porch.

There was no way of knowing how or why she had been in that position. There was slight bruising, just an inch wide, on her right forearm, which could have happened as she was gripped and forced down by her assailant. It was equally possible that she had ducked to try and escape the bullet or simply been caught as she stooped to retrieve her dropped keys.

The person who fired the shot must have been low down too, holding the gun in a horizontal position. It was not possible to say with certainty whether that person was right- or left-handed, though it would've have been easier for someone who was right-handed.

There was a lot of blood at the scene, most related to the aftermath, the loss of blood following the shooting and the work of the ambulance crews. There was some spattering on the porch floor and on the lower part of the door. All that blood was Jill's.

There were three distinctive shoeprints, one of which would never be traced. This was a mark at the front of the porch, not quite complete, which made it impossible to establish which way it was pointing or what size it was. It did not seem to be the print of a leather shoe. The shoeprint had been made when the sole was wet, perhaps from rain or from blood. Its age could not be determined, so it may have been old, or it might have been left that morning. It has never been eliminated. There were no fingerprints of significance.

The police would later conduct searches, on their hands and knees, of Jill's tiny front garden. They would find a nail, a piece of tinfoil, the business card of an antiques' dealer, many hairs and fibres. Wind-blown detritus.

When the bullet and the shell were examined at the forensic science laboratories they would be identified as a single round of 9mm calibre. Not the more common and more powerful 9mm parabellum, but the smaller 9mm, known as a short or a .380. The case was stamped with the manufacturer's mark: 'R-P .380 auto', from Remington in the United States.

The cartridge had not been used before but it did have six indentation marks on its surface. They were variously known as crimp marks, crimping or stab crimping and were not machine made but made by hand, apparently using a gun maker's tools or something more amateur, such as a punch or a nail and an ordinary hammer. Those marks could have been made for a practical purpose, to tighten the bullet in the shell, or they could have been decorative. There was no way of knowing why the marks had been made. No obvious reason. Nothing apparent.

A short round could not have been fired effectively from a parabellum handgun. The gun that had been used to shoot Jill was a 9mm short which was uncommon in criminal usage. The two police forensic science laboratories, one in Manchester and one in London, had over 2,000 unsolved cases involving firearms over twenty years and only eighty-three of them involved shorts.

A short pistol in regular usage was like a back-up pistol, an officer's personal sidearm. This particular short was more unusual because it had left no spiralled scoring marks on the outside of the shell casing. This meant it was a smooth-barrelled weapon and therefore not a regular gun.

Ordinary guns have spiral marks, known as rifling, along the inner length of their barrels to grip the round and send it spinning to its target in a stable trajectory. There were only three feasible explanations for a gun with a smooth barrel and no rifling. It could have been a deactivated gun that had been reactivated, modified to make it incapable of firing in line with the 1988 UK legislation on handguns, and then remodified later to return it to working order. This process required a degree of technical skill. Secondly, it could have been a blank firing pistol converted to fire live rounds but this was unlikely because the typical blank firing pistol, such as a Bruni, used 8mm blanks and could not be readily adapted to take 9mm rounds. The third possibility was a weapon with a 24-inch barrel that had been cut down, back to normal size. 24-inch barrels fell outside the 1988 laws and could therefore be legally owned. Cutting them down made them illegal but easier to use.

Most likely, the gun was a reactivated deactivated weapon. Whatever it was, it was not a normal gun. As Hamish Campbell would say, it was not really a gun at all in the conventional sense. Of all the weapons that could have killed Jill, it had to be a gun that wasn't a gun.

The story the crime scene told could be interpreted almost

anyway you liked. As the work of a professional assassin who had been calm and controlled and precise. Or as the act of someone who had simply been lucky in achieving their purpose so neatly and swiftly. An enraged person, perhaps, in that hard contact, forcing the gun into the side of Jill's head. It felt like an act of anger.

All this information came quickly to Hamish, within the first few days, but he was judicious about making it public, not wanting to disclose everything at once, trying to manage the intense outside interest in Jill's murder and to get the investigation under control, which was, frankly, a challenge in those early stages. He sensed that if the answer did not come soon the inquiry could be a long one. He felt sure that the killer would be somebody in Jill's life – a boyfriend, lover, colleague – someone with a specific motive as opposed to a random act. Money, love, jealousy, revenge, the reasons that drive people to murder.

He would later categorise the case as a 'stranger homicide', which was a rarity, but that was not how he thought of it at the beginning, not at all, though of course you could never rule anything out.

It is standard practice in major investigations for the Senior Investigating Officer to maintain a logbook of strategic decisions, supported by reason and theory, so that those decisions can be reviewed and justified. This ensures that the investigations and the actions of the SIO are accountable. This was Hamish writing in his log on the day after Jill's death, on 27 April 1999:

> The identity of the victim as Jill Dando raises immediate concerns for the motive for the killing. It's clear even without the media's intense speculation and theories (which are already wide and wild) that a precise understanding of events on 26 April must be established quickly . . .

Following the first meeting the main thrust of the inquiry
will be forensic and witnesses . . . within these two broad
lines of inquiry are a range of actions and duties . . . There is
pressure and temptation to conduct immediate and wide-
sweeping inquiries into the varieties of suspect categories
and to explore theories. My view is that this is not the time.
Evidence is sought now or it will be lost for ever.

It was like an ambush. Jill's murder had been a surprise to
everyone and why would that not be true of the Metropolitan
Police and the Serious Crime Group at Kensington. You went
along, you do this murder, that murder, bit tricky, takes a few
weeks then suddenly, boof. This. There were only twelve or
thirteen people in the office. Hamish was still only a chief
inspector.

If you just calmed down, took it one step at a time, that would
be OK. But above him, as Hamish could tell, there was unease at
times.

Just as the media and the public were putting forward their own
theories, some of them presented as hard facts in the papers, so the
Met was theorising too. Senior officers came to Hamish to tell him:
'It'll be to do with Farthing's gynaecology work,' or 'It'll be to do
with *Crimewatch*.' None of this was very helpful or constructive,
whether it came from outside or from within the Met. Hamish was
just desperately trying to sort out the initial bits of work.

His log for 28 April, the Wednesday after the Monday murder:

Real requirement to take calm, measured assessment of
this murder . . . Press interest is enormous and almost

overwhelming. My decision remains to focus on the crime scene, get evidence, which is coming, and to secure a subsequent conviction.

Theories and speculation must be put to one side at this stage. They are causing a distraction now. Reinforce this thought process and record it for there is a danger of the murder investigation becoming swept away in a hysteria of media hype. The concern is that 'something must be done now' syndrome to produce a result. The inquiry team is building up daily and an enormous amount of work being tackled but there are no short-cuts . . . It is my assessment this murder is a protracted investigation . . . My investigative strategy will bring order from chaos and speculation.

The inquiry, which would eventually involve more than forty officers, was assigned a randomly generated name, Operation Oxborough, and entered into HOLMES, a snappy acronym for the lumbering title of the UK's police computer programme, Home Office Large Major Enquiry System. HOLMES was a DOS-based programme, an antique by the current standards of technology. HOLMES 2, which would work in Windows and have greater capabilities in terms of tracking and cross-referencing information, was still in development.

HOLMES was intended to streamline the flow of information through inquiries and make them less vulnerable to human error or oversight. It had been born out of the disastrous Yorkshire Ripper inquiry in the seventies, which had been buried in paperwork and repeatedly missed its target while women continued to die. The Ripper inquiry had relied on indexed filing cards, thousands and thousands of them ('Sutcliffe, P.' had been tucked away in there somewhere several times), which had given the inquiry offices a distinctly Victorian appearance.

The essential vulnerability of HOLMES was that all the information still had to be typed into the system. Information was received and recorded in longhand on Message sheets, and the Messages were typed on to the computer to generate Actions, which were allocated to officers to pursue.

It was Message 16, on 26 April, that generated Action 1, to TIE – trace, interview and eliminate – a man identified by an anonymous caller who had reportedly stated his intention to kill Jill Dando. The man had recently been released from a psychiatric hospital. He had nothing to do with Jill's death.

One day, many months later, in one of those somebody-must-have-done-it conversations, Oxborough's Detective Inspector, Ian Horrocks, would say to Hamish, 'Why don't we go back to the first 500 calls, that would give us the first week? Surely if someone's phoned in about a suspect there's a good chance he'll be in there somewhere?' So they looked at the first 500 calls, which took them up to about 6 pm on the first day.

After the trial the Met issued a single A4 sheet, a press release of statistics relating to the inquiry: 5,000 people spoken to, 2,400 statements taken, 10,500 actions generated, 7,000 pieces of information received, 80,000 phone numbers checked, 14,000 e-mails examined . . . For most of the inquiry Hamish had one typist to rely on. Sometimes two if he was lucky. It was a continuing dilemma: what to type in straightaway and what to leave until later, how to prioritise when you didn't really know what you were looking for.

Moving outwards from the scene, the investigation focused on the two sightings of a man leaving Jill's house heading west, towards Fulham Palace Road and Bishop's Park. Neither Richard Hughes, Jill's next-door neighbour, nor Geoffrey Upfill-Brown across the road was able to describe him in sufficient detail for an e-fit picture to be created.

Within five minutes of those 11.30 sightings, another Gowan Avenue resident on his way to work found himself walking alongside another man who was wearing a dark suit. That was on the north side of the street, near Fulham Palace Road. A woman parking her car on the corner of Gowan Avenue also noticed a man coming towards her. He, too, was dressed in a dark coat, which was flapping open, and maybe a red tie.

At about 11.45, Joseph Sappleton was waiting at the bus stop outside 389 Fulham Palace Road, a couple of hundred yards south of Gowan Avenue. While he peeled an orange to pass the time he was joined by a man who had crossed the road in front of him, as if coming from Bishop's Park. The man was sweating loads, on his face and neck, so that damp was seeping into the collar of his cream shirt. He had a ridge on his nose as if he had recently removed a pair of glasses. He was in his late thirties, just under six feet tall with light coloured hair, wearing a dark jacket and trousers that didn't quite seem to match, brown shoes. He looked like a man who was trying to dress up and had got it all wrong.

The man leaned against the wall. He seemed agitated, though not obviously out of breath. Joseph felt that the man was watching him, which made him a little paranoid, and he wondered if the man was a police officer and was following him.

The bus stop served two bus routes, the 220 and the 74. Joseph was waiting for the 220. A 74 came and went and some other passengers got on, but not the sweating man. Then the 220 arrived, and the sweating man didn't get on that, either. He was still standing there, waiting, as the bus left with Joseph on his way to the social in Wandsworth with the fiver he had just borrowed from his mum.

Joseph Sappleton was able to produce an e-fit as was a woman breakdown recovery driver, Frances Hughes, who had been driving north on Fulham Palace Road in her truck at about the time of the murder. She had seen a man in a dark green suit with a mobile phone in his hand running south on Fulham Palace Road towards Putney. He was south of Gowan Avenue but on the same side of the road. The man was also picked out from CCTV footage at Putney underground station. Frances Hughes herself could be seen on CCTV on Putney Bridge at 11.24, which almost certainly meant that her running man had nothing to do with the murder.

There was another running man on Fulham Palace Road, just by Gowan Avenue, in the minutes after the murder. He was seen by Kenneth Williams, who had just come out of the bookmaker's with a betting slip time-stamped 11.37.02. He had seen the man run across the pedestrian crossing at the top of Gowan Avenue, to the Bishop's Park side of Fulham Palace Road. The man had stumbled as he reached the far kerb and steadied himself first on the bonnet of a car and then on the pole of the crossing before continuing to run south. He was wearing a sleeveless bodywarmer over a suit and was five foot eight to five foot ten, of medium build with dark hair.

A school caretaker watched a man in Bishop's Park as he climbed over the railings by the River Thames and down the steps there to the bank. The same man was also seen by a woman in the park with her child.

There seemed to be a significant number of sightings of Range Rovers, even though they were a common enough vehicle in the area. In addition to the sightings of Range Rovers by people reported in Gowan Avenue in the hours before the murder there were several sightings afterwards, or reported sightings – a 'Range Rover' which was alleged to have turned left out of Doneraile Street into Fulham Palace Road, moving at high speed, turned out to be a Cherokee Jeep.

A man going shopping with his wife, walking ahead while his wife finished chatting to a neighbour, saw a Range Rover down by Fulham football ground on Stevenage Road – an old model, scruffy, with two men inside – and there were two or three sightings around or on Putney Bridge. At least one of these, however, was of a Range Rover that belonged to an Italian restaurateur.

The inquiry was distracted by a series of calls to the *Mirror* newspaper, malicious calls by somebody claiming to know a man with a Range Rover who had been in Fulham that morning and was involved in the murder. The man named in these calls was a landscape gardener and would turn out to have been working in the grounds of a south London primary school that morning. Even after he had been eliminated, the calls continued: 'We know you've been to see him but we still think he's involved.'

All these running and sweating men and Range Rovers were hard to fit together. They could mean that Jill's death was the work of a team of two or more people. They could mean that there had been a planned pick-up by a Range Rover which had gone awry afterwards. They could be nothing to do with her death at all.

The investigation was under constant internal pressure to produce new information for the media. Towards the end of the first week, Hamish had the Sappleton and the Hughes e-fits ready but was resisting demands to release them.

The Metropolitan Police was also in the middle of the investigation into the London nail-bombing campaign, and that inquiry wanted a Dando-free day of attention to its own appeals for help from the public. One way or another, there had been Dando press conferences on Monday, Tuesday and Wednesday. Hamish also wanted some breathing space and could live without a Thursday bulletin.

He wrote in his log for that day, Thursday 29 April: 'Delaying the press conference for twenty-four hours will not detract from the investigation (certainly not for twenty-four hours) and will also allow us to get a clearer understanding of witness issues, e-fits and photos to release.'

In fact, the day's delay did not assist very much in those terms. Pressure to feed the media could sometimes push you to release material which was unhelpful. Hamish had two e-fits and a CCTV still of a Range Rover. He was already pretty sure the Range Rover had nothing to do with it. It was just a Range Rover on Putney Bridge. He had four or five other pictures of Range Rovers and could have produced four or five pictures of any other make of car that would have had about as much relevance.

There was talk of producing the two e-fits, even though they were obviously two distinct individuals, and neither had been in Gowan Avenue. In the end, Hamish said, 'No, let's just release the Sappleton e-fit and the Range Rover still.' He tried to make it clear that Friday, and later on *Crimewatch*, that this was only the sweating man at the bus stop. But as he well knew, in people's minds the distinction was lost and the e-fit became the face of the killer. The Range Rover became linked to the car speeding out of Doneraile Street, which was not a Range Rover at all. It was a mistake, with hindsight, to release that e-fit and that still. His hand had been forced by the pressure.

Within the month they would stop raising Actions on all Messages that related to the e-fit or to Range Rovers, though the Messages still came in and had to be logged. It didn't stop people calling. By now, so far as Hamish was concerned, Range Rovers had nothing to do with the murder.

The suspect pool was burgeoning, more suspects than they could ever hope to find and eliminate. Low-grade suspects for the most part, but even so, the workload was mountainous.

It was the inner group that caused them the most concern. Hamish could not tell you how bogged down they had become by that group at times. For example, he had decided to take blood samples from all Jill's boyfriends going back over five years. They all matched traces found in her home. One of the men had neglected to mention his brief sexual relationship with Jill – they were platonic friends, he had said. He had automatically raised his own profile as a suspect by his deceit, which was intended to disguise a different kind of guilt. He had nothing to do with Jill's death, none of them did, but each had their own particular circumstances, their individual role and timing in Jill's life, which sometimes overlapped. The blurring, as Hamish called it. If you were looking for a motive, what might it be? Could they have done it? How did the timings fit in?

Alan Farthing had been married before. His ex-wife, Maria, was a suspect. So was Alan. Alan and Jill had been a week or so away from signing off on a new mortgage, with life assurance cover, making wills which would have made him the sole beneficiary of everything. An instant millionaire. As Hamish said later – this would have made it more difficult to discount him as a suspect.

Simon Bassil had access to and experience with guns at the South African game reserve. Bob Wheaton, of course, he was a suspect, even Jenny Higham, on the grounds that she might have been jealous of Jill in her new happiness with Alan, which Jenny had orchestrated in the first place.

Jill's life was disclosed through the testimony of friends, family and colleagues, through her diaries and correspondence and the long list of names, contacts – 486 of them – in her Filofax. There were no apparent secrets, no little compartments where mysteries might lie, though there were times when Hamish considered that the darkness of Dando might still hide something of that sort, that the darkness lay within her.

Her mobile telephone records showed a couple of calls to one of those sex-chat lines in the months before her death. Just two calls in all her phone records. Even so, that was curious but, on closer examination, was nothing more than a bit of messing around, jokey calls made to pass the time on a journey once, on a train.

There was an old friend from the West Country who had joined the police in London and called Jill out of the blue, after an apparent silence of years, just six weeks before her death. Then she had called him back two weeks later. That was explored and explained. He was traced, interviewed, eliminated.

Then the policeman was arrested and charged with stalking offences which had nothing to do with Jill but prompted the inquiry to reconsider him as a suspect. He went back into the mix of those long conversations in Hamish's office.

There was further darkness in the many people who seemed to have an unhealthy interest in Jill or her murder. There were 140 suspects in that category.

A man in Shepherd's Bush, an undertaker who drove an old-fashioned hearse, seems to have gone to a lot of trouble to make a suspect of himself and claimed he was the sweating man in the e-fit, the man at the bus stop. He said he had been driving in and around

Gowan Avenue that morning in his hearse. He was the only other person who was formally arrested in connection with Jill's murder, four weeks after her death. When the police searched his home they found a set of spectacle frames with no lenses, an MOT certificate for a Range Rover, some BBC correspondence, an estate agent's aerial photograph of Fulham and a dark threequarter length coat.

The man had a history of confessing to serious crimes, none of which he had ever committed, though he had been convicted of an offence relating to a false claim for reward money. He was six foot four, significantly taller than the man at the bus stop. There was no hearse on any nearby CCTV footage. That was the one vehicle you couldn't see.

There was another man who was under suspicion for a long time who lived in Fulham and had a history of pursuing women on the Internet. He would first meet them in chat-rooms and had travelled to Canada and Australia in pursuit of the relationships he formed.

Five months before Jill's death he had called another J. Dando in Earl's Court. He seemed to have been phoning round to try to locate Jill and the inquiry team wondered why that was. He had also left Fulham after the murder and gone to Australia.

Oddly, for me, he lived in the same road in Fulham that I had been living in for ten years at the time of Jill's death. His house was just across the road from mine though, typical Fulham, I never knew him. I moved to a new home elsewhere in Fulham not long before the police turned up at his address. I heard about it from my old neighbours.

Somehow, it became a tabloid 'fact' that this man had a shrine to Jill in his home, but there was no shrine – just the odd newspaper cutting and a lot of pornographic magazines.

The police were unable to satisfy themselves that he had nothing to do with Jill's death. He had been in Kensington High Street just after midday but had no alibi beforehand, so he fell within the 'killing time'. Even though he was slightly shorter than any of the witness descriptions, he could not be dismissed.

Eventually, Hamish went to Australia to interview him.

The man told the story of how he had previously been in Canada, living with a chat-line conquest. The woman had started taking advantage of him, using his credit cards. He had returned to London and to the chat-rooms, meeting a succession of different women there. He went to Australia and carried on talking over the Internet. More women.

One day he was in the chat-room and a dialogue screen popped up. 'Hello, remember me?' The names of all the women he had been talking to since Canada scrolled past and at the end there was the name of the Canadian woman. She had been posing as all the other women too. The story sent a chill through Hamish. But the man did not have any interest in Jill and was finally eliminated.

A third suspect unknown to Jill, who had a link with Range Rovers, was pursued and followed and wondered about for some months before he, too, was eliminated.

This was Hamish writing about suspects in his log, later, on 28 February 2000:

Make further enquiry into the suspect types in an effort to narrow down the way forward in this investigation. Consider again the merits or otherwise as to why Dando's murder was or was not the work of a contract killer. The suspect pool remains enormous and without a definite steer one way or the other it will continue to remain so . . . We've sought assistance . . . but we must perhaps do more. My notes set out some of the ideas and tend towards loner and away from contract.

As Hamish said in his notes, while they continued to target both fronts, a loner or a contract killer, one was clearly wrong. 'Who is this man we seem to have missed?' Hamish would type the additional notes at home over the weekends and attach them to the log.

The investigation had first been reviewed after a month, a fresh team of officers brought in to examine the work done so far, in accordance with recently established guidelines for major inquiries that were not resolved.

The review had not found any flaws, but the senior officer had said to Hamish, off the record, 'Don't lose sight of the loner.'

Hamish had employed the services of a clinical psychologist, Adrian West from the National Crime Faculty. They had done some work together before, on another case which Hamish had investigated that remained unsolved, which was a continuing source of concern to him: if that case had received a quarter of the publicity of the Dando case, it might have got somewhere.

This was the murder of a twelve-year-old girl, Katerina Koneva, who had been strangled by an intruder at her home in Hammersmith in May 1997. The intruder had been discovered by Katerina's father as he returned home. He had jumped from a first-floor window to escape and had been chased for some distance by Katerina's father before disappearing. Katerina's father had been unaware of the attack on his daughter until he came back and discovered her body. She had been strangled twice. Two other local girls of the same age had been followed by a man of a similar description, but he had not been found. Katerina's death remained a mystery. It featured again on *Crimewatch* while I was writing this, in October 2001.

Adrian West presented Hamish with a report on the Dando case in June 1999. Among his observations about the possible profile of suspects, he wrote: 'Previous police notice or intelligence for communication with, following, harassing other public/celebrity figures, especially Princess Diana. As perpetrator might then have had to mourn and establish another icon.'

West sometimes thought the inquiry was being distracted by red herrings but, as he would acknowledge, he was not the detective, he was the adviser.

In January 2000, two police officers went to the United States, primarily to see if Remington could offer any further information about the bullet and the shell casing. They visited the LAPD's stalking unit and another officer, an accredited profiler from the Crime Faculty, DS Simon Wells, went to meet J. Reid Meloy, a forensic psychologist based in San Diego. Meloy is generally regarded as the leading authority on the subject of stalking and had recently published the first academic work on the subject: *The Psychology of Stalking: Clinical and Forensic Perspectives*.

Unsurprisingly, in its general absorption with fame and success, the United States was far more familiar than Britain with stalkers of famous people. The designer Gianni Versace had been killed by a kind of stalker, and John Lennon by his 'admirer' Mark Chapman, in 1980. An actress, Theresa Saldana, had been attacked with a hunting knife by a man who had been stalking her. Few American celebrities escaped the attentions of obsessives. Stalkers were invariably unable to form anything but distorted attachments to others, or unable to let go. The archetypal stalker was not a celebrity admirer but a spurned boyfriend, possessed by jealousy or bent on revenge.

A British forensic psychiatrist, Richard Badcock, would say that in the many cases he had studied, the female victims of stalking usually had an extra quality, some 'otherness', a vivacity, perhaps, which unwittingly drew people to them. With people who achieved fame, of course, such a quality could be the reason for their success in the first place, or simply the allure of their celebrity.

The people they incited, stalkers, could be extraordinarily determined and inventive in their stalking habits, which could become all-consuming and demand considerable time and effort. It seemed to me that they sometimes deployed remarkable imagination. But Badcock would say this was not imagination at all. They lacked imagination but were fuelled by fantasies, often of power or control.

Though they threatened and intimidated, usually on an ever-increasing scale, the one thing that stalkers weren't was invisible. Most stalkers were known to their victims, or if they weren't they were not usually difficult to trace. One woman television presenter I spoke to had been targeted by the self-styled Beast of Eastbourne, who anonymously sent her obscene postcards and, finally, a box of chocolates booby-trapped with a toy snake. He had left the till receipt from Sainsbury's inside the package and it carried the serial number of his loyalty card, which instantly disclosed his name and address.

Reid Meloy was briefed on the Dando case by DS Wells and thought that Jill's role on *Crimewatch* might hold the answer. He thought it could be a third-party 'hit' – a contract killing. He was also struck by her likeness to Princess Diana and thought this, too, could be of significance.

The police discovered that Jill appeared to have been pursued by the so-called 'utility stalker', somebody who had made three calls in one day to the domestic services such as gas and electricity a couple of months before she died, pretending to be Jill's brother and trying to make changes to the details of her accounts. The police spent a great deal of time investigating this, chasing down the details and the connections. Hamish spoke about it during one of his irregular press briefings. The 'utility stalker' turned out to have been a tabloid reporter.

The calls had been made on 1 February, the day after Jill's engagement to Alan had become public at their engagement party.

In addition to wasting investigative time, the tabloid papers ran a seemingly endless series of articles about the inquiry and the people supposedly responsible for Jill's death. There was the killer bought gun in a pub in Birmingham story, killer was hitman dispatched by Russian Mafia godfather whose advances Jill had rejected on a *Holiday*, the killer escaped on a coach to Belgium, the killer was Ealing Vicarage rapist . . .

Such articles, in a way, reflected the ongoing mystery and the shortage of hard facts to report, the information vacuum which had to be filled somehow, and any old nonsense would do.

There were lots of phoney leads that never appeared in the papers, people writing in or posting e-mails claiming responsibility, in one or two cases, children having a game. An elderly resident of Shrewsbury wrote and confessed to the Bishop of Stepney, and told the bishop that he was next; a letter to the BBC said the author had killed Jill and would never be caught, and was traced to a woman living in a seaside town. A man wrote to the *Sun* revealing that he was the hitman, paid £45,000 for the task, and was writing to absolve himself before he committed suicide. He had been a serving prisoner on 26 April 1999.

Each of these many letters or e-mails was anonymous and had to be traced. Other anonymous messages had been given a low priority, but you could not do that with direct claims of responsibility, however unlikely they might seem.

At any one time, the inquiry had many hundreds of Actions queued and waiting to be pursued. Even at the end there would be 1,500 or so left undone. Each one a mini inquiry all of its own, many of them TIEs, rated and prioritised according to a system of grading which Hamish had established.

By November 1999 the inquiry was floundering in the suspect pool. Hamish wrote in his log: 'We're at the stage of the inquiry where we must make further inroads into the suspect pool. They cannot all be seen and 90 per cent of them will be uninvolved, possibly 100 per cent. We have to determine which ones are more important than others. Why should we follow one person more swiftly and vigorously than another? Who will we see first?'

He developed a new set of criteria and distributed it at a team meeting, while writing in his notes, 'It may well turn out that the suspect is only referred to once and is a low priority, but that is the choice we have to make.'

These were the criteria:

Has he had access, or does he have access, or does he show an interest in firearms?

Is he identified by more than one separate or disparate source?

Has he an interest in, obsession with or is he an over-keen fan of Jill Dando who is not family, friend or work associate?

Is he nominated as looking like the e-fit?

Has he got a criminal record? In particular firearms, violence, contract, murder, stalker.

These were for office staff to apply before allocating the actions. There was also a series of codes, elimination codes which ruled out suspects on the transparent grounds of having an alibi, or of being black or Asian, or otherwise outside the race code, or too tall or too short or too heavily tattooed, or physically disabled in some obvious way.

Hamish explained all this too, in his notes, explained why he was not including Range Rovers, which had long since seemed irrelevant, and why he was excluding the report of Adrian West, which defined the possible profile of the killer as a stalker. Hamish did not want to close down the options; 'stalker' was a broad term, and it could be dangerous to use this as a basis for evaluation.

The suspects were scored and re-evaluated in a matrix system according to the number of categories into which they fitted, being mentioned by more than one source, criminal record and so on. Actions were allocated according to the scoring. There were six pages of names in the high-priority list with eight to twelve points. Barry George was in the low-priority list with one to three points. That was where he started, because he was only known to the inquiry then as Barry Bulsara. There was no criminal record in the name of Bulsara and his history would not have been disclosed by the initial check on the PNC, the Police National Computer.

Many of the names put forward came with serious criminal histories attached. There was no question that those people deserved a higher priority in the system.

In fact, an Action had first been raised in the name of Bulsara on the nineteenth day after Jill's death. On 15 May 1999. Action 1637. TIE Barry Bulsara. That name had been the subject of a series of Messages and, as it would turn out, George had already been the subject of other Messages. Mostly anonymous and not all of them yet typed into HOLMES.

Action 1638, raised on the same day as number 1637, TIE Barry Bulsara, was to TIE a man living at 4 Crookham Road who had been identified in an anonymous call which was logged as Message 1283 two days after the murder. The caller said the man who lived there was very strange, mentally unstable, and had air-guns and a crossbow. 'If you go in his house,' she said, 'you'll see all the Queen posters.' Barry George actually lived at 2b Crookham Road. The woman did not give his name', so her Message was never linked to the others and was given a low priority because of its anonymity.

There was no cross-referencing system in HOLMES which would automatically have helped to make the connection. HOLMES 2 had better search facilities and might have done the job more efficiently, but there was no guarantee that it would. George was simply sitting in the system, unnoticed. Just as Peter Sutcliffe had sat in the card indexes all those years ago, albeit for a much longer period of time. Sutcliffe had been found in the end by chance, but it was Hamish's re-evaluation of suspects that finally turned up Barry George.

Action 1637, TIE Barry Bulsara, was finally allocated to Detective Constable John Gallagher on 24 February 2000, eight and a half months after it was raised. It was Gallagher's 200th Action of the inquiry, or thereabouts, and he had twenty-five others outstanding. He began by reviewing the Messages that had prompted the Action in the first place.

The Messages had come from the offices of HAFAD, Hammersmith and Fulham Action for Disability, a charity agency, which was in Greswell Street, less than ten minutes' walk west from Gowan Avenue.

Barry George had visited those offices on 26 April at some time between late morning and lunchtime. An unknown time which could not be verified in any way and would be the subject of considerable dispute. He had returned two days later and it was this second visit that prompted the first phone call to the police later that day, from Lesley Symes, the director of HAFAD, which was logged as Message 599. She would not give George's name – which HAFAD knew as Bulsara – because of client confidentiality, but she said he had a mental health problem, and that he had visited at about eleven o'clock on the Monday morning inquiring about a taxi card, a concession giving the disabled free rides from local minicab companies. He had returned early on the Wednesday, and been quite stroppy and assertive, asking the staff to recollect what time he was there on Monday. He was about thirty-nine and had short, dark hair. Lesley would later change her mind and say the first visit had been at about midday.

The next call had come on 12 May 1999, from HAFAD's finance manager, Elaine Hutton, who first thought Barry George had visited the offices at about eleven o'clock and later became reasonably certain that it was around midday. By now the HAFAD staff had seen the e-fit and thought it looked like Barry George, though of course the e-fit was the sweating man at the bus stop, not the man who killed Jill Dando. In this call, which was logged as Message 1284, Elaine Hutton gave George's name, as Bulsara, and his correct address.

There was another call a week later, Message 2271, this time from Susan Bicknell, the newest member of the HAFAD staff, whose first day as a welfare rights worker had been on 26 April – and whose first client had been Barry George. He had obviously been a challenging client, with his carrier bag of papers, from which he had produced many hospital letters and various medical notes in support of the various illnesses and instances of mistreatment by the medical profession of which he complained. He had been agitated, particularly when she told him he could not be seen that day. He had just carried on talking. She remembered looking at the office clock on the wall as she got up from her desk to deal with him and it had been 11.50 am. They had been together for fifteen or twenty minutes or so and he had left with an appointment booked for the following day, which he did not keep.

Susan Bicknell said in her call to the police that she didn't think he looked like the e-fit. But he had been flustered, so perhaps he had witnessed something.

HAFAD called the police for the fourth and final time in mid-June. Message 3024. It was Elaine Hutton again, asking whether the police were going to come and take statements, and this time giving Barry George's date of birth.

DC Gallagher went to HAFAD on 2 March and again on 6 March.

If it wasn't apparent then, it certainly was later, in court, at the trial, that there was considerable disagreement between the HAFAD staff about what had happened and when. The receptionist, Rosario Torres, was sure that Barry George's visit had been during lunch, between 12.30 and 1.00 pm. She was equally sure that Elaine Hutton had dealt with him, not Susan Bicknell. And she didn't think he looked like the e-fit either.

The only consensus seemed to be in their perception of Barry George as odd, strange, unstable, agitated, upset and, broadly, in their description of the clothes he had worn, which were very different from the clothes worn by the man – or men – seen by witnesses in Gowan Avenue.

Though Elaine Hutton could not recall what he'd been wearing,

Susan Bicknell said it had been a loose, dark, blouson-type jacket over a yellow shirt and dark trousers. Lesley Symes had the impression it was dark clothing, like jogging trousers and an anorak-style waterproof jacket. Rosario Torres remembered a yellow shirt but nothing over it.

DC Gallagher went to Scotland Yard and to the divisional intelligence offices at Hammersmith police station. There he found traces of Barry George – a criminal history – and references to the various names he had used. DC Gallagher then went to Crookham Road and called at 2b, but there was no answer. A neighbour told him Barry had just gone out. She also said Barry was related to Freddie Mercury. DC Gallagher went back half a dozen times over the next five weeks, left a note asking Barry to contact him, but heard nothing.

Barry's flat in Crookham Road was about half a mile from 29 Gowan Avenue, a walk of less than ten minutes. If you turned right out of number 29, then right on Munster Road, left at the junction with Fulham Road, Crookham was the second turning on the right and number 2 was the first house on the right. 2b was the ground-floor flat. He had lived there for fourteen years and had told people he was seeking to have a blue plaque assigned to the building on the grounds that it was the birthplace of the playwright John Osborne, best known for his 1950s plays *Look Back in Anger* and *The Entertainer*.

This might have sounded like a Barry fantasy, of which there very many, but in fact it was true. Crookham House, as number 2 was known, had been built in 1885, had been a nursery for some years and, from 1905 to the 1950s, had served as the Crookham Nursing Home, where John Osborne, son of Nellie Beatrice and Thomas Godfrey Osborne, had been born there on 12 December 1929.

After leaving HAFAD in Greswell Street that Monday morning, or afternoon, Barry had walked to the minicab office of Traffic Cars on Fulham Palace Road, five minutes away, a little north of Gowan Avenue. He had asked for a free ride to Rickett Street, to the office of Cancer Colon Concern, in the far east of Fulham, near Earl's Court.

Ramesh Paul, the Traffic Cars controller, remembered Barry arriving at about one o'clock. He had laughed at his request, told him to fuck off, that it was a £4 fare and £4 was like £400 to one of his drivers. Barry had lingered in the office and, by coincidence, a call had come in with a request for a minicab to collect a parcel from Rickett Street. 'You're in luck,' Ramesh said to Barry, and he got his free ride after all.

Ramesh had called the police later that day and told them about Barry. He described him as having blond hair. Message 201.

Barry had returned to Traffic Cars on the 28th and begun asking Ramesh lots of apparently stupid questions: whether he remembered him from Monday — which of course Ramesh did; what time it had been; what Barry had been wearing. Ramesh could not remember the colour of his shirt. 'Look up at the sky,' Barry had said. 'What colour?'

'Blue,' Ramesh had replied.

'No, that's not the colour. What colour is the sun?'

'Yellow,' Ramesh had said eventually. 'Yes,' said Barry. Ramesh thought he was a total nutter, going on about Jill Dando's death and not wanting to be blamed.

Ramesh had written '1.15 pm' on the back of a Traffic Cars business card and given it to Barry and when Barry had left he called the police again, this time describing Barry as having mousey hair. Message 489.

These messages had been actioned and statements had been taken in May 1999 from Ramesh and the driver who had given Barry his free ride. But of course there was no way then of linking them to the Barry who had been at HAFAD. His hair was black.

DC Gallagher briefed Hamish about Barry for the first time on 5 April 2000. It was recorded on an old collators' card that Hamish had dealt with Barry once before, in 1988, when Barry had dyed his hair blond and was going by the name of Paul Gadd, the real name of Gary Glitter. Hamish had no recollection of him and even now, as just one more suspect, Barry was of no special significance. Gallagher was told to carry on and eliminate him.

Hamish had been thinking about organising a seminar to try to gather some new thoughts on the case and on 6 April he decided to go ahead. He had tried this once before, in the Katerina Koneva case, and had found it helpful.

There would be senior police officers at the seminar, from outside London, psychologists, pathologists, profilers, analysts from the National Crime Faculty. He would hold the seminar near Birmingham, not in London. It was still Hamish's perception that provincial forces demonstrated more commitment to the investigation of murder.

It might sound a lot, having forty-five officers on this inquiry, but in Norfolk or Devon and Cornwall there might be as many as one hundred officers involved and it just seemed a more structured process, in which things were less likely to get overlooked. It was not an exact science, investigating murder, but the better the structure, the safer the process would be. The seminar was scheduled for the end of April.

DC Gallagher and a colleague finally caught up with Barry George on 11 April, waiting for him at the benefit office in Fulham. He was walking with a limp and began to tell DC Gallagher about his recent bicycle accident and the officer had to interrupt him to explain that he was investigating the murder of Jill Dando and to ask why he hadn't responded to his note. Barry said he had assumed it was about the bicycle accident and passed it on to his solicitor.

Barry did not want to be interviewed at his flat because it was messy, so they went to Fulham police station. DC Gallagher knew by now that Barry was epileptic and wanted an appropriate adult in attendance. He called social services, but they would not send somebody out unless Barry had been seen by a doctor, and no doctor was then available. DC Gallagher did not want to lose Barry now, having waited so long to find him, so he proposed going to Barry's mother's home in east Acton, so that his mother could act as the appropriate adult.

As they drove north on Munster Road on the way to east Acton, Barry said he had told the police on the day that he had seen a Range Rover in one of the streets near Gowan Avenue. The inquiry would search later for any record of this event and find nothing. No police officer who had been at the scene on 26 April 1999 remembered him or had made a note of the information.

During the interview, which was transcribed as a statement, written in longhand by DC Gallagher and signed by Barry, he told the officers he had left home at about 12.30 or 12.45 on the 26th. He had walked to Greswell Street, going west on Fulham Road and through Bishop's Park into Stevenage Road. He had been seeking advice on housing benefit claims from HAFAD and had gone from there to a minicab office, where he had been given a lift to Cancer Colon Concern, so that he could pick up an information pack on

bowel cancer and bowel problems. He had walked home afterwards through Fulham, and stayed in until early evening when he
had visited his neighbour across the road and been told of Jill
Dando's murder. He had never met Jill Dando and hadn't known
where she lived until after her death. He said he used to be in the
Territorial Army and was taught to use a self-loading rifle, but
had not had access to firearms since. Barry said he had been wearing either his suit and overcoat, with a white shirt and red tie, or
jeans and trainers.

After the statement had been taken, the officers took Barry
home to Crookham Road, and he showed them the coat he thought
he might have been wearing. The officers could not get through the
hallway because of the clutter of boxes and bags. Barry clambered
along to retrieve the coat, and held it up so they could see it.

His statement gave the inquiry the connection to Traffic Cars,
and the clothes he might have worn that day fitted at least some of
the descriptions of men seen in Gowan Avenue. There was enough
now to justify the issue of a search warrant and, a week later, officers from the inquiry and a specialist search team known as Polsa
went to Barry's flat, forced an entry in his absence and began to
search. The flat was a complete tip. They took a Polaroid of the
bedroom without even realising there was a bed there, buried
beneath piles of boxes and bags and assorted accumulated stuff.
They returned the following day and continued searching, this
time recording the search on a video camera.

When Hamish saw the condition of Barry's flat he wondered
how he could ever manage to appear on the streets as smartly
turned out as he did. He speculated for a while that Barry might
have a second, secret address where he went to wash and shave and
dress.

Eventually the entire contents of Barry's home would be removed. Everything. It would be stripped down to floors and walls. For now they concentrated on anything that might be significant, and there was plenty to choose from.

They found the coat, a dark blue cashmere coat which Barry had bought from Cecil Gee in December 1988 for £199.50. They found jackets and trousers and yellow t-shirts and various items of military clothing.

There were hundreds of newspapers, and not surprisingly some of those included articles about Jill, in particular newspapers published after her death. There were four copies of the same edition of the BBC in-house newspaper, *Ariel*, also published after Jill's death.

Two mobile phones, notebooks, cards and correspondence containing references to the BBC. An envelope containing six notes of condolence written by staff of local shops on Fulham Road, which Barry had collected after Jill's death.

Two notes written by Barry with similar wording: 'Although I did not know Jill Dando personally, my cousin Freddie Mercury was interviewed by her back in 1986. I was present with him, so for this reason I feel it poignant to bring together the situation of Jill's death and my coming to Christ . . .'

An SAS knife, a variety of magazines and papers relating to weapons, most of them some years old. A notebook containing a list, handwritten by Barry, of firearms and prices. Two photocopied pages from the firearms for sale section of *Exchange & Mart*, February 1987. A shoulder holster.

Dozens and dozens of rolls of undeveloped film, a total of 2,597 photographs of 419 different women who Barry had followed and photographed without their permission, and a picture taken by

Barry of himself wearing a respirator and holding a Bruni starting pistol, which was broken, exposing the spring. He was holding the gun in clenched hands, in the style of an SAS marksman. Another picture of him, wearing a balaclava holding a replica Heckler & Koch machine-gun which the police would work out had been taken in the back yard of Crookham Road. Several pictures taken of the television screen, showing presenters or newsreaders, none of whom were Jill. A picture of the doctor's surgery at 21 Gowan Avenue where Barry had once briefly been a registered patient.

An Olympus camera.

Only one of those 419 women was ever identified. She came forward to tell the police she had been followed by Barry. He had turned up once at her home address and she had been ter-rified by him. She was shown the blue folders of photographs and recognised herself, pictures of rear views of herself walking along the road. She had no idea she had ever been photographed by Barry.

He was now soaring in Hamish's points system. Firearms, men-tioned by more than one source, interest in Jill Dando, criminal record, said to look like the e-fit.

There was some discussion in the inquiry about having his clothes photographed, to see if they might be recognised by wit-nesses. There would be some dispute later about who had authorised this but on 28 April DC Gallagher went to the exhibits store and took the coat, a dark jacket, dark trousers and red tie to the photographic studio at Amelia Street in Walworth, south London – the studio where Jill's front door had earlier been recre-ated. It was used by the Metropolitan Police and firearms were sometimes photographed there.

Exhibits were logged and bagged and sealed and not supposed to be opened because they might contain important forensic evidence which could be contaminated by exposure to the ether. All these items of clothing had yet to be examined at the forensic science laboratory.

DC Gallagher unwrapped the items at the studio and they were draped over a tailor's dummy, together with one of his own white shirts, to be photographed.

Afterwards he took the clothes back to the store room at Kensington and they stayed there until 2 May when they were taken to the forensic science laboratory in Lambeth. The photographs were never shown to any witnesses.

On 30 April 2000, just after the first anniversary of Jill's death, and the second *Crimewatch* appeal, Hamish was writing about Barry in his log:

> There is nothing wholly compelling about the link between Bulsara and Dando. However, our appeal was for obsessive behaviour against Dando or other women. The latter is far stronger. Nevertheless we could have searched his property and found no link whatsoever with Dando or any interest at all. He could simply have fitted the e-fit and behaved oddly at the centre and again, made no comment on Dando. But he did not. There is a link. There may be more to be found . . .
>
> Bulsara matches every one of the criteria to a very strong level . . . For this reason we must concentrate resources on either eliminating him from the inquiry or obtaining the requisite proof and evidence to show that he is responsible.

In the midst of that report Hamish articulated his frustration that the police had not arrived earlier at Barry, had not acted sooner on the HAFAD messages and had been slow to make the link with Traffic Cars. It was all hindsight, of course. But it was a failure of the inquiry or the system, and that was what he wrote, that there was a failure.

They began surveillance of Barry in May which lasted for just over three weeks until his arrest on 25 May. He spent a lot of time out and about, following and sometimes approaching women, which was what he seemed to have spent years doing. His major pastime and preoccupation.

A static camera was placed outside his home to record his comings and goings. He was seen hopping up and down the front steps and sometimes vaulting from the front wall on to the window ledge to gain entry to his own home. He went to the West End, to Kensington, Victoria, Wimbledon, Chiswick, Putney and Tooting. He chased buses he never caught. He also spent hours in Internet cafés, in particular EasyEverything in Kensington High Street. He grew a goatee beard and a moustache.

The inquiry officers wondered where he was going on the Internet and what he was saying to the women he approached, and Hamish decided to place an undercover officer in EasyEverything to see what would happen and if it might produce any useful information. He chose a young, attractive police woman and gave her strict instructions not to ask any leading questions. A previous murder inquiry, into the death of Rachel Nickell on Wimbledon Common, had used an undercover woman officer to befriend and correspond with the key suspect, Colin Stagg. The use of the officer had compromised the trial and been the subject of considerable criticism by the judge. Hamish was anxious not to repeat that mistake. 'The shadow of Rachel Nickell looms large,' he wrote in his log.

They waited until they guessed one day that Barry was on his way to EasyEverything, and then the policewoman went along there, just a few hundred yards from the inquiry offices in Kensington. Sure enough, Barry came in, looked around, and went and sat down at the terminal next to hers and began a conversation. He was very polite and said nothing untoward, and when the officer left, he did not follow her. She asked him just one pertinent question, about firearms websites. 'Oh, don't talk to me about guns,' he said.

There was some enthusiasm afterwards to take this strategy further and place the woman there again, but Hamish was not prepared to take the risk.

Hamish writing in his log again, 8 May:

The work during the last week has not diminished Gadd's importance as a key suspect in this inquiry. There is a temptation to see anything remotely suspicious as evidence of his involvement and interpret his clearly unusual behaviour as suspicious . . . This is dangerous and unwise.

However, from the limited surveillance that's already been conducted, it is clear that he leads an extremely isolated lifestyle. If he is responsible it would go a long way to explaining the absence of any good information in this case. He does not appear to have a strong social link with anybody at all . . .

It is safer perhaps to start from the premise that Gadd is *not* responsible for the murder of Jill Dando and then to look at his behaviour and actions and words both before and after the event and decide whether such behaviour is more or less consistent with the actions of an innocent person, a disturbed person or possibly a guilty person.

Officers returned to Barry's home for a further search and this time he told them they couldn't come in. One of the officers pushed him gently but firmly out of the way. They had a search warrant. Barry asked the police why they had returned and they showed him his handwritten list of firearms.

'That's from when I was in the TA,' he said. 'I have only handled weapons there under strict supervision. I have still got a healthy interest in the military, as you can see.'

The search went ahead and more newspapers were taken away as well as another notebook, with the name Steve Majors – yet another Barry pseudonym – on the cover, containing another hand-written list of firearms. A copy of *Soldier of Fortune* magazine from 1983. A Queen Productions company badge.

They did not find, and never would find, any CDs or other evidence of Barry's supposed admiration for the music of the rock band Queen. Hamish would conclude that he was actually not so much of a Queen fan. The interest seemed entirely focused on Freddie Mercury and Barry's fantasy role as his cousin. Bulsara was Mercury's family name. It was not Barry's.

On 19 May, two days before his seminar was due to start, Hamish had a phone call from the forensic scientist, Robin Keely, who told him he had found a single particle of firearm residue in the inside pocket of Barry's Cecil Gee coat. The particle was consistent with residue from the scene. The scientist could not say with certainty that it had come from the scene – it could have come from another firing of a similar bullet – but it was consistent.

Coincidentally, Hamish had worked with Robin Keely on another case that had placed reliance on a single particle, a shooting in the Emporium nightclub in central London in 1997.

That case had involved a contract hit by two men, £500 for one and £400 for the other. They had shot the wrong man in the nightclub by mistake and only been linked to the crime by a particle found on a surgical glove in a hotel room they had used before and after the shooting. They had not been picked out by the many witnesses on identification parades, so the prosecution case had relied heavily on the particle. The man who had worn the glove had been convicted.

After the call from Keely, Hamish knew that Barry George would be arrested and possibly charged with Jill Dando's murder. He went ahead and held the seminar over the following Sunday, Monday and Tuesday, in a hotel at West Bromwich. He did not tell the gathering about Barry until the last day, when he briefly described the circumstances of the case against Barry and asked what they would do next if they were him.

No one at the seminar had thought Jill's murder was a contract hit. Not in a million years, the people from Northern Ireland had said. Not with that weapon and that round. It just wasn't professional.

Other thoughts had emerged before he mentioned Barry: in the absence of any other motive perhaps it was Jill's celebrity status that had provoked her death. The assailant a lone male, maybe, with anger against women, a misogynist, insecure, violent temper, previous difficulties with women, with the opportunity to loiter during the daytime.

Was the doctor's surgery a few doors away significant, could it be a class thing? Had the killer been institutionalised? Owned firearms. Subscribed to firearms magazines. Had he a history of indecency and sex offences?

Many of these thoughts were right on the button. They were Barry to a tee.

After Hamish had described Barry to the seminar, he made further notes of the responses. The one that stood out was 'Beware of making things fit.' Of course Hamish knew that already, but it was an important reminder all the same. He had always known this would be a tricky case to pursue in court. As time went on, eroding forensic evidence and the potential for identification, all that was left were the possibilities of a confession – and if you had killed Jill, why would you want to confess? – or of retrieving the weapon. What you would be left with was circumstantial evidence, indirect evidence of guilt. The particle was quite a bonus.

Barry was arrested two days after the seminar, on 25 May, at 6.30 am. He was taken to Hammersmith police station in handcuffs and changed out of his clothes into a paper suit and then interviewed, irregularly over the next four days, for a total of seven hours and fifty-three minutes.

The Polsa teams moved back into his flat and cleared it out. Forensic scientists came in and sucked up dust and fibres and peered with fibre optic cameras behind walls, under floorboards and in cavities. They found no forensic trace whatsoever of guns or the residue of guns.

By the time of the trial the police had counted 762 newspapers, eight of which contained articles about Jill before her death and forty-six of which had articles after her death. None of those articles was marked in any way but there was one photograph of Jill and Alan which had been torn from a newspaper. Barry's defence lawyers would go through his possessions at the police store and find a further 154 newspapers and magazines with no mention of Jill.

The police did find the Traffic Cars' card with '1.15 pm' written on it by Ramesh Paul, various items of additional military clothing, some SAS epaulettes, and military magazines and books, *Ninja – The Invisible Assassins* and *Constructing Secret Hiding Places*, a book about military ambush.

There were many long and meticulously handwritten lists, of music production facilities and sound studios. A list of vehicle registration numbers, among which were a couple of cars connected to the late Princess Diana.

In all this – in 104 boxes that went from 2b Crookham Road to the exhibits store in Mandela Way off the Old Kent Road – there was no reference to Jill Dando, no piece of paper with her name or address or anything about her, except those few articles. There were many more articles about Freddie Mercury and about Princess Diana, as you might expect in any random assortment of newspapers from recent years.

Barry George never looked guiltier than when the video recordings of his interviews were played in court and, though they seemed to be conducted in a fairly plodding, understated fashion they were in fact effective at trapping or leading Barry into many lies.

Hamish did not conduct the interviews himself, not until he stepped in at the end after Barry had stopped speaking. Instead he assigned the role to DS Mike Snowden, who had interviewed with Hamish on the nightclub shooting case and was one of the officers on the inquiry who had always thought a loner was probably responsible for Jill's death. The second officer was DS Eric Sword.

Barry was supported or watched over by an 'appropriate adult', a duty social worker, Françoise Lemir, and represented by his new solicitor, Marilyn Etienne, who had a partnership on North End Road in Fulham. Hamish watched the interviews via a video link, from an office on the top floor of the police station.

He would always wonder why Barry answered questions for so long before finally exercising his right to silence. In the tactical game of criminal justice, 'no comment' might have served him better and left the inquiry with a more difficult task.

Barry was often ill or complained of being ill and was repeatedly seen by doctors during the four days of interviews. He spoke mostly in a deferential and pedantic fashion, a pseudo legalese, punctuated by bursts of verbal aggression, as if he were appearing in a television police drama.

MIKE SNOWDEN: Can you remember on the day what happened once you'd arrived at the front door of HAFAD?
BARRY GEORGE: I don't recollect exactly what happened, no sir. But they had at some point engaged with me in dialogue.

He was slippery too, elusive and, no doubt, frustrating and irritating to interview. In the construction of Barry as the man who had shot Jill, he went to HAFAD to establish an alibi and returned there two days later to reinforce that alibi. Though, of course, at this stage, he was saying he had been at home all morning and not left to walk to HAFAD until early afternoon, which was no alibi at all for the time of the murder.

MS: Did you go anywhere else after you'd left your home before going to HAFAD?
BG: No.

MS: How long would it take you to walk that distance?

BG: Which distance?

MS: The route you've shown me from your home to HAFAD.

BG: Approximately about fifteen to twenty minutes.

MS: Had you made an appointment?

BG: I had no appointment with them, sir.

MS: Did you know that you would need an appointment?

BG: On initially seeing them no but later they made that known to me, yes.

MS: But at that time you didn't know you needed an appointment?

BG: Which time?

MS: When you went on the 26th?

BG: I did not know.

Barry seemed not to want to say Jill's name.

BG: I've spoken to her [his neighbour, Mrs Smith] and we've discussed the aftermath of what had happened, obviously on the television, media stories.

MS: To do with?

BG: To do with the case that is being investigated.

MS: To do with this case?

BG: Yes.

MS: To do with the death of Jill Dando?

BG: Yeah. That was the aftermath.

He was reminded of the two notes found in his flat, in which he said he had been born again as a Christian and had been present when Jill Dando once interviewed his cousin, Freddie.

MS: Was Freddie Mercury your cousin?

BG: No, totally not.

MS: Were you present at any interview that took place between Freddie Mercury and Jill Dando?

BG: No, not at all.

Jill never had interviewed Freddie Mercury, so far as it was possible to check. She had participated in a television charity appeal for Comic Relief in which she was one among a number of television personalities who sang along to the Queen song, *Bohemian Rhapsody*.

'Mama, just killed a man, put a gun against his head, pulled the trigger, now he's dead,' as the song went . . .

Barry said he had never seen Jill Dando in the flesh in any shape or form.

MS: Have you ever owned a firearm?

BG: No, sir.

He was shown the picture of him wearing the balaclava and holding the Heckler & Koch replica. He was asked if he recognised the picture, which had been taken at the rear of his home.

BG: Yeah, I recognise the scene and basically that is SAS but more than that . . .

MS: So you recognise the background of the picture? Where it's taken?

BG: No. I can only assume that's the SAS base at Hereford but that's all . . .

MS: Is that you in that picture?

BG: No, sir.

MS: Is that you holding that weapon?
BG: No, sir.

He was shown the picture of him holding the handgun and asked if he recognised that. It could be anyone, he said. He was told the picture had come from one of the rolls at his home, pictures which he had taken.

BG: How could I take a picture of myself?
MS: Exactly. Have you ever owned or possessed a handgun?
BG: Not a handgun, no, sir.
MS: Mr George, this weapon is the type of weapon similar, could have been used to murder Jill Dando. Here is a picture of you holding that weapon. Where is that weapon?
BG: It was . . . if it's the same one, it is a replica.

Barry admitted now that he had once owned this gun and that it was now with a friend, David Dobbins. It was not a gun, it was a replica gun, he insisted.

Hamish sent officers out in search of David Dobbins. He had known Barry in the mid-1980s when they had both lived in bed-and-breakfast accommodation, the Stanhope Hotel. Barry used to say he was Tommy Palmer, ex of the SAS. (Tommy Palmer was a genuine SAS soldier-hero who had died on active service in 1983.) Barry had the Heckler & Koch replica and the blank-firing Bruni, neither of which fired live bullets. He would show them off sometimes – he had once crashed into a room firing off blanks, dressed up like Tommy – but he was secretive with them too. Another resident, Susan Coombe, would say that she once saw a handgun, in a box beneath his bed, a gun with a silver handle, nestling in a soft scarf.

The police believed that this was a third gun, which had gone untraced. This third gun, or the possibility of its existence, would weigh heavily at the trial.

The other two had been stolen by David Dobbins and some friends later, in 1986 or 1987, after Barry had moved into Crookham Road. They had gone there one day to see him and he was out, so they had broken in and stolen the respirator and the two replicas, not seeing or taking any third gun in a box. The Heckler & Koch had ended up in David Dobbins's little brother's toybox. The Bruni was broken anyway and no longer fired even blanks. During the interviews and later at the trial it would be argued that the Bruni was not broken but modified with the implication that Barry was capable of creating or modifying a gun, though no gun expert could say that the broken bit of the Bruni represented any kind of purposeful modification.

Mike Snowden began to play tough with Barry, told him he was lying about guns, had bought guns and used them and was lying because he matched the description of Jill's killer and had owned a gun similar to the gun that was used. Barry said he wasn't lying and had bought only a replica. In that case, said Mike Snowden, you must have modified it. No, said Barry, he wouldn't know how to do that.

He admitted that he had been a member of a gun club but said that was many years ago and he had not been accepted as a full member.

'Why not?' asked Mike Snowden.

BG: I don't recollect that, sir, and if it still exists then there shouldn't be a problem ascertaining that. I have no objections.

MS: Well, if you can't remember which name you used we don't know who to ask for, do we?

BG: It's not necessarily the case. You could ask, is a person under these names?

MS: Which names do you use? Which names have you used?

BG: All from the start?

MS: Yes, please.

BG: Barry Michael George, Steve Francis Majors, Thomas Palmer, Barry Bulsara, Barry Michael George again.

He had missed out Paul Gadd and also an earlier claim that he was the cousin of Jeff Lynne of the Electric Light Orchestra.

MS: Is there a reason for that? Do you tell lies, Mr George?

BG: No, sir.

MS: Are you Freddie Mercury's cousin?

BG: No, sir.

MS: Have you told people you were Freddie Mercury's cousin?

BG: I have done, sir.

MS: Is that a lie, Mr George?

BG: No. Exaggeration maybe, but not a lie, sir.

MS: What is your interest in Jill Dando?

BG: I don't have an interest in Jill Dando, sir.

MS: Have you ever had an interest in Jill Dando?

BG: No, sir.

MS: Do you know who Jill Dando was?

BG: Until after her death. I had no idea until then.

MS: Before Jill Dando's death you had no idea who she was?

BG: That is correct, sir.

ms: But since her death you know who she is?

bg: Obviously because it's been widespread throughout the media.

The police would later have two witnesses who seemed to suggest that Barry knew who Jill Dando was. A woman who had once visited Fulham and found herself attached to Barry as she came out of Parsons Green tube. She had been a little lost and he had offered to show her the way and as they walked up Munster Road he had indicated one of the side streets – almost certainly Gowan Avenue – and said a special lady lived down there, a friend. He intimated that she was well known and said he couldn't really talk about it.

Then there was the woman in the jewellers' shop in Carnaby Street who he had once, in the mid-1990s, been regaling with tales of celebrities he had met through his association with his cousin, Freddie Mercury. Princess Diana, the lady from *Crimewatch*. 'Do you mean Jill Dando?' the jeweller had asked. 'Yes,' Barry had said.

Barry told Mike Snowden he had never met Jill Dando at the BBC though he had once worked there as a messenger and used to see quite a number of celebrities. He was asked when he had worked at the BBC. 'From May to September 1976,' came the swift and very exact answer. He could not remember any other jobs he had held.

He was shown the photograph of the doctor's surgery at 21 Gowan Avenue and said he didn't recognise it, except as one of the many surgeries he had attended. Mike Snowden told him it was four doors from where Jill Dando had been murdered and reminded him that he had been a patient there in 1996. Barry said he couldn't recall that and Mike Snowden said he was lying. Barry said he had genuinely forgotten. He had been dealing with a number of medical situations and he had forgotten. He couldn't remember exactly how many doctors he'd had in the last ten years but it was fair to say a number.

He was asked about following women and denied following women. The blue folders of photographs were produced, showing all the women he had followed and photographed, sometimes as many as seventeen pictures of the same woman in a sequence.

Mike Snowden returned to guns and tried to establish, working backwards over the years, when Barry had last fired one. Not last year, not the year before. '1997?'

'No, sir.'

'1996, '95, '94, '93, '92, '91, '90?'

'No sir, no sir, no sir.'

He couldn't recall 1989. With the new information from David Dobbins, Mike Snowden went back over the guns he'd owned. Barry still said he had only ever had those two guns and Mike Snowden said he thought he was lying.

MS: It seems to me, Mr George, you certainly possessed at least two weapons, two firearms, if not three, whether they be replica, blank-firing or imitation weapons. That's right, isn't it? At least two, if not three. Is that right, Mr George?

BG: Only those two, sir.

MS: Did you kill Jill Dando?

BG: No, sir.

And then, after some brief further exchanges:

MS: Was that you leaving the scene of the crime, Mr George?

BG: No, sir.

MS: The police took your three-quarter length coat from your flat at the time of the search.

BG: Yes, sir.

MS: A firearms expert, firearms laboratory, has also examined that coat. Did you kill Jill Dando?

BG: No, sir.

MS: The inside of your coat pocket has been found to have a trace of percussion primer discharge residue. Did you kill Jill Dando?

BG: No, sir.

MARILYN ETIENNE: I did ask you if any forensic analysis had come back and you didn't indicate to me anything about any firearms residue or any other type of residue being found.

MS: Thank you. How do you explain the firearms residue in your coat pocket, Mr George? The coat pocket, the three-quarter length coat that you may have been wearing on the day that Jill Dando was killed. How do you explain it?

BG: I can't explain it. I have no knowledge about it being there.

MS: Of course you haven't. But how did it get there, Mr George?

BG: I have no idea, sir.

MS: Isn't it possible that it got there because you were at the scene of the crime and you were the person that shot Miss Dando? Wouldn't that explain how it got there? It's consistent with the firearms residue found in the cartridge at the scene of the crime. Could you explain that to me?

BG: I cannot explain that, sir.

That was it then. Barry exercised his right to silence. Marilyn Etienne said that the police had enough to charge him if they chose to.

Over the weekend Barry had taken part in an identification parade for Jill's neighbour Richard Hughes and the bus-stop witness, Joseph Sappleton. Neither man recognised him. Sappleton picked out a different person in the line-up. Identification remained an important issue and the Metropolitan Police had asked newspapers not to publish any photographs of Barry after his arrest.

This was a concern for Hamish as he considered whether or not to charge. The alternative was to release him on bail, or even without bail, and that would leave the newspapers free to run their photographs and that would make it impossible to hold any further identification parades. There was also the more mundane consideration of where Barry would go, his entire home having been emptied, his name and address widely published by the media.

Hamish discussed this with a senior official from the Crown Prosecution Service, Alison Saunders. He knew that everyone was waiting and wondering what he would do. He thought about Barry and decided, yes, I do think you should be charged, yes I do think you killed her. Though he might have thought differently without the residue.

Barry George was charged with the murder of Jill Dando at 18.43 on Sunday, 25 May 2000, one year and twenty-nine days after her death.

Twelve

In the midsummer of 1997, Jill was on the *Queen Elizabeth II* bound for New York, a crossing of six days, with only three and a half days of filming for *Holiday*. She had just cancelled her appointment at the onboard beauty salon, which promised to take up to eight inches off your hips with a combination of electrodes and a coating of gunge, as Jill described it. She had cycled nine miles on an exercise bike in the gym that morning.

And now she was sitting in the lounge writing a letter to Liz Johnston-Keay. She told her about having a flirty time on the dancefloor with the ship's doctor, and about sharing a bottle of champagne in her cabin with an old friend from Radio Devon, Colin Parkes, who was also working on board. She remembered that she had been meaning to tell Liz all about Cliff's party, which she had attended a few days before she her departure.

It was usual for Sir Cliff Richard to have a summer party and it regularly featured a surprise or something special, sometimes arranged by his friends. This year, his PA Roger Bruce and Roger's partner Alan had planned, on the cue of a fired rocket, for an entire boys' choir in smocks to appear out of the woods at the end of the grounds and proceed across the lawn singing angelic songs before switching into 'Jailhouse Rock'. A fifty-piece band of Scouts and Guides had followed them later.

Jill told Liz all about this, describing Cliff's home, Charters, as 'absolutely gorgeous', mock-Georgian she supposed, with lovely big windows. She had taken Simon Bassil with her to the party. 'I couldn't really exclude him,' she wrote, 'especially as the invite said Jill and guest.'

She was, she wrote, still bowled over by Sir C. One of his friends had told Jill after the party that Cliff had spoken 'very warmly' about her. 'We shall see.'

Cousin Judith would hear from Jill about her encounters with Cliff: how they had accidentally brushed hands while at dinner and he had glanced at her and she had been left thinking there was hope. She really thought there was a chance, for a while. Some people were willing to question Cliff's sexuality but Jill would shush the doubters, never countenance the idea that he was anything other than straight.

Jenny Higham remembers being with them once at lunch, in that post-Bob phase, thinking that if it was ever going to happen it would happen around this time. But nothing ever did happen. Jenny remembered Jill and Cliff and Gloria Hunniford sitting together discussing cosmetic surgery and its merits, and whether or not they ever would succumb. Gloria would say she talked about it all the time, was still talking about it. Jill certainly talked about it, increasingly, as she noted the accretion of lines around her eyes.

Jenny imagined that Cliff and others in a celebrated position must spend a lot of time and become very adept at brushing aside people who attempted to become close to them. It was probably second nature to them.

A number of Cliff and Jill's mutual friends felt they became much closer and more intimate after Jill began her relationship with Alan and those yearnings for a different kind of intimacy with Cliff had passed.

Cliff had been appearing at the Hammersmith Apollo in *Heathcliff* earlier in the year and Jill would often recommend local restaurants where Cliff and his PA Roger could go after the show for supper. Jill sometimes went too. They liked Chutney Mary, an expensive, colonial-style Indian restaurant on the New Kings Road. One night, Cliff and Roger went to Jill's for supper and she cooked. Jill had also invited Eamonn Holmes, her former colleague, who was now a presenter on the ITV breakfast show *GMTV*.

'Hi, Eamms,' Jill would greet him when she called. The only person he knew who called him Eamms. She would invariably be calling from the BBC newsroom, whiling away the time between or before bulletins, not catching up on the news but catching up with friends. 'Right,' he would bark. 'What do you want? This had better be fucking serious.' He always swore. He was an Irish Catholic. And she would start to laugh. 'Why do you always laugh at everything I say?' he would ask. He often felt a bit like her court jester, so this invitation was typical. She was having Cliff over for supper and wanted Eamonn there to keep him amused while she was in the kitchen.

Eamonn did not mix in showbiz circles, was not out for dinner every night with Cliff or Gloria or whoever. He would call his wife later to say, 'Guess who I'm having dinner with tonight?' He and his wife were both fans of Cliff. So Eamonn asked Jill what time.

'About eleven.'

'What? I'm up for work at four! Why would I come out at eleven?'

'But Cliff doesn't finish till then. Oh Eamms, please, please.'

He relented.

He arrived before Cliff and found Jill busy in the kitchen, with Heart FM on the radio. Eamonn hadn't heard it before, but he liked it and listened to it regularly after that. He noticed Jill had her *Radio Times* covers up on the wall in the hallway. He would've put them in the loo or somewhere out of sight. A typical Fulham house, he thought. How much did you pay for this? He thought those London prices were so stupid. And you didn't even get a free parking space outside.

Cliff had changed out of his costume when he arrived with Roger, but was still in his make-up and hair extensions. Jill was in and out of the kitchen and Eamonn was telling his stories. There was this gossipy tale about life at GMTV, which Eamonn would not wish to repeat in public. Cliff was in fits and Eamonn was just getting to the best bit, swearing away – '. . . and then I just fucking said to this guy—' – when Jill stood up, pushing her chair back from the table.

'Eamonn Holmes,' she said. 'How dare you.' He thought for a moment she was joking, then he realised she was in earnest and guessed she must be taking exception to his mockery of the subject of the story, but that was not it, either. 'How dare you,' she said. 'Don't you ever swear in this house. Don't you ever swear in front of me.'

'Oh, for fuck's sake,' said Eamonn. How dare you spoil my punchline? he thought. It seemed to him that he'd been swearing all night and in front of Jill ever since he'd known her. Cliff said it wasn't a problem for him, but Jill was quite huffy about it, went out to the kitchen and there was a pause before she returned and said, 'I'm sorry. If it's OK with Cliff, it's OK with me.'

Everything was fine again then but Eamonn thought it was an absurd incident. Jill playing the God-squad card because of Cliff and her crush on him. That was how he saw it. Jill really didn't like people swearing. Perhaps she didn't usually notice it in Eamonn's company and was more conscious of it and embarrassed by it because Cliff was there.

By the time they left it was about two hours before Eamonn was due to get up and go to work. As they stood on the doorstep, Eamonn, Cliff, Roger and Jill, Eamonn said, 'Well, here is the picture the press would love now, isn't it? Jill Dando at two o'clock in the morning with a bunch of men on her doorstep.'

On a later occasion, Jill and Eamonn went to Wimbledon together, had a few glasses in the Lanson champagne tent, sat and watched the tennis, chatted and flirted, as they usually did. They fell to talking about their contracts and Jill said she was on a great deal at the BBC. 'Three thirty k,' she said. Eamonn had said, 'Fucking hell, I'm asking for a pay rise tomorrow.' 'Just think,' she said, 'of the life we could live on our combined salaries.'

Jill asked Eamonn if he wanted his own chat show and he said nothing would fill him with more dread. 'You're only there to be shot down. Besides, it's all got to be different these days. You have to be different. You have to be a comedian, Clive Anderson or Graham Norton or Frank Skinner. No, the secret of survival in this business is to stick with a format programme, go with the format. It's the format that's good, and by association you are good. Don't put yourself out on a limb.'

But Jill was not convinced. 'I really love the idea of *The Jill*

Dando Show,' she said. '*The Jill Dando Show*. That's what I really want.'

I don't see that, thought Eamonn. Not a good idea.

Jill was not exactly sitting around that year, waiting for the flowering of a relationship with Cliff. She was busy, busy at work, busy in life, travelling, socialising, dating, having a ball. This was the year she called Judith on the way out of Buckingham Palace, having just been chatted up by Prince Andrew. The year that her mobile phone service provider called out of concern, because her voicemail had been interrogated twenty-four times in one day, which was just Jill picking up her many messages. She was addicted to her mobile phone, to keeping in touch and checking her voicemail to see who was keeping in touch with her. As Judith says, she was discovering that all these men were interested in her, and she was in her element.

As the police inquiry would discover afterwards, her male friendships were not clear-cut, separated and ordered through the months, but bumped against each other in a cats' cradle of dates that could have become far more complicated and difficult to manage than they apparently were. The men were barely aware of each other's existence, each in their own compartment of Jill's life, and if she ever felt guilty or bothered about this, I never heard of it. The men didn't seem to worry, either, not the ones I spoke to. They just enjoyed Jill and their time with her.

She was lonely sometimes, too. Nothing is ever quite straightforward and underlying sadnesses or vulnerabilities are not simply erased by having some fun. She was still searching for that soulmate, knight on the white charger or whoever he was. Undoubtedly still seeking to fill the void of her mother's loss. She gave an interview to the journalist Danny Danziger, published in *Cover* magazine, based on the theme of the 'yellowing clipping'. Jill's clipping was a corner of a page from the *Daily Mirror* that Jill's mother had cut out and kept in the front of her Bible in her bedroom drawer. Jill explained in the interview that she was sure her mother had put it there for her to find after her death.

Jill now kept the Bible in her living room, the clipping still inside. She could not look at it without becoming emotional, or read it aloud without crying. This was in 1997, which was twelve years after her mother's death. The clipping was from a once regular column, 'Kingsley Amis On Poetry', featuring the poem 'Remember' by Christina Rossetti, a Victorian poet who had lived in London. 'The finest of our women poets', according to Kingsley, and 'a deeply religious high-Church Anglican'. The poem had been written as an address to a suitor whom she had rejected on grounds of conscience and from whom she had parted in great sorrow.

> Remember me when I am gone away,
> Gone far away into the silent land;
> When you can no more hold me by the hand,
> Nor I half turn to go yet turning stay.
> Remember me when no more day by day
> You tell me of our future that you planned:
> Only remember me; you understand
> It will be late to counsel then or pray.
> Yet if you should forget me for a while
> And afterwards remember, do not grieve:
> For if the darkness and corruption leave
> A vestige of the thoughts that once I had,
> Better by far you should forget and smile
> Than that you should remember and be sad.

Jill told Danny Danziger how she and her mother used to go to church together. Her mother always sat at the back, she said, because she had a 'phobia' about people looking at the back of her head. A self-consciousness, you might say, not really a phobia.

Not long after she finished with Bob, Jill had said to Jenny Higham that she would go out with anyone who asked her so long as they didn't have two heads. Say yes to everyone, accept the offers that came along. She was trying out dating again and also said to Jenny she would go for lunches, because lunches were safer and there was less expectation that you would end up in bed together afterwards.

The pool of prospects was quite small really, in the place that Jill now found herself, emerging fully formed and famous from her relationship with Bob. 'Don't go out with all those media sycophants,' Jenny would tell her.

Much as Jill revelled in being famous, it was a double bind in the quest for relationships, since she always worried that people were interested in her only because she was on television, and worried too that her fame set high expectations which would be dashed when men got to know her and found out what she was really like, how ordinary she was.

Still, she seemed to manage. She had given an interview earlier that summer of 1997 to Jan Moir in the *Daily Telegraph* in which she spoke of men not wanting to have sex with her – 'They just want to take me to a nice wine bar for a nice glass of wine.' That was the image of her, the public face of Jill Dando, a perception which she seemed content to sustain. It obviously served a purpose but it was not quite the full picture.

'I hope you're not including me in that,' Jan Knott told her next time he saw her. He was still living in hope and determined to declare his feelings.

An author and journalist who wishes to remain anonymous was briefly in a relationship with her during this period. They had met when he interviewed her and then he was having dinner one evening with a girlfriend in a Chinese restaurant in London and Jill was there with Simon Bassil and came over and spoke to the journalist in friendly terms, which flattered and pleased him.

He may have called her or she may have called him, he can't remember, but they arranged to have dinner together and then began a relationship based on sporadic and short assignations. The most time they ever spent together was a couple of nights.

It had obviously suited them both. The journalist didn't go out of his way to tell colleagues and friends he was dating Jill – not wanting to trade on her name – and he never met any of her friends, either. They didn't bring each other into their lives, they were just together for a while.

He said it was a bright and breezy affair, and oddly unemotional too, which made him and, he assumed, Jill realise it was not going anywhere, which it didn't. She would call him at his office sometimes, and his colleagues would tease him mildly for being in a liaison with a woman who was thought to be such a goody two-shoes. She was often just back from somewhere when they met and tired. The journalist sensed an air of apology about Jill, that she was sorry she wasn't cleverer than she was.

He could see that she was interested in reading books that stretched her and was tempted to recommend some, but then didn't want to get caught playing the Svengali, particularly since the relationship did not look likely to endure. It just petered out.

The journalist never inquired and had no awareness that Jill might be seeing other men and did not seem concerned by this.

He was quite posh this man, especially by journalistic standards, occupying the middle- to upper middle-class world that Jill drifted in and out of; the world of minor royalty, a Fulhamy world, or part of it, of matchmaking suppers and dinners.

There was the man with a double-barrelled name and a home in Belgravia, who took Jill away on a country house weekend where she felt socially ill at ease, which she spoke about afterwards in less than flattering words. She could meet that way of life on certain terms, as her celebrity self, at charity functions, at lunches with Sophie Rhys-Jones, with whom she became friends, but it was more difficult when she was just herself – a step too far from Weston.

At a reception after the BBC Proms at the Albert Hall, Jill met Michael Dobbs, another journalist, by now also a successful writer of political thrillers (such as *House of Cards*) and a politician. He had been deputy chairman of the Conservative Party for a year after Jeffrey Archer. When I mentioned to Jeffrey that Michael had known Jill, too, perhaps rather more intimately than he, Jeffrey made a snorting sound. 'Really?' he said. 'How interesting.' If he'd known that, he said, he might have tried a bit harder himself.

Michael Dobbs was single in this period of his life and when he bumped into Jill again at another reception, this time at the Ritz, a travel industry function, they talked longer and she seemed fresh, unstarry and untainted and had a curiosity about other people that was not usual on the media circuit.

They did not see each other very many times, a dozen in all perhaps, before that winter, when Jill went off to Australia with Alan and everything changed. It seemed to Michael that they might have seen each other a great deal more often, if Jill's diary hadn't been packed with the burden of work, especially the travelling for *Holiday*, which had certainly become burdensome by now.

When they did go out it was generally to dinner, to restaurants where Michael would feel invisible, seeing the diners' reaction to Jill's presence. He only remembered being noticed once, at Christopher's in Covent Garden when two men came over and told him how lucky he was, being out with Jill.

He was almost apologetic, telling me how nice Jill was and fun and easy to be with. 'You must have heard that from everyone,' he said, which of course I had. He could not recall flagging conversations or moments when he thought he ought to change the subject because Jill was struggling. ' I know it sounds mushy,' he said, 'but the truth is that ever afterwards she was never far from my thoughts.' That was the impression she had made upon him.

During their time together he was beginning work on a new book, *Whispers of Betrayal*. Jill was interested in his work as a writer and often took his books away on her *Holiday* trips, sometimes sneaking them into shot, just for fun. He was still working on the book when she died and decided it to dedicate to her and donate some of the royalties to the Jill Dando Fund.

Michael could tell that he was meeting Jill at a fundamentally exciting period of her life, when she had arrived professionally, had negotiating power and financial security and ahead of her were all the possibilities that kept her in thrall. There was no doubt she wanted to find a partner and start a family but she remained ambitious too.

They went to plays a couple of times, to the opening night of *The Letter of Resignation* at the Comedy Theatre, an account of the Profumo affair. It was late when they came out, keen to find a drink and they slipped into a low-life pub nearby and ordered glasses of champagne and Michael had one of those moments: what am I doing here in this down-at-heel pub, drinking champagne with Jill Dando? She was perfectly happy. The Ritz or the pub, it was all the same to her.

There was another man Jill knew whose professional embarrassment I'll spare, a doctor – nothing to do with Jenny Higham or Alan Farthing – whose company she enjoyed and he was keen on her, and they went out a few times and he had hoped she would be his date for New Year's Eve, but it was not to be.

They met up again at a party, after which they went back to Jill's home and slept together for the one and only time. It was the kind of thing that would certainly have made him very anxious after her death, which is undoubtedly why he was less than forthcoming about it to the police.

Jenny Higham had held a party at her home way back in October 1996, to celebrate qualifying as a consultant in obstetrics and gynaecology at St Mary's. Many of her colleagues and friends had been there. Jill, she remembered, had been wearing a vibrant orange suit. She and Bob were just leaving as Alan Farthing arrived.

It was an event which Alan told me he could clearly recall and Jill, to her disappointment, could not remember at all. Jenny had already noted Alan's curiosity about her friendship with Jill, which she didn't routinely discuss at work, and his occasional references to having seen her on television.

Alan had returned to London a year earlier with his wife Maria, a nurse. They had been in Australia for eighteen months where Alan had become skilled in the new technique of laparoscopy – keyhole surgery – in gynaecological cancer surgery. This was a developing area of gynaecology with few specialists and Alan's experience had helped to secure his appointment as a consultant at St Mary's. He had been offered a consultancy in Australia at the same time and so events might have taken a very different turn.

Alan and Maria separated in the summer of 1997, after nearly seven years of marriage, and that August Alan moved to his new home in Chiswick.

Jenny and Alan had become friends through working together and, not long after this, Jenny went round to Alan's one evening, to see his new home. 'I'll put a CD on,' she said. She rifled through his collection of CDs, which was unashamedly middle of the road: Celine Dion, Abba, greatest hits, compilations.

The following night, or maybe the night after that, Jenny was going out with Jill and went to Gowan Avenue to meet her and went to put a CD on. Celine Dion, Cliff, Abba, assorted compilations . . . she realised there was a 70 per cent overlap with Alan's collection.

It dawned on her then how alike they were in other ways, with their West Country backgrounds, both religious and quite restrained. These people, she thought, are potentially very compatible.

Jenny was not in a rush to be a matchmaker. She'd had her fingers burned a couple of times in the past and knew that when mutual friends were introduced and it didn't work there could be some fall-out. On the other hand, she had introduced a relative to her current husband, so she was at least willing to give it a try. All you could do was bring people together and see how they got on.

Knowing that Alan was quite battered and bruised by his recent separation, Jenny decided to leave it for a while. Then, in October, Jill was standing in for a week for Esther Rantzen, who was on sick leave from her eponymous show, *Esther*. It was just a few weeks since Jill had participated in the BBC's live coverage of Princess Diana's funeral.

Jenny usually went to the studio to see Jill working at least once in any series and Jill invited her to come along and be in the audience for *Esther*. Jenny decided this was the best moment and said she would bring this bloke along from work. Didn't make a big deal out of it, but let Jill know he was a colleague and available.

She decided not to say anything about it at all to Alan. She arranged to meet him for a drink after work at the Landmark Hotel on the Marylebone Road, not far from St Mary's. There were two entries in her diary for 22 October 1997: '8.15 pm, Jill, BBC' and, a later addition, 'Alan – 6.30 pm, Landmark'.

Alan recalled turning up at the hotel and after a quick drink being told there was a taxi organised. He wanted to know where they were going and why. Jenny said they were going to see Jill recording an *Esther* as members of the studio audience. Alan was not so impressed at the prospect of appearing on television, but went along and sat through the programme, which was on the theme of shyness.

As Alan heard later from Jill, she had got a colleague to peer out beforehand from behind the scenes and size him up and report back to her. A test which, as he coyly put it, he had evidently passed.

He was quite shy himself afterwards when they went down to a restaurant on Shepherd's Bush Green, where Jill had booked a table, quite unnecessarily, since it was almost empty. Alan sat there in near silence while Jill and Jenny talked. Jenny could see that Jill was quite wired from work, the *Esther* was not exactly a walkthrough for Jill, requiring considerable preparation and being important too, since Jill hoped one day to have her own eponymous show. 'Charming but distracted,' Jenny would say of Jill that evening.

At the end of the evening, Jill did ask Alan if he'd like to come to her birthday party, on 9 November at the Cannizaro House Hotel on Wimbledon Common. Alan said yes he'd like to go, then afterwards he realised it was the same day as a friend's fiftieth that was being celebrated at Wasps Rugby Club during a European Cup match. Alan was keen on rugby and didn't feel he should let his old friend down, despite Jill's invitation. He talked it over with Jenny and she gave him Jill's number and he called to explain and apologise.

Jenny was sure he thought he'd blown it with Jill, but they had both indicated their willingness to meet again and Jenny was prepared to give it one last try so she invited them both round one evening in late November.

There was certainly no commitment at this stage and Jill must have been preoccupied with her birthday party which she was anxious should be a success and, in her way, was at times convinced would be a complete failure, with no one turning up, or those that did not talking to each other. She had never hosted a big function on her own before, and it seemed to Jenny a bit like a coming out party, a declaration of independence.

Jill had called Jan Knott earlier in October and met him for dinner while she was working down in Canterbury. That was when he brought up the *Telegraph* article about men and wine bars. 'Did you see that?' she said. 'Yeah, I saw it. I hope you're not including me in that.' Even though they had not seen each other for a while they had kept in touch with cards and calls and, seeing her once more, Jan again felt strong feelings for Jill. He didn't mention Simon Bassil and neither did Jill. She invited him to Cannizaro

House and sent him a handwritten invitation, 'Jill's birthday drinks and canapés, 12 noon onwards'.

Jan went to the party and had a thoroughly good time, talking to Jill's father, who he had met on the Boxing Day trip on Concorde, discussing football with her brother Nigel and discovering a shared enthusiasm for Brighton football club with Des Lynam. Cliff was missing but he'd sent a huge bowl of flowers, which were on display. Jan was one of the first guests to arrive and immediately noticed a man he gathered was Simon and wondered what Simon was doing there and wondered then what he was doing there himself.

At some point he was sitting on a sofa next to Jill with some of her family, and Simon came up and took a photograph of Jan and Jill together and Jan was very confused. He became even more confused when she suggested that they meet up after the party and she called him at his hotel and invited him back to Gowan Avenue, after Jan had seen Simon leaving on the drive back to his home on the south coast.

Jan and Jill drank some red wine and he stayed there one last time, the last time they saw each other. He left unable to speak his feelings to Jill. All he could say was that he was going skiing in January and would love her to join him. She said she might very well do that. Instead, he had a letter in January saying she'd met someone new and how she felt about him. She said some nice words about Jan, too, by way of an ending.

He wondered if Jill had been testing her feelings for him that evening after the party. Or maybe she was just lonely and wanted his company. She had sent him a note the day afterwards, thanking him for his birthday gift of a cruet set and for making the effort to come to the party. 'I'm slightly regretting the later over-indulgence but, hey, you only have a birthday once a year . . . Thank you again, Jan, for all your kindness. With love, Jill x.'

Of course, Jan was happy for Jill in her new happiness with Alan, but he always regretted his own failure to come forward and wondered if he had missed the chance of a more permanent relationship. Probably not, he concluded. Even so, he grieved when Jill died, and felt even greater regret then, like a double loss.

I couldn't help wondering how the party would have gone if Alan had been there. Those things were unknowable. Jenny said Jill had a kind of impatience about her . . . not impatience, but she wasn't going to be messed around. She wasn't into playing games and being cool by this stage. If something was going to happen, then it had better happen: she wasn't going to hang around waiting.

When Alan and Jill got together at Jenny's home in late November, they all had a glass of champagne and went to the pub across the road, Jenny, her husband Ed, Jill and Alan. Alan was more at ease now, and more talkative, and as they left the pub to go back to Jenny and Ed's, Jill whispered to Jenny, 'Very nice, very nice.' At the end of the evening Alan nobly offered to give Jill a lift home, and she accepted. As he dropped her off he invited her out to dinner and she accepted. Their relationship began with that first date, on 23 November 1997.

Alan had planned a house-warming party in Chiswick which Jill could not attend because she was going to be away for *Holiday*. But she called from Hong Kong during the party, pretending to be a neighbour complaining about the noise, which confused the friend of Alan's who answered the phone. Jill Dando calling might have been strange enough, but Jill Dando calling and pretending to be a neighbour?

When she returned from that trip she invited Alan to go away for the weekend and share the Jaguar XK8 which she had been given the chance to test drive. It was her ideal car and she would soon be thinking about buying one. They went to the Cotswolds, the first of many weekends away, and while they were there Alan mentioned that he was going to Australia over New Year. It was already mid-December, and he couldn't believe Jill wouldn't already have plans, but he asked her anyway, 'If you're free, why don't you come along?' To his amazement and delight, she said yes.

Alan then had to rapidly rearrange his Australian schedule, downgrading his fortnight with friends in Adelaide to one week and finding a hotel which would be suitable for Jill, the holiday queen. In fact, Jill made inquiries, too, and found a resort. So they ended up staying in Alan's choice, the Intercontinental in Sydney, for four nights, watching the New Year's Eve fireworks over the harbour bridge, and then took a seaplane north to the secluded and rather luxurious resort, Headlands, at Broken Bay.

There was a photograph of the fireworks over the harbour bridge in the New Year's Day edition of the *Sydney Morning Herald*. Alan later tracked it down and had a print made and framed, which he gave to Jill on Valentine's Day. It was the most romantic moment of the trip, watching those fireworks, and it became a symbol of their relationship. Something which they always planned to repeat. They had promised that night to be back there for the Millennium, though, had she lived, Jill had been due to present the BBC's coverage of the Millennium.

They did return to Sydney, just under a year later, but that was for work, when Jill was filming for *Holiday*. Alan was asked by the crew to be in a shot at the Opera House. 'Just stand there and, as Jill walks past, look at her like Richard Gere looking at Julia Roberts in *Pretty Woman*,' he was instructed. Alan had no idea what that meant.

After their few days at Headlands at the start of 1998, Jill flew back to London and Alan went on to Adelaide to see his friends. Jill seems already to have had a sense of a future with Alan by then. Both Jenny and Judith recall her vacillating beforehand about whether or not to go to Australia. There was the rival New Year's Eve offer from the other doctor. Jill had joked then about her two doctors. It was uncharacteristic and entirely healthy, that she should do something so impetuous, going off to Sydney with a man she barely knew. She was full of the trip afterwards, and showing the first signs of the glow that everyone said enveloped her, in her love for Alan.

He was with Jill the following month when she went to Weston for Jack's eightieth birthday, which was celebrated with a lunch at the Commodore Hotel. He was in the spotlight with all Jill's surrogate mother figures, Auntie Esme and Liz Johnston-Keay, but they both approved. Another hurdle crossed.

Then, in March, they went to see Judith in France for a long weekend's skiing at Serre Chevalier. Judith's friends Richard and Vicky were there. In just over a year, Richard Quinn would be calling on Alan at St Mary's to tell him of Jill's death.

They returned on the Monday and were due to dinner the following Saturday with Jenny and Ed and Jill's old friend and colleague Suzanne Yates and her husband, at Sarastro's restaurant in Drury Lane.

They were getting ready in Chiswick, at about six o'clock, when Alan's doorbell rang. He answered it. 'Who was that?' Jill called when he had closed the door. It was a reporter from the *News Of The World*, a sheepish female reporter, asking Alan if he had any comment on his new relationship with Jill. 'No, certainly not,' said Alan. 'That sounds very intrusive.' The reporter apologised and left. Jill called Jon Roseman, which prompted further calls and the discovery that the *News Of The World* was planning to publish pictures of Jill and Alan kissing on the ski slopes. The pictures had been taken by Jason Fraser, who was a chief tabloid skulker well known in that business for his long-lens scoops.

A reporter called on Alan's ex-wife too. She did not then know of Alan's involvement with Jill.

Alan and Jill both felt uncomfortable at the thought of having been spied on. But that was not Jill's main concern. By the time they reached the restaurant she was really quite upset, as Jenny could tell. Jill was never good at disguising her true feelings, pleasure, irritation, annoyance, embarrassment, boredom, distress, it always showed in her face to those who knew her.

Jenny could see she was trying to front up but was obviously distracted and upset. They went off to the loo and were there for about twenty minutes while Jill cried and said she was sure that would be the end of Alan, how good it had been so far and now the press were bound to destroy it. Everything was spoilt.

When she had listened, Jenny tried to reassure her. A relationship wasn't a bus. Alan hadn't just got on board to jump off the first time a couple of pictures were published.

After the meal Alan and Jill were dropping Jenny and Ed home and stopped at King's Cross Station to pick up the first edition of the paper. They were the front-page splash. Though fortunately, as it turned out, it was a dummy splash by the *News Of The World* to disguise the bigger and more salacious story that replaced them in the later editions: a tale of indiscretions by Newcastle United executives.

Alan thought the effect of the pictures might have been more damaging if they had not been together for a few months by then and he'd had time to get used to this bizarre world that Jill half-occupied.

In his business, any publicity was bad publicity, as he would always say, was always saying. You were not supposed to draw attention to yourself. In Jill's business it was almost completely the opposite.

Naturally, some of the St Mary's staff plastered copies of the picture on notice boards. One or two colleagues phoned to say they thought Alan must be the first gynaecologist from the hospital to appear on the front page of the *News Of The World*.

He had known from the start that he was bound to get caught in the light that shone on Jill. But he was nervous of the professional impact and determined not to project himself in any way and impressed upon Jill the need to be diplomatic in interviews. She could sometimes say more than she needed to and regret it later.

He'd attended his first public function with Jill before they went to Australia. 'Carols With The Stars' at the Albert Hall. They had walked through the assembled ranks of photographers slightly apart – certainly not holding hands or anything, as Alan was anxious to make clear – Alan looking very respectable in black tie. That was important to Jill, somebody who looked the part. And it was important to Alan that Jill should not feel she had to look after him at these functions, that he could hold his own in the general hubbub of superficial conversations. He could do superficial conversation, no problem, he said, but it was sometimes difficult to sustain for an entire evening. He remembered another early event, the *What Car?* Awards, sat at a table for dinner, sure that his neighbour was working overtime to keep the flow going. He felt uneasy too in those early days, not being her established or recognised partner. Sitting there patiently while Jill was whisked off to be photographed with the company chairman or whoever it was. For all those people knew he could've been hired in for the evening. So maybe a little bit of recognition wasn't such a terrible thing.

And, of course, it was exciting and fun too. He and Jill hardly ever had quiet nights in. Or if they did it might be to watch Jill on television, which could be quite surreal, having her sitting there next to you while she was on the screen.

They were always making the most of their time together. Going out for dinner on their own to talk or catching up with friends if they were both in London and Alan wasn't on duty at the hospital; going away for weekends, at least once a month, attending the many functions and occasions.

Quiet nights in would sometimes seem highly desirable. As Jenny observed, they never settled into any kind of routine, which would cause Jill a little anxiety as their marriage approached. What would it be like, being normal together?

'Jill brought Alan to the party,' said Jenny, 'and it was all high days and holidays.'

When she reflected on it, Jill felt betrayed by the *News Of The World* story. Someone must have told that photographer where and when they would be in France. It couldn't just be coincidence. She began to be suspicious, called Judith, even asked if she thought Richard and Vicky could inadvertently have said something to somebody. Which was out of the question. The sense of paranoia lingered and was further stoked by Jill's reappearance in the tabloids the following Sunday.

Jill had been receiving letters for a while from an elderly man in Kent, John Hole, who wrote to other celebrities too but was currently targeting Jill. She generally received many letters via her agent or the offices of *Crimewatch*, *Holiday* and *The BBC News*. Most of it was fan mail and entirely innocuous and even though stalking was increasingly an occupational hazard she had never ever been threatened or felt threatened.

She was not threatening either. Many of the letters that came were requests from wives for personal notes or messages to their husbands who adored her. She went to the trouble once of making a tape for a man at his wife's request. She got the name wrong and the wife was most upset. She was meticulous about replying. Cliff's friend Robin Williams offered to help her out once with her correspondence and she was grateful but still not quite satisfied with his letters, which she made changes to before sending on. She did not have a secretary.

Zoe Taylor, Jill's *Crimewatch* assistant, still remembered the words of one note from Hole: 'I was waiting for you at 6.30 after you did the report. I remember thinking how lovely you looked in your pale lemon suit.'

It was after a note from him appeared on the mat at Gowan Avenue that Jill became concerned. She discussed it with Alan and talked to people on *Crimewatch*. The BBC had its own investigations unit – composed mainly of retired police officers – to deal with just such circumstances. She went and explained it to them and an officer said, 'Don't worry, we'll pay him a visit, we'll deal with it.'

That following Sunday both the *Sunday Mirror* and the *People* had stories about Hole and his interest in Jill. 'STALKER GRIPPED BY TERRIFYING OBSESSION.' 'LOVESICK LONER.' 'DANDO PEST.'

Jill had not spoken to the newspapers and had hardly discussed it with anyone, had certainly not disclosed the man's identity. She suspected that the investigations unit had been responsible for the leak and felt her confidence had been betrayed by the very BBC department that was supposed to help her. She wanted to make a formal complaint but that seemed more likely to cause a greater fuss and incur further publicity. So she said nothing, while the suspicion and paranoia festered.

Thirteen

Here is a single sheet of A4 notepaper, headed 'QUEEN, Queen Productions Ltd', with the company crest and the company address: 2b Crookham Road, London SW6 4EQ, England. Fax 0171 381 4953. At the foot of the page, the directors are listed as the three surviving members of Queen, B.H. May, J. Deacon R.M. Taylor, plus B. Bulsara. Here, too, is the registered company number and VAT number, the genuine numbers of the genuine Queen Productions, which is not and never has been based at 2b Crookham Road, SW6 and does not and never has had a director called B. Bulsara.

There is a page of text on the sheet, handwritten in spidery capital letters, sloping slightly to the right, in the same hand that had written the endless lists found in Barry's flat. It is undated, but the words are a kind of psychological self-portrait which slips back and forth between the first and third person. Barry on Barry. Paul. Steve. Thomas.

Past lives – explain your current emotional complexes. My mother with whom a psychic link exists even when not present physically, and by accepting myself, my true compassionate nature can help others in so many ways.

Being so emotional I'm very moved when coming into contact with people. I have a warm, kind and sympathetic nature and understand the insecurities of others. Often you wear your heart on your sleeve but wish your feelings were not so apparent.

Moreover you're naturally kind and tender, taking into account other people's feelings and needs comes instinctively. I have a strong need to be constantly active, I tend to work long hours and play competitive or aggressive games.

I am easily inclined to become angry also, especially with close friends and I sometimes incite anger without realising it.

At times I am stunned by the depth and intensity of my feelings and those that I can unwittingly stir up in other people, especially women.

Sometimes my behaviour or strong reactions lead to a chain of events beyond my control. For example the issue of control and secrecy in relationships can lead to their destruction.

There is no easy solution to this problem. There will be a time when I am driven to understand and explore the depths of my complex emotional nature.

Delving into my subconscious or my past can be a painful process but I may feel it necessary to cleanse myself, to bring my repressed feelings to the surface or get to grips with any irrational guilty sentiments. Through this personal therapy I may start to insist that feeling [sic], both my own and those near me are brought out into the open.

Home life does it's extremes [sic], even a few crises from childhood. Personal privacy, especially with family issues is important to me. But my experiences and instincts enable me to see the potential in people.

There is some nonsense in there, of course, but some insight, too. Barry could drive people to distraction. He claimed that one of the many GPs he had seen had physically attacked him once in the surgery. And during the trial one of the psychologist experts who was assessing him was apparently drawn into a shouting match with him in the middle of an interview, their raised voices clearly audible way outside the private room in the Old Bailey.

There seemed to be two public perceptions of Barry George. Early on, after his arrest, when the newspaper reporters went knocking on doors in his area, canvassing local opinion, and he was portrayed as the harmless eccentric, the urban equivalent of the village idiot. Then, after the trial, when the newspapers could write what they liked with impunity, he was a dangerous monster. He tried to kill Di too, as the *Sun* put it, inaccurately describing how Barry had once been arrested in the grounds of Kensington Palace with two knives. (In fact he was outside the grounds with one knife, though it was in the middle of the night and he did have a 50-foot length of rope coiled around his waist. A Thomas Palmer fantasy, no doubt.)

If you had gone out on the streets of Fulham in search of the polar opposite of Jill Dando, you would almost certainly have ended your search when you bumped into Barry. And you would almost certainly have bumped into him, since that was where he spent much of his time. He was only a year older than her, born in the mid-April of 1960. He had achieved almost nothing and, it's safe to say, had known little happiness or security in his life, and considerable pain and sadness.

Where Jill was vital and alive, accomplished, fulfilled, brimming with hope and expectation, Barry was aimless and troubled, barely even himself. He was dogged by various illnesses, physical and psychological and imagined (though no less real to him). He could go blind without being blind. Hysterically blind. He could go mute without losing his voice. Hysterically mute – a condition known as aphonia. It was not surprising he fantasised. Where else could he go for some respite, except out of himself? Like so many people who are disordered and dysfunctional, Barry was plagued by his past.

Barry's Auntie Elizabeth would say that his parents were inadequate parents, physically and emotionally punitive with their children. His mother, in her view, could not cope and would rather go out than care for her children. During Barry's adolescence, Auntie Elizabeth says, before his father left, the family home was a war zone.

Dates and timings are cloudy and obscured by the passage of years and perhaps a preference to forget. Barry says his father had left home when he was eight, around the time that he was sent away to board at Heathermount, a school for children with special needs which nowadays focuses on pupils with disorders associated with autism in general and Asperger's syndrome in particular.

Alfred George himself has said that he and his wife, Margaret, had separated after their son Barry went away. Alfred maintained contact with Barry until 1974, when he went to Australia with his new wife, Barbara. He moved to Australia to escape abuse and hassle from his ex-wife and because he had seen an advertisement for a job as a prison officer in Melbourne, and applied and had been accepted.

Alfred and Margaret were married in 1954 and their family home was Creighton Close on the White City Estate, north of Shepherd's Bush and close to BBC Television Centre. They had three children: Michaelina, who was known as Michelle, Susan and Barry. Alfred had been a bus driver in those days and, in addition to being a prison officer, was also a fire officer and a special constable. He had been in the Army on National Service after the war.

Susan later spent time in locked psychiatric wards. Like Barry she was a diagnosed epileptic. She died in April 1986 when she choked after swallowing her tongue during a seizure, while in the early stages of pregnancy. Michelle appears to have emerged relatively unscathed from her past. She left home early and moved to Ireland, married, had children. She supported Barry throughout the trial, just as she had sometimes been his surrogate parent in childhood and would recall him as overactive, hyperactive, incapable of sitting still or concentrating on any task for any reasonable length of time.

Although it was never diagnosed, he probably suffered from ADHD, Attention Deficit Hyperactivity Disorder. His father said he realised early on that Barry was mentally slow and the local social services identified him as ESN, or educationally subnormal, in the jargon of the period. He was expelled from a school in Shepherd's Bush after punching a teacher who had caned him for something he hadn't done, according to his father. He went to a special school nearby before going away to Heathermount.

Barry would agree that he had been caned at school but said he had never been suspended or expelled. At Heathermount he experienced quite a lot of bullying from other children and felt he was unpopular, already a loner, even then, frequently picked on and picked last for team sports. He described being asked to leave the school, for no apparent reason, and said this was his first rejection. In reality, he must have been quite an old hand at rejection by this stage, being sent away by his parents, his father leaving him to begin a new family, being constantly rejected by his peers.

His job at the BBC, as a messenger, May to September 1976, was a source of great pride to him. He had found the job himself, without any help from careers officers or anybody else, and that was an achievement. It was the only position for which he had ever applied and been accepted. He had never had a full-time job. His application to join the Metropolitan Police had been rejected.

Auntie Elizabeth always wondered what Barry did with his time. She thought he slept late and was out till all hours. She only ever heard him talk about one friend, somebody in Chiswick, whose name she didn't know.

Barry cut up his letter of rejection for the Metropolitan Police and used the crest to make a fake warrant card, and used the warrant card to pretend he was a detective from Hammersmith on inquiries. When he turned up at a woman's home in Kingston the real police were called and he was arrested. This was in 1980, when he was twenty and embarking on a criminal career, though he was already on record as being suspected of lurking in the gardens of women's homes, in 1977.

In court Barry pretended to be pop musician Paul Gadd, the cousin of Jeff Lynne, pretending to be a police officer. He pleaded guilty as charged and asked for five other similar offences to be taken into consideration. He was fined £5 on each count.

Laughter during supper at the home of Robin Williams, with the group of friends Jill came to know through Sir Cliff Richard. A guest has just accidentally beheaded three of Robin's terracotta soldiers.

Jill and Alan Farthing at their engagement party with Cliff Richard. Chiswick, January 1999.

A black-tie dinner at Cliff's house, January 1999. Left to right, seated: Jill, Robin Williams and Cliff, and behind them, Alan Farthing and Bill Latham; Abass Khadra and Pia Hoffman; Chris Wood and Tony Ferrari; Stuart Lord, Malcolm Reeves, Roger Bruce and Alan Osman.

Jill touched by royalty. *Above*: With Sophie Rhys-Jones, later the Countess of Wessex, with whom she became friends. *Below*: Jill and Alan are introduced to the Queen in 1998.

Jill poses with Desmond Lynam outside the BBC Television Centre. Des suggested they could become the 'Richard and Judy' of the BBC.

Jane Lush's *Holiday* leaving party in 1998. Jill arranged the surprise appearance of Sir Cliff Richard.

The last images of Jill, recorded by CCTV cameras in Hammersmith less than an hour before her death.

Detective Superintendent Hamish Campbell, who led the murder investigation.

Barry George, found guilty in July 2001 of the murder of Jill Dando.

ALPHA/STEVE FINN

REX FEATURES/TIM ROOKE

Some of the floral tributes left outside the gate of 29 Gowan Avenue.

Nigel, Jack and Vanessa at Jill's funeral.

Alan and Jenny Higham speak to the press after the conviction of Barry George.

Sir Cliff Richard and Gloria Hunniford launch the Jill Dando Rose, which raised funds for the British Heart Foundation after Jill's death.

Meanwhile he had been accused and acquitted of an indecent assault, and committed another indecent assault on a woman who worked at the benefit office in Kensington. He had asked her out for a drink as she left work and she had ignored him. He had followed her to the car park and tried to kiss her and touch her breasts inside her jumper. She had hit him with her briefcase and driven off.

Later that same night, in July 1980, he was alleged to have put his hand up the skirt of a woman who owned an off-licence in Baron's Court. He was convicted of the first charge, cleared of the second and given a three-month suspended sentence.

That summer he tricked the local paper into running a story that he was Paul Gadd, cousin of Jeff Lynne, who had just become the British Karate champion by smashing forty-seven tiles with his foot during the championships at Crystal Palace. None of this was true. Not even the bit about the championships. When the paper realised this, sometime later it ran another story about Paul Gadd the hoaxer. It quoted a karate expert – 'forty-seven tiles, impossible' – and checked Barry's credentials with Jeff Lynne who said he'd never heard of him.

Barry almost certainly took secret pleasure in his deceptions; no doubt the deception, putting one over on somebody, was part of the purpose, but the only other source of pride and achievement for him after May–September 1976 was his single performance as a roller skating gala stuntman, leaping across a row of double-decker buses in front of a crowd and the television cameras of Anglia regional news. This was on 21 September 1981.

A reporter from Anglia's news programme caught up with Barry in rehearsals just before the event. He was dressed in a red outfit with lots of padding. The name 'Steve Majors' on his shirt.

He was filmed leaping from a low ramp over four chairs and landing unsteadily on his skates.

'Aren't you a nutter?' the reporter asks him.

'No. I do stunts every day of my life and for the last eleven years I've not had one accident. I think that's a good track record.'

'But you haven't tried this. You've no idea what it's going to be like, and you're just going to go out there on Saturday evening and have a go?'

'Yeah,' says Barry, 'because I can trust my knowledge and the knowledge of the universities throughout the world that have been involved in the calculations.'

'So you've never actually done anything like this before?'

'Never in the world. It's never been done.'

'But haven't you had a go on a mini ramp or something, just to have some practice?'

'No, not at all.'

At this point the reporter cracks up, laughing.

It is the big night: a floodlit scene, scaffolding festooned with pennants. It is very windy and wet.

'Conditions on top of the 150-foot tower were described as impossible and the organisers officially asked Mr Majors to cancel his roller skate jump over four buses but with a crowd of 5,000 at the Long Eaton stadium, the stuntman decided to go ahead.' There is a shot of drum majorettes. 'In the heavy rain, and winds at gale force, I asked him why.'

'Because I've been planning this for four years,' explains Barry.

'I thought about it four years ago, been training for four years. A year ago I told a lot of people in London that I was going to do it. I'm not going to let them down now.

'The chances are you're going to end up in hospital.'

'Chance I'll take.'

Barry is seen receiving a good luck kiss from a young black woman. There is a shot of an ambulance on standby. He climbs up to the top of the ramp. He is miked up, and can be heard saying, 'I feel confident . . .' There is a shot of men hurriedly covering the gaps between the last two buses with wooden boards. Barry takes off down the high ramp, gains no elevation at all as he jumps and crashes into the newly placed boards, flies head-first on to the lower ramp, somehow gets back up and skates into waiting arms and a cry of 'Well done, lad.'

'A hospital check later revealed a fractured femur and a dislocation to his spine,' the reporter says. Barry is seen giving a last, triumphant wave to the crowd.

A few weeks later Barry enrolled, as Steve Majors, in the 10th Battalion Parachute Regiment of the Territorial Army. He left just under a year later having failed to complete his basic training.

The following year, he was stopped three times by the police in the early hours of the morning in residential areas around west London. On one occasion he claimed he was on a TA exercise. On another occasion, when he was not stopped, he attacked a twenty-year-old woman on her doorstep after walking with her to her parents' home in Acton. She had told him she was studying German and he had used a German phrase to her. He put his hand over her mouth when she screamed so that she thought she would suffocate. He pulled off some of her clothes and tried to rape her. He then seemed to panic suddenly and apologised before running off.

He joined the Kensington and Chelsea Pistol Club as a probationary member. His application for full membership was rejected and he left.

On 9 January 1983 he was stopped by police while acting suspiciously in Palace Gate, Kensington, near Kensington Palace. The following night he was arrested in the early hours, after being found crouching in the bushes next to the wall of Kensington Palace. He said he was on a training exercise. He was wearing military clothing and carried a rope and a knife. He was held overnight and the police had to search his home by torchlight because the electricity had been cut off. They found SAS paraphernalia and some manuals relating to explosives. 'It appears he's a bit of a fanatic about the military,' wrote the reporting officer.

Later that month he was being questioned on another matter and was asked if he knew German and repeated the phrase he had used with the student he had attacked. He was then arrested and charged with rape. He later pleaded guilty to attempted rape and it was this offence of which he was convicted when he appeared at the Old Bailey. He was imprisoned for thirty months, plus the earlier three months that had been suspended from the indecent assault.

He later claimed to have served part of this sentence at HMP Grendon, a specialist therapeutic prison – the only one of its kind – primarily for people convicted of serious violent and sexual offences. 'Doing a Grendon' in prison-speak is sometimes thought of by inmates as a bit of a soft option by comparison with the normal routine of jail but Barry would say, 'they didn't take prisoners [sic] in the group therapy and there was no backing out. They went for the jugular.' He had learned there that no means no, he said.

Oddly, after he was charged with Jill's murder, no record could be found of his time at Grendon. Though this does not necessarily mean he was never there. His name might just have been lost in the system.

It was on his release in 1985 that he lived in bed-and-breakfast accommodation in the Stanhope Hotel for a time, acquiring the imitation guns and being seen with the apparent third gun in the shoebox. He moved into Crookham Road that year and for a while he seems to have stayed out of trouble.

His sister Susan died in 1986 and his father returned from Australia for her funeral, which Barry did not attend. His father had been home before for a couple of years and there had been sporadic contact between them, after no contact at all for eight years. They had met at Michelle's wedding in Ireland to which Barry had apparently hitchhiked. He had seemed to his father then to have the mental age of a thirteen-year-old, even though he was in his early twenties.

Alfred had visited Barry while he was on remand in Brixton Prison accused of rape and Barry had told him he had stopped when the girl said no. His father terminated all contact with him again after that. He didn't want Barry around his daughters in his second family, he said. He bumped into Barry in the street a couple of weeks after Susan's funeral and noted the expensive looking camera around his son's neck. Barry said he was keen on photography. Barry had asked for some money, and his father had given him a fiver and they had parted. They had not spoken again after that, though his father had written occasionally and sent birthday and Christmas cards.

In 1989 Barry met and married Itsuko Toide, a young Japanese woman who was studying in London. In newspaper interviews after Barry's conviction she would say that he had raped her and physically assaulted her during their turbulent time together, before she left and returned to Japan. The police had often been called to their marital home, at 2b Crookham Road, and she had pressed charges of assault against Barry on one occasion, only to withdraw the allegation later.

She once ran to a neighbour's home in a panic and said Barry was trying to kill her. Then Barry appeared at the neighbour's door, calm and relaxed, as if nothing had happened.

His family and others assumed that Barry had married the woman as a marriage of convenience, for immigration purposes. There was a story that she had run off when immigration officers turned up at the flat, though this may have been Barry's explanation for his wife's absence.

There were other clues that suggested Barry was interested in Japanese women and their culture. There was the suspicion of an earlier assault on a Japanese woman who had run screaming and in tears from a room she had been in with Barry. There was the more benign evidence that he had once worked voluntarily in a Japanese community centre and there was the account of the librarian at Fulham Library who could recall Barry asking for his help in the reference section because he was thinking of creating a Japanese ambience in his flat and wanted to research the styles of decoration. When he was stopped on the street by police in 1990 Barry said he was escorting some Japanese students. The reporting officer noted on the collators' card: 'This individual is a most strange character.'

Hamish Campbell arranged to interview Itsuko Toide after Barry had been charged and then travelled with a police woman to Japan. They were on the train to her home town when the message came through that she no longer wanted to be interviewed. They went to see her solicitor who was helpful but said Itsuko was adamant. Itsuko was quoted later as saying that she had been expecting a woman to interview her. Hamish suspected she may have been more interested in the financial rewards of being interviewed by the newspapers.

There was a new allegation of indecent assault. Barry was arrested and put on an identification parade and not picked out. Another officer's note on the cards: 'This subject is known previously to me. Not mentally defective. He is a Walter Mitty character. Often has documents. A persistent, pathological liar.'

He was stopped with an £800 Canon camera at Fulham Broadway. He was stopped at four o'clock in the morning outside a lingerie shop on the Fulham Road.

When Sophia Wellington left work at the BBC late one night to walk down Wood Lane to the bus stop on Shepherd's Bush Green, walking quickly because she felt nervous, alone at night, Barry attached himself to her and introduced himself as the cousin of the late Freddie Mercury. Sophia must have been carrying a BBC bag because Barry asked her if she worked there and she said she did and he said he didn't like the BBC because of the way they had treated Freddie and his family over his illness (Mercury had died of an AIDS-related illness on 24 November 1991). Barry gave her his business card which described him as a singer-entertainer and had a logo of a man juggling. She kept it for a long time and then lost it, or threw it away. He seemed respectable to her, in his crombie-style coat, with his Mediterranean complexion. He looked like he could've been Freddie Mercury's cousin.

Barry had his head superimposed on to a photograph with Freddie, his fantasy cousin. He chatted to the woman in Go Gay, his local dry cleaner on the Fulham Road, and told her he was the secretary of the Freddie Mercury Fan Club. He gave her a copy of the photograph, which he signed, 'from Barry Bulsara'.

He was again suspected over an allegation of rape, involving a

French woman, though nothing was ever proved. He must have been busy in this time, prowling, taking the many photographs, following and approaching women, attaching himself to them, spinning them his yarns. Stalking them.

In 1997 he was noticed by police officers on the beat in Kensington, approaching a woman who was alone and talking to her. The officers followed him, all the way down to Earl's Court, and watched him constantly looking around, apparently in search of other women. When they eventually stopped him he told them he was Barry Bulsara and they ran a check on his name and found no trace on the PNC. He was known to the police then by the name Steve Francis Majors. The reporting officer made a note requesting a follow-up on a collators' card: 'This man has previously followed.'

It was the year that Princess Diana died and Barry told his aunt that he would be watching the funeral from the roof of Buckingham Palace. She thought he had watched too many episodes of *The Professionals*, with his constant references to friendship and association with famous people or the SAS or the security services.

When his mum got a £200 phone bill they realised most of the bill had been notched up with one telephone number, the Leeds number for a sex chat-line. Barry said it was the number of his girlfriend.

Though he could not apparently manage the regularity and consistency which a job would have required, Barry's hallmark appeared to be regularity, or, more specifically, obsessive repetition. The repetitive behaviour of meticulous list-making, of the thousands of photographs that he never even bothered to develop.

It was not just women he returned to, over and over. He was

always in the library, on some research. In the months before his arrest he seems to have been planning to return to study, in the field of new technology. He researched colleges at the library and collected many brochures which the police found at his flat. He haunted the local housing office with complaints and requests, was troubled for a long time by a bathroom refurbishment in his flat which had not gone according to plan. He went frequently to BBC Television Centre, often late at night, to collect a copy of *Ariel* or the *Radio Times*, as did other former employees.

And then there were the surgeries and hospitals and sundry medical professionals who Barry sought out and sought to burden with his complex medical history. There was little record of Barry's childhood problems but he had been born with a cleft palate, which left the legacy of a hare-lip and a slight impediment in his speech. He had been identified as suffering from epilepsy at an early age. Epilepsy revealed itself through brain scans, EEGs and Barry had undergone five of these in his life and four of them had shown the grossly abnormal patterns associated with severe epilepsy.

At the time of the trial he was said to be suffering from petit mal seizures which were distinct from grand mal seizures and were like brief absences during which the sufferer might appear to be day-dreaming. They were quite rare in adults and could be caused by hyperventilating, perhaps as a result of anxiety.

Before the trial Barry had never really been properly examined by a psychiatrist, though his mental state had been a constant source of concern, to him and others, throughout his life. Appointments had been made and not kept by him, though Barry would say he had cried out sometimes for psychiatric help and it had been denied him even while he was in 'desperacy'. He had been embittered by this, as he often felt bitter that nobody cared or bothered. He experienced feelings which were almost over-whelming, which he could not identify. Not anger though. Definitely not.

There were notes in a referral from 1987, from a neurologist who had been investigating Barry's long history of shaking attacks, to a consultant psychiatrist: 'Mr Palmer' (Barry) was complaining of many stresses, saying he could sometimes lose control and lash out at people. The referral observed that while he was at boarding school it had been noticed that he had trouble distinguishing fact from fantasy and had begun modelling himself on Gary Glitter, going by the name of Paul Francis Gadd. Then he had joined a stunt team which jumped over double-decker buses on roller skates, as Steve Majors. Now he was Thomas Palmer and he wanted to talk to somebody about the stresses he felt had been building up since his childhood.

The various neurologists who saw Barry could not always tell which of his seizures were real and which were functional, in other words, not organic but created to serve a purpose, whatever that purpose might be. There were references to shaking dating back to 1979, when Barry could not control the movements in his arms and head, sometimes for a whole day, and would suffer severe headaches. His poor personal hygiene was also recorded.

He often presented himself at the A&E departments of Charing Cross and Chelsea and Westminster hospitals, sometimes with fits, or the fear of fits or with other urgent complaints. He was in the latter A&E seventeen times between 1994 and March 1999, as Barry Bulsara, weak, in pain, depressed, suicidal on one occasion (though not really, he told the doctor, the thought had simply crossed his mind). He seemed slow sometimes, unkempt. He complained of not being taken seriously on previous visits and became 'very angry' when told his breathing difficulties were stress-related hyperventilation.

In March 1999 he had bowel problems, had not had a bowel movement for six months, he said. An X-ray was scheduled but he left the hospital before it could be taken.

In 1994 he had turned up at Charing Cross unable to speak, for the previous six weeks. He was examined and said to be suffering from aphonia with no organic cause. He went for speech therapy where it was noted that he spoke in a whisper and expressed his meaning with odd gestures. He was said to recognise that his condition might have emotional roots and that he might benefit from counselling for the trauma of his marriage breakdown and his recent bereavement. (I don't know who it was that had died. Perhaps it was Freddie Mercury.)

From May 2000 onwards, during the period of his remand at Belmarsh Prison and his ensuing trial for murder, Barry was seen on numerous occasions by two consultant forensic psychiatrists, three clinical psychologists and an eminent neurologist specialising in epilepsy. Some of these acted for his defence and others for the prosecution. The issues they raised would become key issues at three moments during the legal process.

There was uncertainty about the exact nature of his conditions, though not much doubt – none at all, in the expert opinion of the neurologist – that he continued to suffer from epilepsy. There was no doubt that he suffered from personality disorders, the question was, which disorders? He could be suffering from ADHD or Asperger's syndrome. He could be doing a lot of faking.

He went blind for a week of the trial, in its early stages before the jury had been called. He was cured by one of the psychologists using hypnosis. He vomited bile in prison which, on closer examination, appeared to be some kind of washing-up liquid.

He was pedantic, rigid, persistent in his complaining and sense of grievance. This could be explained by Asperger's syndrome, a form of autism, which might also explain his behaviour with women, or some of it, since Asperger's sufferers could find it difficult to make appropriate social approaches and responses. There could, on the other hand, be some overlap with ADHD and some of his patterns of behaviour could be explained by a passive-aggressive personality disorder.

He was tested and found to have an IQ of 76, which was borderline, being just above the grading for 'mental handicap' or 'learning difficulties'. There were tests of his memory and his routine ability to function. He professed himself baffled and confused during these tests and his scores were low even by comparison with people who had suffered brain damage. Perhaps he had brain damage too. Perhaps it was hereditary in some way, given what had happened to his sister Susan.

When he was asked to recite the alphabet, Barry began: 'Alpha, Bravo, Charlie, Delta,' and then stopped. He was told that only the letters were required. He said, 'A,B,C,D,E,' and then stopped again. He was asked to continue and refused, saying, 'Trust me, I know the alphabet.'

There was evidence of a depressive personality disorder and of post-traumatic stress disorder. During one interview Barry declared, apparently for the first time, that he had himself been the victim of an attempted rape, a male rape, while at Heathermount, when an older boy had approached him with his penis in his hand while Barry was in a toilet cubicle. He had been terrified when the older boy tried to hold him and pushed past him to escape. He had never felt able to report it.

It's almost axiomatic, of course, that someone who sexually abuses, as Barry had done in the past, has been similarly abused themselves, in some way, at some stage. Such an incident, however far in the past, could continue to be a source of stress, post-traumatic stress.

Barry said during this interview that he had only ever had a sexual relationship with his wife. Then he later said that he'd had a lot of girlfriends but was not a superstud. He was described as being 'lit up' as he said this and added that he'd had sexual inter-course with twenty-five different women. He could not explain the contradiction between the two statements when it was pointed out to him.

Bitterness and rejection were recurrent themes in many of the interviews. His pride too, at being a BBC messenger from May to September 1976. He said the name changes he had undergone were because of police harassment, except for Steve Majors, which he'd used for his stuntman persona.

Another psychologist found evidence of a histrionic personality disorder, which was characterised by excessive shows of emotion and need for attention, the manipulation of others and the extreme concern with appearance and presentation. Also, a narcissistic personality disorder, involving a grandiose self-image, overconfidence, overvaluation of personal achievements and arrogance. She thought it probable that Barry had a paranoid personality disorder as well, a condition suggested by his suspicion, distrust and resentment of others. She assessed him against a checklist of recognised psychopathic personality traits and found that he scored highly by the standards of prison inmates.

She further identified a somatisation disorder, in which illnesses are exaggerated, and a factitious disorder, in which they are feigned 'in order to assume the sick role'.

This was the psychologist who raised her voice with Barry. Her assessment took place during the period of Barry's blindness.

Barry was an elusive subject for the professional consideration of the experts. He defied consensus. It really was very difficult to work out what was wrong with him. Perhaps it would become clearer through extended assessment over a longer period of time. He was ill though, one way or another, it couldn't all be a sham. And in a bell chart of life he would be way down the line from the middle quartile, the norm.

Guilty or not, it is hardly surprising that Barry would attach himself to Jill's death and talk about it and involve himself in the event of it. Guilty or not, that was exactly the kind of behaviour you would expect from him. Obsessive and repetitious.

He collected the condolence cards from the local shops and went to the local housing office to suggest that the council erect a memorial in Jill's memory. The customer service officer on reception would say that he must have seen Barry in there thirty or forty times before.

Barry claimed he had taken flowers to Gowan Avenue and given them to a policeman to place outside number 29. There was a receipt for flowers, dated after the murder, among the papers taken from his flat, but there was no trace or record of any flowers being handed in or laid at Jill's gate. It was typical, too, that he left the condolence cards lying around in his flat, never did anything with them.

He had a conversation with a journalist from the *Mail on Sunday*, who was walking around Fulham that week looking for people to talk to. He told her he was Freddie's cousin and she gave him her number thinking that he might be a useful contact in the future. (What a future scoop: 'My conversation with Jill's killer.')

On a bus going down Shepherd's Bush Road to Hammersmith, Barry struck up a conversation with a female passenger and told her he was on his way to a memorial service for Jill where he was going to speak in his capacity as Freddie's cousin, who had once been interviewed by Jill. The woman, Vicki Murphy, thought Barry said that he and Jill went to the same church. He had a piece of paper in his hand, the text of his speech, which was probably the note found in his flat, in which he linked Jill's death with his own 'coming to Christ'.

Barry had been attending the Fulham Baptist Church on Dawes Road (which Jill had never attended) for about three years. Within a month of the murder, nearly a year before the police got to him, he told a member of the church fellowship: 'They think I killed her.'

'Killed who?'

'Jill Dando.'

'Who thinks you killed her?'

'Them at the cab office, everyone.'

'Did you kill Jill Dando?'

'No.'

Another member of the fellowship, a serving police officer, recalled discussing Jill's murder with Barry soon after it had happened. He could sense that Barry was upset, but then so were lots of other people. Barry said he had seen a red car going up and down the street before the murder. The officer said he would report it to the inquiry team and Barry had not seemed perturbed by this.

That previous winter the officer had been on night duty in Victoria and had stopped a group of people, among which had been Barry. Everyone had been searched and Barry had seemed embarrassed, perhaps because someone from the church had caught him in possession of a large number of the prostitute cards continually plastered in London phone boxes.

The officer would later say that in early 2000 Barry had been making inquiries at the church about being baptised, reborn, just as Jill had been in Weston so many years before. By this time, it was too late for Barry to be purged and cleansed. He was about to be arrested.

He took to sitting sometimes in a local hairdresser's called Jazzy G., chatting to the staff and customers. Always talking. He did this in other Fulham salons, seemed interested in young black women, sometimes looking after the customers' children, even taking them over the road to the park. He was considered quite safe and reliable, albeit a little odd. It helped no doubt that he was Freddie's cousin.

There was a conversation in Jazzy G. late one afternoon, not long before his arrest, when he seemed a little troubled and two of the women, the owner and a member of staff, were quizzing him on what was wrong and he started saying he was being followed by the police and the press, suspected of Jill's murder.

He told them he had told the police he'd seen a Range Rover. He then told them he hadn't actually seen the Range Rover and they said, 'Well, no wonder you're a suspect.'

The young woman from Jazzy G., whose name was Lenita, eventually got irritated with Barry and asked him outright if he had killed Jill. He looked at the floor and played with his hands and didn't answer so she asked him again and then again. It looked as if his lips were moving but there was no response. When he finally looked up she told him he was stupid and had got himself into that situation.

He told the librarian at Fulham Library that the police had switched from regarding him as a witness to treating him as a suspect. He wanted to give the librarian's name to his solicitor as a potential character reference, just as a precaution, though nothing ever came of that.

A local woman, who knew Barry by the nickname Superman, met him in the street and he told her he had gone to Fulham police station to tell them he could help with the murder, and that now he was under suspicion. He might have told her he had been there when Jill was murdered, or maybe afterwards, she couldn't be sure and hadn't really been paying attention. It was just another one of Barry's fantasies. He was harmless enough, it was just that reality would drift off on him.

'You're gonna get yourself into trouble,' she told him.

Fourteen

As her three-year contract came up for renewal in the spring of 1998, Jill was determined that this would be her last year of *Holiday*. She would have left a year or so earlier, but the BBC had cajoled her into continuing – not entirely against her will. She wanted to be on television all the time, after all, and there was still the question of what she would do instead.

Jill was losing her passion for the programme, and if they weren't careful it would begin to show. For all the pleasure and success of it, *Holiday* had played havoc with her life and now she wanted to travel less and be at home more, to enjoy the fruits of that success and to nurture her relationship with Alan.

There was, finally, an alternative in the offing: the prospect of becoming the main presenter of the *Six O'Clock News*, which Jill hoped and believed she was qualified to do.

That would give her the constancy she sought and it would be convenient, too: she would be finished work by seven most days. She used to talk to Jenny Higham about it, and Jenny knew that Jill's ambition to be that main presenter was primarily based on the lifestyle opportunity. The suitability of the job for a career woman who had been travelling non-stop for six years and now wanted to spend more time at home. She felt she had earned it, and she felt she deserved it.

Jill had a champion in the new controller of BBC1, Peter Salmon. In his position, you were looking for that small number of people, iconic faces who could represent the channel, who were adaptable and professional and trustworthy and would embody all the values and virtues of the channel, its approachability, its warmth and its contact with peoples' lives.

There was debate in the air, on-going debate about the BBC and its relationship to its audience. Peter felt that Jill was in some ways central, or emblematic to that debate and about how in touch BBC1 was with its viewers, through its journalism and its programming.

Jill was a girl for all seasons . . . well, not a girl, she was clearly a woman, but with that disarming quality that made people think of her as a lovely girl. Adaptable. And with this transcendent quality so that she was attractive in real life and on television. When her eyes caught the light, she was stunning.

Peter took to her immediately and knew she was a face for the channel. He wanted her for the big events, he wanted her on a special contract, he wanted the channel to have a special relationship with her. He wanted her for the *Six O'Clock News*.

You might have imagined it would be his decision, being his channel, but as he said, how could you fathom the BBC and the process by which decisions were made, even the important ones. It was like peering into the Vatican, trying to work out how they elected a pope.

Bob Wheaton understood the BBC, especially from the news

perspective. He was on the sidelines now, looking on, though Jill continued to turn to him for advice. With John Birt as director-general, he said, news was like the praetorian guard and had a power all its own, with a direct line to and the special interest of the DG.

The chief executive at news during this time was Tony Hall, who had overseen John Birt's command for a major review of all news programmes. That was just one of the reviews that were then taking place. The BBC was awash with reviews. This was the Programme Strategy Review, which Tony thought of as the ugliest title imaginable. This review was delayed and a long time coming.

When it eventually emerged, the review concluded, among other things, that the *Six* was top heavy with presenters, something like twelve or fourteen different faces over the year, in its two-handed format. Jill was then doing sixty days a year on the *Six*.

According to Tony Hall, audience research indicated that this excessive number of presenters had to be narrowed down; that viewers wanted to associate the BBC with just a small group of people.

Others who knew the content of the review would say that Jill was clearly identified as a popular choice to be one of that small group, perhaps even the main presenter of the *Six*.

There were other issues in the debate that followed. Two presenters or one? London-oriented presenters, or presenters who more reflected the regional diversity of the UK, if not quite its ethnic diversity?

The BBC was preoccupied with devolution and how that should affect its future. In Tony Hall's view, the debate was traumatic, fiercely contested. Should Scotland and Wales have their own main news programmes and not just the regional opt-outs? The agreement in the end was for a continuing UK news with an eye to the future of digital broadcasting, and its possibilities for diversity of choice. That meant trying to integrate the regional news programmes and placing greater emphasis on regional awareness. That meant regional presenters.

Of course, it was a popular subject of internal gossip and debate among the news staff, and especially the presenters, many of whom were concerned for their own future. Nicholas Witchell said he always thought the new main presenter of the *Six O'Clock News* would be someone from the regions. That was his understanding, right from the beginning of that protracted and uncertain argument.

He didn't want the job, he wanted to go back out as a correspondent. But he didn't think it should be Jill either and he made his view known and a colleague told Jill. They stopped speaking to each other after that, a source of great sadness to Nicholas when she died.

That newsroom was not always an easy place in which to work. Presenters watching each other's careers, their progression and the directions they took with keen interest, sizing and assessing and judging each other's abilities and their disposition to the accretion of celebrity.

Nicholas felt that fame had turned Jill's head. That her plausibility in news was affected by some of the choices she made, which is almost certainly true.

It cannot have helped her case, for instance, that she appeared on an edition of *Blankety Blank* in May 1998. Just as it cannot have helped that John Birt had been perturbed earlier by her appearance on the cover of the *Radio Times* in a short leather skirt.

She was becoming a regular in the pages of *Hello!* and *OK!*. As Tony Hall acknowledged, that was not the place you would expect to find senior BBC journalists. It did not reinforce her integrity and authority with the news audience. Tony Hall felt that her commitment to news was diminished.

Jill had sought to straddle the two worlds of popular

programming and serious television journalism. And it was a seri-ous business presenting the news, taken very seriously by those who were involved. *Crimewatch* might look to the viewer like a serious programme or a semi-serious programme at least. But that was not how it was perceived by the people in news.

In many ways, those worlds were opposing worlds which even *Crimewatch* could not bridge and Jill had been seduced by the fame that went with her success in popular television. There were prob-ably people in news who envied her that success but the truth was that the limited credibility she had always enjoyed within the news environment was gone.

News was especially sensitive at this time to accusations of 'dumbing down'. The debate about the new presenter seeped into the newspapers and Jill's name was invoked and Tony Hall wrote to her to reassure her that this media criticism played no part in the BBC's deliberations.

Jill hated being associated with the idea of dumbing down and did not like being thought of as blonde equals bimbo. It was her Achilles heel: she knew that many of her news colleagues did not respect her credentials as a journalist and considered her their intellectual inferior. She was once stung by a tabloid newspaper columnist who questioned her journalistic abilities, and she wrote to the columnist to point out her background in newspapers. Jill always took pride in her early experience and routinely cited it as evidence of her qualification to work in broadcast journalism.

For most journalists, a job as a reporter on a provincial weekly newspaper such as the *Weston Mercury* was no more than a stepping-stone and would not carry much weight at a national level. For Jill, it was all she had, the keystone of her journalism. She had almost always worked as a presenter after that.

Being caught up in the arguments which were now being aired in public in a gossipy fashion was a torment. She felt exposed and humiliated among her peers. Yet the stakes were high now that she was committed to leaving *Holiday*. Not getting the *Six* would leave a vast hole in the middle of her contract and her future.

She muttered about going to ITV if she wasn't wanted and seemed almost in despair, talking about giving up television altogether. Jane did not take that possibility too seriously, but losing Jill to ITV was a genuine concern, especially to Peter Salmon.

Peter was continuing to argue his corner for Jill and had enlisted other senior BBC executives such as Will Wyatt and Alan Yentob to fight for Jill too, against news.

The whole point about the BBC's news presentation, Peter felt, was that viewers were turned off by it, especially younger viewers, who found it remote, stuffy, male, old. He knew that ITN was lining up Trevor McDonald to perform a similar role as its primary news anchor and he wanted a big hitter too. He wanted Jill, which would send out a signal that BBC News was changing with the times.

News seemed preoccupied to the point of obsession with Jill's ability to perform in the big interview. The concern that she was lightweight. Could she handle a live interview on the *Six* with the chancellor or the prime minister or a foreign leader or whoever it might be? Obviously not.

Peter Salmon couldn't see the problem. These were rare events anyway and, if needs be, the BBC had its army of correspondents who could step in with their expertise for those specialised occasions. Jill would be the figurehead, the team leader, backed up by the correspondents. Audiences trusted her and felt safe with her; they thought she was intelligent, even if news didn't. Peter suspected that the resistance to Jill was about snobbery. Presenters feeling or being made to feel like ventriloquists' dummies, as Martyn Lewis would say. Lost without an autocue to read from.

The view of Jill as inadequate was by no means universal in news. Her old friend and colleague Suzanne Yates was sometimes senior duty editor on the *Six*, and always happy to have Jill presenting. Jill might have stepped off a plane and come straight in to read the news. They would sit down to go through the scripts at 5.30 and Jill would be across all the detail, picking out the inaccuracies.

Then she would go down to the studio and Suzanne would feel safe with her there, knowing that if anything went wrong, if a feed went down, Jill would smooth the moment and fill in without flapping. Suzanne respected Jill's brain. She had a good brain, read good books. She just thought it was a mistake doing those frothy programmes and exposing herself in those magazines such as *Hello!* or *OK!*. They undermined her and, as Suzanne warned her, they increased her vulnerability to nutters.

Martyn Lewis, who had been paired with Jill many times on the existing version of the *Six*, thought her eminently capable of doing the job. Martyn himself was on his way out. He would be called in just before Christmas by Richard Clemmow – 'Tony Hall's hatchet man' as Lewis describes him – to be told, 'Right, come off the *Six*, we would like you to do BBC World. We want you to take on Dan Rather and Tom Brokaw in the States.' This meant working in the middle of the night every night in what then seemed like the graveyard of television. No thanks.

Martyn felt there was much game-playing and sniping and rubbishing of presenters in sly press briefings, in the build-up to the decision on the *Six*. He remembered a BBC PR briefing against himself and two colleagues to a broadsheet media correspondent during the Edinburgh Television Festival. He thought Jill's agent was smart to play the BBC at their own game.

Jon Roseman and Jill agreed a new two-year contract in April 1998. It was settled in detail for the first year and left open for the second year, which would begin in April 1999. That second year's contract did, however, include Jill's anticipated role as the main presenter of the *Six*. Everyone agreed it should be in there because she was likely to get the job. But as 1998 progressed, it became apparent that the new role was by no means certain and, in fact, becoming more uncertain with each month that passed.

Jon could see that the decision lay with news and thought that Tony Hall couldn't have cared less about ratings or popularity. He just wanted his news to be better than ITN's. 'Jesus, if it was just about having serious journalists at the helm, they might as well go out and get the editor of *The Times* to present it,' he said.

Finally, in about October, Jon called Peter Salmon and said he didn't want to be in a position where the BBC announced that some-one else had got the job and Jill hadn't, and she ended up looking like a loser. He wanted four or five weeks' notice so that she could with-draw with dignity. And this was exactly what happened – a face-saving exercise. Roseman's proudest spin, if he said so himself.

In the end, the decision was Tony Hall's. Apparently. Somewhere between Tony Hall and John Birt, it was decided that the presenter would not be Jill. Jon wrote a press release in which Jill said she wasn't going to get into a race with anybody and no longer wanted to be considered. Jon might have been a little over the top in the press release, criticising the BBC on Jill's behalf, because he remembered how Peter Salmon wanted it toned down. A wording was agreed and Jill emerged, publicly, at least, with some grace from a job she hadn't got.

'Who was this Huw Edwards who had been chosen over Jill?' Jon asked. It was said that even Peter Salmon didn't know who he was when his name was first mentioned to him by news.

Jon was angry on Jill's behalf at the way she had been treated by the BBC, and he would remember that when they came to sort out the contract. He was spoiling for a fight, as Jane Lush could tell. She was not at all surprised when he let rip later, over dinner at the Criterion.

Peter Salmon wondered if Jill could be persuaded to do yet one more year of *Holiday* – to fill out the contract – but Jane Lush knew she'd had enough. Jane herself left *Holiday* in September 1998 to become the BBC's head of Daytime Television. There was a party at the Pier in Chiswick, which would soon be the venue for Jill and Alan's engagement party. In a Vienna Ball reversal Jill arranged for Cliff to surprise Jane. He waited in the loo while Jill made her farewell speech to Jane, then everyone began singing 'Summer Holiday' with a lyric newly written for Jane and then Cliff came into the room on cue to pick up the song.

Many people at the party thought at first it was a Cliff lookalike, then realised he was the genuine article. There were more speeches, and then everyone got behind Cliff and sang 'Living Doll' to Jane.

The event was recorded on video. For a long time after Jill's death, Jane found the tape difficult to watch. Jill standing there behind Cliff, just another face in the swaying chorus, flushed and radiant with the excitement of the evening.

During the presentations Jill had given Jane a jokey gift of a teapot adorned with holiday motifs from Harrods. The next day, privately, she went to Jane's office and gave her a second gift, a clock from Cartier. That was a typical Jill gesture, an act of generosity for a close friend and colleague, not wanting to show off by handing it over in front of everyone at the party.

Fifteen

The case against Barry George was first aired in outline during committal proceedings at Bow Street Magistrates' Court in October 2000, five months after he was charged.

There had been rumour and speculation about the case, or the lack of it, ever since Barry's arrest. Conflicting snippets of information had seeped out and not many of them were accurate. I had heard, from a police officer with a remote connection to the inquiry, of a photograph of Barry which showed him holding a gun just like the gun that had killed Jill. Well, that wasn't quite true. I had heard that the police had found a jumper at his home with a forensic trace from the scene, but it had been found on a second search, so it was compromised as evidence because it might look as if the police had put it there themselves. That wasn't quite right, either. Though there was of course a forensic trace, in his coat, and it was, or appeared to be, compromised.

I was sitting on the press bench that day at the committal and heard the case as it was described and thought it was a weak case, and from that point onwards was convinced that Barry would never be convicted. For a while I believed he could not have been Jill's killer. I'm not so sure about that any more – he could have done it – but still I was greatly shocked by the verdict at the end of trial and have difficulty, even now, explaining that verdict.

After some time had passed and I had recovered from the shock and the intense and enervating business of following the proceedings, I realised I must have completely misread the trial and not seen it as the jury and others saw it. I looked back through the scribbled commentary in my notes of the trial – 'This case is about to collapse' (for a long time I thought it possible, even likely, that there would never be a trial at all), 'Another dud prosecution witness', 'Mansfield has destroyed this evidence' and so on – and wondered how I had got it so wrong.

I spent some long hours afterwards talking to Hamish Campbell, who I had first met early on, after Jill's death. He had by now been promoted to Detective Superintendent. He seemed to be a careful and cautious police officer and, for me, his integrity was beyond question. He was convinced of Barry's guilt and, as he made clear, frustrated by much of the post-trial media coverage that suggested Barry had been fitted up or shoehorned into the frame.

It was the inaccurate accounts from people who had not followed the case that got to him most. And there was quite a lot of that. Long articles in the broadsheets purporting to describe the details and getting them wrong; pundits in the broadcast media offering ill-informed opinions.

There was also the final layer of the darkness of Dando, the shadow across the investigation in which he had sensed a degree of internal jealousy. Sometimes he felt there were people who would have been happier if the case had not been solved at all, as he believed it now had been solved.

Inside the Metropolitan Police were some who had greeted the verdict with silence and not a word of 'well done' or 'good work'. Hamish did not feel triumphalist about the conviction but, even so, he noticed the absence of those messages of support, which contrasted with the many others who had sent notes and e-mails of congratulation.

Hamish thought there was disappointment at the banality of the explanation for Jill's death. What, him? Is that all? We want Mafia, lover, Kosovo. Something, anything, dramatic.

In debriefings with the inquiry team he reminded them of the words from Kipling's 'If'.

> If you can bear to hear the truth you've spoken
> Twisted by knaves to make a trap for fools.

Operation Oxborough had finally shone the torch and disclosed the truth, as Hamish saw it, and there were people who didn't like it or weren't satisfied and kicked against it; twisted by knaves to make a trap for fools.

It bothered Alan Farthing too, I knew, the apparent pointlessness of Jill's death, the lack of reason. If George had killed her, no one knew why, and in Alan's mind the matter was not entirely settled. He could not say with absolute certainty that it was Barry George who had killed her, because he couldn't make sense of it.

He described to me how his eyes had met Barry's one day late on during the trial. Barry was in the dock at the top of the stairs and Alan was standing nearby, the court having just risen. Alan's instinct was to look away and then he thought, no, so he looked back and stared straight into him. Barry stared back, then looked away and then looked back at Alan. It probably lasted only two or three seconds, but it seemed much longer to Alan.

He did not necessarily believe what people said about looking into someone's eyes and seeing the truth, but still he thought that Barry could have given him some signal – a shrug of his shoulders, a shake of the head – to say 'I don't know what I'm doing here. It wasn't me.' Instead, Barry's look was blank and then he went down the stairs and disappeared from sight.

Both Hamish and Alan knew how I felt and no doubt had their own views about that. As Alan said to me one day at the court, during a conversation about another unpopular public figure who I was trying to defend: 'But David', he said, 'you don't believe anyone's guilty.'

There's some truth in that though. Put simply, I do tend to identify with the underdog and perhaps this shaded my view of Barry George's trial.

It was fourteen months after he had been charged that Barry was finally convicted:

MAY 2000	Charged with murder.
OCTOBER 2000	Committed to the Old Bailey for trial.
FEBRUARY 2001	Pre-trial legal argument begins at the Old Bailey and is adjourned after four days, for seven weeks.
APRIL 2001	Pre-trial argument resumes and lasts two weeks.

MAY 2001   The jury are called, the trial begins.

JULY 2001   The trial ends with the guilty verdict.

The Old Bailey judge who heard the case sat for fifty-one days of legal argument and evidence and I was there for every hour of every one of them, sat in more or less the same seat on the front press bench in Court 1.

It became a familiar and oddly welcome routine, returning every day. It was stressful and at times sad but it was absorbing and fascinating, the more so because of the many continuing uncertainties that surrounded the case. 'Aren't you bored yet?' one of the lawyers or police officers would sometimes say. It was never boring. Not to me. Well, maybe just once or twice.

Trials can be obsessively repetitious too, just like the behaviour of some defendants. The same evidence gone over and over endlessly – evidence-in-chief, cross-examination of the same evidence, re-examination of the same evidence, legal argument on that evidence, the judge's ruling on the argument about that evidence, closing speeches on that evidence, the judge's summing-up on that evidence. Points were certainly driven home with a sledgehammer.

In essence, the case for the prosecution was based on three principal pieces of evidence: the identification of Barry by witnesses who had been in Gowan Avenue that morning and whether or not that placed him in the street before the murder, the timing of his visit to HAFAD, and whether or not that gave him an alibi; the particle of residue in his coat pocket, and whether or not that had come from the scene.

By the start of the trial, each of the witnesses who had seen someone in the street had attended an identification parade. Barry refused, as was his right, to stand on any further live parades, so the police, as was their right, took video footage of him in close-up portrait looking at the camera, and created a videotape ID parade with the faces of eight other men.

Witnesses sat in a room in front of a television with a police inspector and Barry's solicitor and watched the faces appear in turn on the screen. They were then asked if they could positively identify any of them as being that of the person they had seen in Gowan Avenue. Naturally, these parades were not like live parades where you could see the whole person and ask for them to stand up and turn around. All you could see here was bearded faces.

Only one witness could make a positive identification and that was Susan Mayes, who had been on her way to work at 7 am and seen a man standing by a burgundy-coloured car. The police had tried and failed to trace that car. Susan Mayes identified Barry George as the man she had seen.

Other witnesses thought they might have recognised Barry on the parade but weren't sure. In the footage he had a goatee beard and a moustache. He was not asked to shave before he was filmed, and all the other faces had to be made up with false beards and moustaches to match Barry's. The man – or men – that the witnesses had seen in the street was cleanshaven. It was at least a year since Jill's death.

Terry Normanton, who had seen the man with a mobile phone to his ear, was sure it was Barry, just not quite sure enough to make a positive ID. Stella de Rosnay, who had seen a man from the bedroom window of her daughter-in-law's home, thought it was either Barry or another one of the faces on the videotape, which did look uncannily like Barry. Her daughter-in-law Charlotte de Rosnay said she could not recognise anyone on the parade, and then later said Barry's face had been familiar.

The postman, Terence Griffin, who had seen a man while he was delivering the mail, did not recognise Barry or anyone else from 26 April, but said Barry was the man who had approached him later in Gowan Avenue, when he had returned to the round some six weeks after the murder. This was true. Barry had approached Terence in June 1999 and said he'd just seen someone in the café round the corner who looked like the killer and could he borrow the postman's mobile phone to call the police. The postman didn't believe Barry – obviously thought he was odd – and said he didn't have a mobile phone.

It seemed significant to me anyway that Terence Griffin apparently regarded the person he had seen on the street on 26 April and Barry, whom he had seen six weeks later, as two separate people, though he did say during the parade that they could have been one and the same.

There was perhaps even greater significance in a sighting that the police almost missed. On the afternoon after Jill's death they had taken a call from Julia Moorhouse, who was ringing to report an encounter with a man in a bright yellow jacket, like a sailing jacket, she said. He had a hare-lip and a speech impediment, had been carrying a mobile phone and had made reference to the Territorial Army.

They had met at 12.32 as she walked west on Doneraile Street towards the river. She did not yet know of Jill's death but had seen the police activity around Gowan Avenue and noticed helicopters overhead. She crossed the road to look at them and the man in the yellow jacket came over to look at them too and then began talking to her and attached himself to her and walked with her to Stevenage Road, near Fulham football ground, where she went into a house and he carried on walking. This was about 12.35, she said.

There was a still image from CCTV footage at the football ground which showed a figure in a yellow-ish top walking along Stevenage Road towards Greswell Street, where HAFAD was based. That still was recorded at 12.33. It was a fuzzy, indistinct image, but it created a further link in the continuity between the evidence of Julia Moorhouse and the HAFAD staff and Barry's appearance at the cab office with its fixed time of 1.15 pm. Though Moorhouse did not recall a carrier bag of papers, as some HAFAD witnesses did.

Barry had also made a call on his mobile phone at 12.30, to check the remaining credit on his pay-as-you-go account. A telecoms expert would be called to give evidence in court that he could not have made the call from the HAFAD offices, though it was possible that the call had been made in the area to the west of Fulham.

Julia Moorhouse's message to the police had been typed into HOLMES and remained there unnoticed until a day or two before the trial was due to start, when one of the office sergeants searched the system for 'Territorial Army' and the message came up. The police hurried round to take a statement from Julia Moorhouse and hoped to get her to an identification parade.

Then the trial started and the photographs of Barry appeared in the media and the chance was lost. Julia Moorhouse recognised Barry in those photographs as the man she had met, but the jury could not be told this.

In court, during the trial, Michael Mansfield would pick over Julia Moorhouse's evidence during cross-examination and insist that it was not Barry she had seen.

There was a further parade for a woman, Helen Scott, who had seen a man loitering at the junction of Gowan Avenue and Fulham

Palace Road the night before the murder. He had been looking down Gowan Avenue. She, too, described a Mediterranean complexion. On the parade she ummed and ahhed between Barry and the face that looked like him and picked out the wrong one.

In the strictest terms, you either identified somebody or you didn't. But the prosecution wanted all these half or partial identifications included in the evidence, and this was part of the legal argument at pretrial. The Crown wanted to be able to point up the continuity in the sightings, the similarity in the descriptions, the man with Mediterranean or olive skin.

The rise to prominence in the case of the witness Charlotte de Rosnay was a cause for concern to Hamish Campbell and the Crown lawyers, just as it was a delight to Barry's defence. Charlotte had begun a relationship with one of Oxborough's detective constables, Peter Bartlett, who had taken a statement from her four days after the murder. Both parties had a spouse and children.

Hamish had first heard of it months earlier from a colleague who had seen them leaving a police function together hand in hand. How odd that she should be there. Hamish had spoken to Peter Bartlett and pointed out the danger of such a relationship and its potential legal consequences. The officer had denied any relationship. Then it had become clear to Hamish that there was a relationship and it was continuing. He had spoken to Peter Bartlett again, removed him from active inquiries and prevented him from getting access to the computer files. The officer had assured Hamish then that the relationship would end. They had spoken about it again, because it was continuing. It was still continuing. Of course, it had to be disclosed to the defence and only narrowly avoided being aired in open court.

Later, there was a much anticipated exchange in front of the jury between Charlotte in the witness box and Michael Mansfield, Barry's QC, which was thick with innuendo. Mansfield asking how Charlotte had kept abreast of developments in the case. 'What did the police want from you, so far as you could tell?' He pressed her on who she had talked to about the case. 'No one else? Are you sure?' The jury would have been oblivious to the real meaning of these words. In a way, Mansfield was warning Charlotte, whose evidence anyway seemed a little unreliable. She had not even mentioned the man she saw and later thought was Barry George when she first spoke to the police on the day of the murder.

Mansfield argued at the beginning that the trial should not go ahead because Barry's case had been disadvantaged by the year's time lapse before his arrest. A so-called abuse of process argument. He tried then, and again in front of the jury, to demonstrate that the police had been incompetent in not getting to him sooner. He also argued that the pre-trial publicity about Barry had prejudiced him in the minds of potential jurors. This was becoming an increasingly familiar argument at pretrials, particularly in high-profile cases which had attracted blanket press coverage. It was usually countered by the proposal that juries could be instructed to disregard anything they had read.

In this case, if anything, the pretrial publicity broadly portrayed Barry as someone relatively harmless who could not have committed the murder. The judge ruled that the trial would go ahead and Mansfield then proceeded to lobby for the exclusion of various strands of evidence.

All the photographs of women which Barry had taken had already been excluded by agreement between the Crown and the defence. The test was whether the probative value of evidence outweighed its potential for prejudice. Barry's photographs clearly had nothing to do with whether or not he had killed Jill, but if the jury heard about them, he would seem to them a generally guilty character, perhaps the sort of person who could have murdered Jill, which would be unfair.

There were other witnesses who could testify to Barry's practice of stalking women, and Mansfield successfully argued these out of the case as well. He would've liked all those conversations of Barry's excluded too.

The inquiry had nearly missed another important witness, Vicki Murphy. She had called the police and told them about Barry talking to her on the bus after the murder, when he had said he was on his way to speak at Jill's memorial service. Her message was not typed into HOLMES and might well have been lost for ever if Vicki had not called the police again, after Barry's arrest, having recognised the name Bulsara in the newspapers.

Barry talking about Jill's death, Barry talking to women about the BBC, or that 'special lady', or that lady from *Crimewatch*. They all remained in the case and, in a way, they implied what the other stalking evidence would more obviously have shown, that he followed and approached and talked to women. The evidence of those conversations might have been probative but it was also, surely, prejudicial.

There was no evidence that Barry had stalked Jill. None at all. And next to no evidence that he had any interest in her. You could say that he must have known where she lived, that he must have stalked her in some way or other. But there was no real evidence that he knew. It was only supposition.

Mansfield said that the Crown was trying to prop up the half-identifications from the parades with the one positive ID turning non-identifications into identifications – and he thought they should be excluded. He wanted to destroy the continuity in those sightings but they too remained in the evidence.

He was able to exclude part of the evidence of Richard Hughes, Jill's neighbour who, despite picking out the wrong man on the only live parade, had said the man he saw from his window looked like Bob Mills, a television presenter. Bob Mills, as it happened, did look a bit like Barry. But that was not a reliable way to make an identification.

Any continuity in the sightings came to an abrupt halt at 11.30. Beforehand, the man – or men – that witnesses had seen was wearing a suit jacket. The man that Richard Hughes and Geoffrey Upfill-Brown had seen was wearing a coat, and their descriptions of his hair were different from the earlier sightings.

There was another witness who had attended an ID parade and picked out Barry without going on to make a formal identification and this was a member of the staff of Cope's, the fishmongers Jill had visited a few minutes before her death. He recalled a man who had left the shop while Jill was there and the police wondered if this was Barry. Cope's was just across the road from Barry's home and, in the police version of events, Barry could have gone home and got his coat and his gun and still had time to get to Gowan Avenue and kill Jill. In the absence of any firm identification, however, this was pure speculation.

Michael Mansfield also tried hard to have Barry's first witness statement removed from evidence. Barry said in that statement that he had left home at around 12.30 or 12.45 to go to HAFAD. He had since submitted a new alibi statement in which he claimed he had left home between 10.30 and 10.45.

Hamish Campbell thought that Barry had revised his time to fit in with the timings given by the HAFAD witnesses for his arrival at their office. The new time, if it was believed by the jury, gave him an alibi. The earlier time left him with an unsupported alibi – left him home alone when Jill was killed. And having two alibis might look a bit suspicious, which was presumably why Mansfield wanted the first statement removed from the evidence. That statement was also now contradicted by the evidence of Julia Moorhouse, if the jury believed Julia Moorhouse had seen Barry, just after 12.30.

Mansfield again tried to argue police incompetence or malpractice by DC Gallagher in not following correct police procedures when he took the statement. He lost that argument, too, and Barry was stuck with two alibis.

The final admissibility issue was the single particle from the coat. It was invisible to the naked eye – just a thousandth of a millimetre – and comprised three of the four components found in discharge residue taken from samples of Jill's hair. The typical residue of a Remington 9mm short discharge was composed of lead, antimony, barium and aluminium, all of which were found in the hair sample residue. The particle from Barry's coat pocket was comprised of lead, barium and aluminium – everything except the antimony.

The issue was how the particle had got into the coat. From the gun, perhaps, or from Barry's fingers after he had shot Jill. Or by some other means. Such particles could occur in fireworks, but none had ever actually been found or produced in tests. It could have got there from legitimate gun usage, but Barry was saying he had not fired a gun for some years. The coat had been dry-cleaned many times in Go Gay, though there was no evidence that it had been cleaned since the murder. It could have got there from contamination, from improper handling during the search or, most significantly, during the photographing of the coat at the studio.

During the admissibility arguments the judge said that if the particle was the only evidence against Barry George the Crown's case would not get past first base but, taken with the other evidence, it was really quite significant. Mansfield clearly realised this, and devoted a lot of time to trying to exclude it from the case. The judge ruled against him.

These opening arguments took up three weeks of pretrial time and in the middle of them the case was adjourned for seven weeks after the judge lifted the ban on publication of photographs of Barry and the tabloids went to town, some of them, especially the *Daily Mail*, the *Sun* and the *Mirror*, publishing numerous pictures across two or three pages in the context of 'the changing face' of Barry George, which made him look very dodgy indeed. Any juror seeing those pictures might well think he was a guilty character.

Lawyers for the newspapers had come to court to argue that the ban be lifted and both Mansfield and Orlando Pownall for the Crown had also spoken on the issue. Pownall had raised no objection to lifting the ban, though Mansfield had. It was the judge's decision and, as he and everyone else immediately realised the next morning, if not sooner, it was a serious mistake. Immediately after the judge gave his ruling and removed the ban the court emptied of reporters, all cheerfully going off to call their newsdesks and explain the new freedom.

The judge seemed a little petulant that next morning when the papers appeared, notably terse with Orlando Pownall, as if he was to blame. No doubt the judge felt responsible. His conduct of the case seemed otherwise meticulous, a factor which will probably inhibit Barry George's appeal against conviction.

The judge was William Gage, the Honourable Mr Justice Gage,

who had recently presided over a succession of three trials that had ended without a verdict, with hung juries who could not reach a decision. He must have been hoping this would not be a fourth trial with no verdict either way.

A modified ban on publication of photographs was imposed, allowing for one relatively innocuous picture to be published, but all others blocked.

Meanwhile, Mansfield disclosed that his client was 'devastated' by the newspapers' coverage. And, as I later discovered, Barry was unhappy with Mansfield, too, rigidly and wrongly believing that Mansfield had not tried to stop the ban being lifted.

For much of that day and the next there was toing and froing of the lawyers between court and the judge's room, where they met in secret, in chambers. It was apparent that Barry, to use a phrase Mansfield would employ later, was teetering on the edge of unfitness to continue with the trial. Hence the seven-week adjournment, which also allowed the prejudicial effect of the published photographs to dissipate.

It was when the pretrial began again in late April that Barry suffered his week-long bout of hysterical blindness, which was finally cured by clinical psychologist Gisli Gudjonsson, by means of hypnosis. He continued to appear in the dock during this time and his behaviour – clutching the rail, grasping at furniture – was a source of much amusement to the press, who had no idea what was wrong with him and generally assumed he was shamming.

There were many stops and starts in the sittings as Barry fell prey to further illnesses. The Old Bailey matron was called to minister to him, arriving in court in her starched uniform.

Days passed with only one or two hours' of court sitting having been achieved. The lawyers were huddled in chambers again, and the rumour that the case was about to collapse gained momentum. Instead, it was agreed that a colleague of Dr Gudjonsson's, Dr Susan Young, also a clinical psychologist, would sit with Barry in the dock to help him and watch out for further illness, especially the petit mal seizures which he had been having.

It would not ordinarily have been of significance, but no one could fail to notice that Dr Young was good looking and blonde. As the days went on she became physically closer to Barry in the dock. They were sitting next to each other and she, apparently a naturally tactile person, would touch him reassuringly every so often, or look at him and smile warmly.

There was nothing improper in what she was doing but, as Orlando Pownall well knew, the effect of all this on a jury would be striking. This defendant didn't kill blondes, he made friends with them. Dr Young had to go.

Her presence in the dock was contested by Pownall and Mansfield. Not, of course, on the grounds that she was a good-looking blonde. After all, said Pownall, she might have to give evidence. No, said Mansfield, he would be happy to give an assurance not to call her. No, no, said Pownall; he couldn't possibly ask such a thing of his learned friend.

Dr Young was relieved from dock duty by judge's ruling and replaced by an experienced social worker from south London, Verona Reeves, a black woman, who sat one seat apart from Barry for the duration of the trial, during which time he did not succumb to further significant illness. His epilepsy medication dosage was changed and the judge called ten-minute breaks every hour, for Barry to rest. In the cells beneath the court, some mornings, after he had arrived in the prison van from Belmarsh, and whenever else it was necessary, Dr Young would go through relaxation techniques with Barry to help him to cope.

By the time the full trial began in front of the jury, it was clear what the battlegrounds would be. It still seemed inconceivable that there would be a conviction. Prosecuting counsel Orlando Pownall said in his opening speech that the cumulative effect of the evidence was persuasive of guilt. It would bond to form an unassailable link and identify the defendant as being responsible.

The evidence was circumstantial, but, said Pownall, this did not make it inferior evidence. I thought this was just rhetoric. How could it not be inferior to hard evidence. There was so much missing. Where was the eyewitness, the gun, the evidence that Barry had ever owned or bought or fired such a gun? The proven connection of his interest in, or stalking of, Jill? The fingerprint or shoeprint from the scene that belonged to him, the flecks of Jill's blood on his uncleaned coat in which the particle had been found, the traces of firearms in his uncleaned flat? The motive? Were these things missing because he had been careful or lucky? Or were they missing because he was innocent?

Why didn't the witness sightings before and after the shooting not match in their descriptions? What had happened to the Range Rovers, the burgundy car, the sweating man at the bus stop – never traced – the shoeprint on the doorstep which had never been identified?

There seemed to be almost unlimited scope for Mansfield to challenge and cast doubt on the evidence. This was the basis of his reputation as a leading defence counsel. As one of the court reporters put it, 'He loves to give the police a good kicking.'

On certain days, Mansfield seemed to command the court, soaring in his eloquence and mastery of detail, imperious in his disdain for witnesses, especially the official witnesses such as police officers. He paraded the entire Polsa search team through the court, from chiefs to minions, and bullied and harried and teased from them disclosures about the inadequacies of their search procedures. He apparently wanted them to look negligent or corrupt, or both, and seemed to make a pretty good job of it.

He wore his wig at a jaunty, the-hell-with-it angle and prowled up and down behind the front bench, twirling a gold pen in his fingers. He barked at the officers in the witness box, barely even bothered to look at them. He stopped and leaned forward on his legal folders, peered up and delivered an acerbic flourish. 'Are you really saying . . . ?'

He wore red socks which, apparently, is his personal trademark, as I discovered later in the trial when he approached the press seats for the one and only time, to speak to the actor James Wilby, who, as Mansfield well knew, was sitting there studying him and noting his tics in preparation for a portrayal of Mansfield in a dramatised documentary about the trial.

There were those in court who said that Mansfield's style could alienate juries, who didn't always want to see witnesses manhandled. On balance, his manner seemed more probative than prejudicial. He threw up smokescreens and fished for red herrings, but he could also turn cracks of uncertainty into chasms.

It's often the case in court that the defence is showy and the prosecution is plodding and deliberate, and that was how it was here, with Orlando Pownall, a Senior Treasury Counsel, proceeding in an undemonstrative manner through the evidence. He appeared weary sometimes, and could be wearying to listen to, but he was gentle and warm with witnesses, the antithesis of his learned friend, and generally very thorough. The judge often seemed to want to hurry him along, especially during legal argument, as if the judge was already ahead of him. Pownall would rub the knuckles of one hand in the palm of the other and smile as he composed his thoughts.

In his re-examination of witnesses, Pownall was routinely adept at piecing back together the fragments of evidence that Mansfield had just exploded, so that sometimes it was hard to second-guess what impression the jury would be left with.

The HAFAD witnesses were so confused and confusing that it was almost as if they had something to hide. Perhaps this was the effect of the year's delay. They could not agree who had seen and spoken to Barry or how long he had been there, or most importantly, what time he had arrived. Susan Bicknell seemed most certain about having looked at the time on the office clock, 11.50. But in court she came across as having almost as many problems as some of the clients she was trying to help, such as Barry, which was not good for her credibility as a witness.

There were many hours of evidence from forensic scientists and firearms experts about the type of gun that could have been used in the shooting, about the bullet and its markings and about the residue, and how likely it was that this could have got into Barry's pocket by contamination.

It did not much help the Crown's case that 104 boxes of Barry's property, which had been removed in the final search, had been placed in the police store right next to the cage where all the firearms were kept. This did not directly affect the coat – the coat had been kept at Kensington – but other items had definitely become contaminated, which meant that they were useless as potential evidence and also proved the point that contamination could occur. There was also evidence that the scientists' own canteen in their forensic lab was routinely vulnerable to contamination.

Mansfield tried hard to show how the coat could have been affected. There was evidence of all the items that had been photographed in the studio over the previous year and additional information about the firearms that had been photographed there. There was evidence of how often and how well the studio was cleaned, the detail of the Henry Hoover that was used. Nothing was too minor to mention.

Despite the foolishness of the police in taking the coat to be photographed, it was hard to accept that it had been contaminated. But perhaps the mere possibility of contamination was enough. Mansfield did not need to prove anything. That was the task of Pownall. He needed to persuade the jury beyond all reasonable doubt that Barry George had killed Jill.

To that end, the Crown seemed keen to throw everything in, every potentially damning smidgeon of evidence. A card had been found in Barry's flat with the word 'Roseman' and a phone number on it. Jill's agent, of course, was called Roseman. The phone number on the card bore no relation to the phone number of Jill's agent. Then there was a list of music-production facilities from a music industry publication which contained an entry for Barry and listed his mother's home in east Acton, masquerading as a studio called Xanadu. Even Hamish was obliged to concede, in cross-examination by Mansfield, that this had nothing to do with the case. Such evidence smacked of desperation.

When the Crown's case was complete, the jury was sent home for a couple of days while Mansfield submitted that the trial should not continue, that there was no case to answer. He argued, with legal precedents, that the evidence was tenuous, especially the identification evidence, and that even Susan Mayes' positive identification was based on a dangerously fleeting glance.

He advanced the argument now, which he would develop later, that the sightings might be of another person altogether, a kind of parallel Barry: the sweating man in the e-fit, the real killer. He said it was significant that none of the identifications had related to sightings in the half-hour immediately before the shooting. The killer must have been somewhere. Perhaps he was in a car. He said that the Crown's view of Barry as the calculating killer returning to HAFAD to shore up his alibi did not stand up to examination. Offered 11 am by HAFAD, Barry had said no and stuck instead to 12.30, which gave him no alibi.

The judge disagreed and rejected Mansfield's submission. He said that these points could be put to the jury.

Mansfield then began a new submission: that Barry should not be penalised for not giving evidence. That he was unfit to give evidence. Since the mid-1990s, a defendant no longer had the right to silence without fear of this affecting his case. Nowadays, juries could think what they liked about a defendant who did not give evidence, unless the defendant was physically or mentally unfit, in which case the judge would tell the jury not to draw any inference at all. Expert opinion had to be called on Barry's state of health, and a succession of psychologists and psychiatrists and the one neurologist who had interviewed him were called to give their testimony. Was he shamming or was he really ill?

The neurologist was persuasive of Barry's continuing epilepsy and voiced his concern that the stress of giving evidence might provoke fresh attacks. This seemed to sway the judge, who ruled that Barry was unfit and under no obligation to testify. In purely dramatic terms, this was disappointing. Seeing Barry being cross-examined would have been compelling. It must have been disappointing for the Crown, too. They could not have failed to notice how guilty Barry had seemed in his police interviews, the tapes of which had already been played to the jury.

The jury was recalled and the trial resumed with a powerful opening speech by Mansfield, in which he said that the Crown's case was hanging by the merest of threads. The particle was not only invisible, it was about to disappear altogether as evidence, and without it there would be no case, no link between the crime and the defendant. It was a fine speech, but it lacked the substance of any response to the Crown's claims. It was the kind of speech you made at the end of your case, not at the start of it.

Hamish would say that Barry had no answer to the evidence against him. It became clear that this was right. The defence was simply more of the same, a reminder of the frailty of the identification evidence, of all the people who had been in the street and not seen anyone. A reminder of all the evidence that was either missing or had never been fully explained. The advancement of the theory that the shooting was a Kosovan-related professional hit.

Kosovo had been there from the beginning, considered early on and not given much weight by the inquiry. Jill had made a BBC charity appeal on behalf of Kosovan refugees not long before her death, which had prompted an angry letter to her agent's office from an anonymous viewer. Allasonne Lewis had opened the letter and thought it a racist diatribe against the Kosovans and thrown it away.

NATO had bombed the Serbian broadcasting headquarters three days before Jill's murder, killing several employees. There had been a series of anonymous calls to the BBC after her death, linking it to the conflict in Kosovo and making further threats to other BBC employees, including the head of news, Tony Hall.

Michael Mansfield sought to create his own continuity of evidence from all this and had found, in among all the case papers amassed by the inquiry – the defence had access to everything – a police intelligence report that suggested Jill's murder had been a hit ordered by the Serbian military figure Arkan. He had further evidence that bullet crimping was a trademark of some Yugoslavian arms manufacturers (though that, of course, was machine crimping, not hand crimping).

The theory looked weaker later, after the full text of the intelligence report had been read out in court. It was made clear that the report was based on information from an informant, who said that Jill had also been killed because she possessed highly damaging information about a north London crime family.

In the end, there was no evidence that Barry had not killed Jill. Nothing to say it wasn't him. The burden of proof remained with the Crown, but an alibi, or anything, might have helped his defence. It might have helped if he had given evidence. Seeing him laid bare in that way might have enabled the jury to understand his aberrant behaviour and separate it out from the act of murder. In their minds the two – the behaviour and the event – must have become entwined.

There was nothing to show he was capable of murder – certainly nothing in the evidence – and the jury could not be told of his previous convictions. Nothing except the well of anger evident inside him. For me, that anger made it just possible to envisage him on Jill's doorstep. Otherwise, the evidence seemed full of holes. It could just be a series of coincidences. Perhaps there was a parallel Barry the inquiry had missed. I didn't know but, not knowing, I could not have convicted.

Nearly all the crime and court reporters seemed to think he was guilty and most, though not all, seemed sure he would be found guilty. They drifted in and out of Court 1, following other trials. Jeffrey Archer was in the Old Bailey now accused of perjury. We would see him strutting through the halls sometimes, looking chipper as ever. Before him, the attention was shared by Jane Andrews, who had once worked for Sarah Ferguson and was now accused of murdering her partner, Thomas Cressman. I had seen her in the building sometimes, too. She looked in agonies of stress and fear. Like her, Archer would be found guilty.

I was not entirely alone in doubting Barry's responsibility for Jill's death. Those of us with an exclusive interest in the trial of Barry George were bonded by our continual presence. There was Helen Phelps from *Crimewatch*, who was working on the BBC's night-of-the-verdict documentary; Ingrid Kelly from *Tonight With Trevor McDonald*, who was assembling the actors and the script for the drama documentary on ITV; Brian Cathcart and John McVicar, both of whom were writing books.

John seemed to vacillate in his opinions about Barry's culpability. He was working with Benjamin Pell – who was widely known as Benji the Binman because of his habit of acquiring documents from dustbins. Benji sat every day in the public gallery, writing furiously on loose sheets of A4 paper which he carried to court in a plastic bag. He and John would huddle in the local cafés at lunchtime and discuss the case. Alan Farthing was warned not to throw away any revealing rubbish for a few months, during the trial, during Benji's interest in the trial.

Brian was very doubtful that Barry would be convicted. Ingrid did not think he was capable of murder. Helen would have liked to go back to *Crimewatch* every night and proclaim his guilt with certainty, but she didn't seem very certain. We even sowed seeds of doubt into the mind of Nicholas Witchell, who was also there nearly every day, with his black leather bag containing, in its zip-up side pocket, a cellophane-wrapped black tie, which he carried everywhere in his capacity as the BBC's royal correspondent, in case the Queen Mother should suddenly die.

BBC news lost interest in the trial during its middle phase, but Nicholas still turned up. On good days, days of dramatic evidence, he would get notes passed forward from his producer: 'Live at 1', or '1.15 for the *Six*'.

There was often time to fill and people would read newspapers beneath the bench, or write their reports or play silently with their mobile phones, or do their expenses. One television reporter needed someone to fill in a blank taxi receipt. John McVicar was happy to oblige.

We were amused sometimes in the afternoons by the endless procession of guests who would appear on the far side of the court after one of the Old Bailey's judges' lunches. All kinds of people, mostly elderly and very smart and soon bored, apparently, since they never seemed to stay long. They were probably off to catch ten minutes of Jeffrey Archer. Betty Boothroyd, the politician, was there one afternoon. Vera Lynn. Michael Parkinson, all looking curiously, discreetly, at Barry.

Mostly, our group – the Dando Squad, as McVicar called it – sat around, at lunch, in breaks, at breakfast sometimes, and coffee after court, endlessly poring over the details of the case, their meaning and their impact on Barry's potential guilt. We watched the jury and tried to guess who was for and against him. It was just a game, I had no idea. I simply couldn't believe they could be sure he had killed her.

The judge summed up for two days after the closing speeches, which themselves took three days. Mr Justice Cage tried to guide the jury through the evidence. They had to be sure, he said, at each step.

He had proposed earlier to Mansfield and Pownall that he would tell the jury to acquit if they were not sure on any one of the three main planks of evidence: the identification, the HAFAD timing and the particle. Mansfield was quite happy with this, but Pownall said it was too heavy a burden to place on the Crown with regard to the particle. The judge relented and said he would tell the jury merely that, if they did not accept the particle, the case was severely weakened.

He summed up carefully and did not betray any bias towards a favoured verdict. He said that the three planks could be supported by the lies Barry had told, if they believed he had told lies. The judge also told the jury to shut out any feelings of sympathy for the victim. As Mansfield had put it, they must not convict simply because they felt someone had to pay for the death of Jill Dando.

Jill had been oddly absent from the trial, objectified in the evidence of how she had died, but by and large missing, despite the regular presence of Alan and Nick Ross and the occasional presence of a friend or relative. Alan was clear that his prime reason for being at court was to represent Jill, because no one was there for her. Right or wrong, it was something he felt he owed her, and he didn't want to let her down. All the same, he had maintained a discreet presence – at the request of Michael Mansfield – sitting in the far corner of the court, virtually hidden from the jury by the dock and, at one stage, before they were removed by a Crown lawyer, a strategically placed pile of defence box files.

When the jury were sent out, we waited. There was a sweepstake in the press rooms downstairs and we signed up, to guess how long the jury would take to bring back a verdict. The jury outpaced the lot of us. They deliberated for thirty-two hours over five days, spending four nights sequestered in a hotel.

They had a day off on the Sunday before they brought in their verdict on the Monday. As I heard later, ten of them went out on a day trip and one stayed in the hotel to watch the Grand Prix on television. That may have been a clue as to how things were shaping up in the jury room, in that most secret of places.

One juror had already been discharged because of a family bereavement, which left eleven. They had asked to see Barry's witness statement and the tapes of his interviews. At 4 pm on the Saturday they sent a note to the judge saying they were stuck, which meant they were divided in some way. The judge called them in and said he would accept a 10–1 majority verdict but that he would still prefer a unanimous one. It appeared that wasn't enough to break the impasse, because still no decision was forthcoming. I was sure by now – another misreading – that there would be no verdict, which would mean a whole new trial.

Late on the Monday afternoon, the jury asked to see Barry's coat. I did not know about this at the time but Hamish Campbell heard of it and said that he then knew the verdict would be guilty. They would not be bothering with the coat if the majority thought he was innocent.

Sure enough, half an hour later, just after 4 pm, Barry George was found guilty by a 10–1 decision. 'Did he say guilty?' someone behind me on the press bench said as the foreman made his announcement. There was a loud gasp from Barry's sister Michelle. It seemed to me that Barry did not flinch. He alone, apparently, of those around him, believed he would be convicted. The verdict was a shock to the defence too.

Barry's previous convictions were read out from the witness box by Hamish. The judge told Barry he was dangerous and unpredictable and then said, 'You may go down.'

Many of the jurors were in tears, or appeared to have been in tears, as they left the court later. Those five days in that room, after a long and intense trial, must have been almost unbearable. I went over the road with Brian Cathcart for a drink which we both needed.

Nick Ross invited Alan, Jill's brother Nigel and his wife Vanessa and others who had been there at the verdict back to his home for champagne. Jenny Higham did not go. There was not much to celebrate and people soon drifted away. None of Jill's friends or family, certainly not Alan, had ever expressed any vengeful thoughts about Jill's killer. The loss was the only thing that mattered; that and the growing need for an end to the business of her dying.

It seemed to me that Barry's conviction was not much of an ending. No answer, no explanation, the inevitability of an appeal; the unease, in some quarters, at the verdict, a continuing media interest – documentaries, articles, books.

Sure enough, Barry's lawyers immediately announced that he would appeal. Three senior judges will hear the appeal over three days in mid-July 2002. The admissibility of identification evidence will be one of the central issues.

Barry, meanwhile, was moved to Whitemoor Prison to begin his life sentence. It was there that he was tape-recorded apparently confessing to the murder. The existence of the tape, supposedly an accidental recording by a cellmate, was disclosed in the *News Of The World* in early April 2002. The tape was made available on a telephone 'hot line'. Listeners could decide for themselves how valid his 'confession' really was.

Sixteen

After the engagement, when those magazines came calling, there really was no contest. *OK!* was offering more than twice as much as *Hello!* for the exclusive rights to cover the Jill Dando wedding. That was the way of things at the time: *OK!* the aggressive upstart, muscling in on *Hello!*'s territory, poaching its celebrities, spoiling its exclusives with sneaked pictures, outbidding it in the dealmaking.

Jill does not seem to have agonised overmuch about entering into such an agreement, though others cautioned her against it.

Both magazines routinely paid the famous people who featured in their pages. They were then innocuous, unthreatening, unchallenging articles with no hint of scandal or salaciousness; no mockery of their subjects, who usually spoke through unadorned question and answer interviews and were depicted in flattering, glamorous photographs, all of which they could approve before publication.

If there was an intrusive element in this form of journalism, it was an intrusion with which the subjects were complicit. Disclosing the privacy of your home, or your wedding, or your newborn baby to readers, as celebrities casually did in those articles, might make you seem more familiar, break down barriers which less stable readers might be tempted to cross, but at least you were paid for it. Sometimes handsomely. At least you knew what you were doing and retained a degree of control that was rarely available in the mainstream press.

It must have been flattering merely to be asked, a signal that you had reached a certain status of public recognition. You were famous, you were going to be in *Hello!* or *OK!* and be even more famous. A temptation that must be difficult to resist.

When Sally Magnusson's agent called and said *Hello!* wanted to feature her, which happened just the once – she had recently interviewed Charles Spencer, the brother of Princess Diana, so some of his stardust must have settled on her, she assumed – Sally said, 'No, no way.' She went on: 'And don't tell me, now or ever, how much they're offering.' She knew how it worked, how you'd start thinking, house, mortgage, children . . . and before you knew it, you would've been seduced. You would have sold yourself. People always assumed the celebrated were rich, too, and didn't need the money. But however rich you were you could always be richer. There was always the bigger house, the bigger car, the private schooling.

Sally talked to Jill about her wedding and wondered how she could go along with it. Sally was enormously fond of Jill and loved seeing her so happy in her love for Alan. She knew how important her wedding day would be, how precious and special. So why invite *OK!*? They would take it over: it would no longer be her wedding.

But this was the place that Jill now occupied, where it was quite natural to see your wedding in *OK!* She had become a star and even while she was ordinary, and craved ordinariness, and wanted a husband and a family, she was also the celebrated Jill Dando who took pleasure in her fame and embraced the attention whole-heartedly.

She was not alone in that world. Gloria Hunniford's wedding had been in *Hello!*. Her wedding had been one of those that prompted *OK!* to run a spoiler. All the more reason for Alan and Jill to go with *OK!*. It was less likely to be spoilt by the more sedate and respectable *Hello!*.

Cliff thought those magazines harmless. He would allow them into his home – he had allowed them into his home and been photographed by them there, alongside Jill and Gloria and his other friends. They were not nasty, those magazines, and for all that they entered your home and took it away with them, there was something posed and unreal about it. Not the real you. The real you remained unknown to the public. So far as Cliff was concerned it was the rest of the press that were the problem. The press that speculated and theorised about you and presented that speculation as if it were fact.

There was quite a lot of discussion between Jill and Alan about the *OK!* deal. In the end, they were both quite clear why they were doing it. For the money, naturally, but, ironically, for the privacy too, because any wedding involving someone as famous as Jill was bound to attract the press, the hoards of photographers and snoopers. And now it would be *OK!*'s job to keep them away, to hide the wedding from all prying eyes except its own. As Alan said later, you would almost have paid them to do that. The difficulty with this, it became apparent, was the extensive protective measures that the magazine required.

The deal was brokered by Jon Roseman and was worth £120,000. Jon was still not flavour of the month in the Farthing–Dando household, following his performance at the Criterion dinner with Peter Salmon. On the other hand, it was a pretty good deal. In this instance, oddly, Jon was representing Jill and Alan. Jon had once been offered only a tenth of that amount by *OK!* for the engagement and wedding of another client. 'Forget it,' he had said. He had told his accountant: 'Listen, no client does it to be in *OK!* magazine. They do it for the money. If they ain't gonna pop the money, what's the point?'

Jill and Jon had never fallen out over money. Unusually she paid Jon an agreed amount at the beginning of every year, up front, as his fee. With most clients, you accounted once a month, paid their dues and took the commission as a percentage off the top. That was not how it was with Jill. Very unusual but it worked for both of them. In addition, as with all clients, he took 20 per cent of all corporate, that is non-broadcasting, work. The *OK!* deal was a corporate. This gave *OK!* the rights to an exclusive interview with the newly engaged couple, to a set of engagement photographs, and then later the exclusive coverage of the wedding.

Alan was anxious about being drawn into any public role and would have kept out of it altogether if he could. On the other hand, he was now Jill's partner and it was part of Jill's business to give something of herself away. He did not want to give anything of himself away and did not want Jill to give anything about him away either. Jill did remind him that they were being paid a lot of money.

They agreed that Alan would not speak in the engagement interview and would appear in just one photograph. It was arranged that this session would take place in a room at Claridge's on Valentine's Day.

Jill was away for most of early February, in Malaysia for *Holiday*, back for two nights, then off filming for her new series, *Antiques Inspectors*.

Antiques Inspectors was a spin-off from *Antiques Roadshow* which Jill very much wanted to present: a format programme, fixed and enduring in the schedules. Unfortunately there were no current presenter vacancies on *Roadshow*. *Antiques Inspector* was not the greatest programme in the world. Still, Jill was enjoying learning about antiques and was close at hand, as and when *Roadshow* became available.

With Jill away, Alan became a reluctant participant in the contractual negotiations with *OK!*. The contract the magazine wanted them to sign was unacceptable. It was full of details about how the wedding would be conducted: a security guard in the bridal car, blacked-out windows to hide the wedding dress, a ban on any guest bringing a camera, sight of the guest list and right of veto. Not the wedding they wanted. They rejected the contract and there then began a tortuous exchange of faxes and phone calls between *OK!*'s lawyers, Jon's lawyer and Alan. By the time Jill came back from filming nothing was resolved. They went out to dinner on the Saturday night before Valentine's Day and still nothing was resolved. When they returned home there were more calls and faxes. By now they had both had enough and were willing to walk away from the deal. It was still not settled by about 1 am, so they gave up and went to bed. The appointment at Claridge's was for 10 am the next morning.

In their minds, Jill and Alan had set out their plans for the wedding and if they were agreeable to *OK!* then the deal was on. If not, then, thanks but no thanks. Clearly, however, Jon Roseman and his lawyer and *OK!* were not going to give up that easily.

The phone was ringing again the next morning, *OK!* calling from the hotel, eager to keep them in the game, saying they might as well go ahead and get the engagement spread done at Claridge's. They could resolve the details later. So, well past 10 am, Jill and Alan drove to Claridge's and went up to the penthouse suite where the pictures were taken. Alan sat silently next to Jill while she was interviewed.

Jill went away again the following day, leaving Alan in charge of negotiations. It was about now that he felt he was beginning to exasperate Jon's lawyer. Alan thinks the lawyer assumed they were playing hardball, holding out for more money, being self-important celebrity types. Alan suspects he felt he had spent long enough trying to appease them and now it was time to put Alan in his place. The lawyer told Alan he had his priorities all wrong. It seemed to Alan that the lawyer thought he was trying to manipulate Jill, do Jon's job for him. It was Jon's job to represent Jill, not Alan's.

When Jill and Alan finally met the editor of *OK!*, Martin Townsend, their anxieties were allayed. What *OK!* was doing, of course, through its lawyers and contracts, was zealously protecting its investment. Martin was far more relaxed. All he wanted was to prevent seeing pictures of the wedding published elsewhere first. As long as Alan and Jill accepted a share of responsibility for that, there would not be a problem.

There would have been no blacked-out car. Jill would have worn a Lindka Cierach shawl, or coat of some kind, over her dress on the way to the church.

The wedding was fixed for 25 September. Cliff had already offered to make his garden available for the wedding but Jill and Alan had politely declined. Alan was particularly resistant to this.

He was still trying to keep both feet on the ground. Didn't want old friends and colleagues to think he was jumping on the celebrity bandwagon. They had, however, agreed to accept the use of Cliff's Bentley as the bridal car and the services of Cliff's gardener, Mike, as chauffeur.

Jill had considered returning to Weston for the wedding, in general discussions with Alan about where it should be held. Should she do what many girls did, and go home to get married, or was she an independent woman with an established life of her own? She no longer thought of herself as that Weston girl. She had moved on and was not about to go back. The obvious choice was the local parish church – not even the Baptist church – All Saints, on the edge of Bishop's Park by Putney Bridge.

Alan went to see the vicar – Jill was away – and was surprised and pleased to discover that he had never heard of Jill Dando. Very refreshing. Except that he then proceeded to make derogatory comments about another celebrity wedding at which he had officiated, and the magazine photographer who had turned up to cover it.

They plumped for a reception at Claridge's and then began to consider the food and music. Alan thought it seemed a bit excessive, Jill's talk of three bands and three meals in three hours, or however long it would be, along with umpteen different toasts. Planning weddings really was quite a fraught business, but Jill had waited a long time for hers, and wasn't going to be short-changed on splendour.

The wedding date coincided with the golden wedding anniversary of Judith's parents, Aunt Esme and Uncle Ken, which would be the previous day, September 24. Jill, anxious not to upset Esme and Ken's plans for their celebrations, spoke to Esme about it and there was no difficulty on that point. Esme was less happy, though, that Jill was getting married in London and spoke to Jill about it in plain terms. How did she expect her elderly father and the rest of the family to get up there? Where was this church, where was Claridge's? Why wasn't she coming back to get married in Weston? Why didn't she want two young girls from the family as brides-maids? It was an echo of Esme's feelings about the engagement and about Jill's life slipping away from her, not feeling a part of it any longer, Jill caught up in this new celebrity world.

Jill was quite upset after one phone conversation with Esme and said it made her feel bad. But this was the way of nearly all families, especially when a wedding was being planned.

As it happened, Judith agreed with her mother about the wedding and challenged Jill herself about why she was getting married in the parish church in Fulham. That church had no meaning for her, so why do it? On the other hand, it was apparent to Judith that this was saying something, namely, that Weston had even less meaning to her. Judith also sensed that Jill was trying to have a wedding which matched a certain image of herself that existed in her mind's eye. Perhaps that image was not quite fully formed, not quite the real Jill, and perhaps she was not quite sure what she wanted. These were minor tensions and frictions, but Jill still wanted Judith to come up and stay in the week before the wedding to help her get organised, in addition to being joint chief bridesmaid with Jenny.

Alan had started a pink folder labelled 'wedding' which contained correspondence with the vicar, Claridge's, details of bands, details of florists and a guest list of names which he had typed, drawn from the engagement-party list, Jill's Filofax and Alan's own address book. The list was confined by the size of the room at Claridge's to 230.

Then there was the matter of the wedding dress which was also progressing uncertainly. After the fitting at Harrods, Jill went to Lindka Cierach and discussed it with her and Lindka produced the sketch of a proposed design, together with two fabric samples. Jill took the sketch and the samples with her in mid-April when she went to Jenny's for one of their M&S evenings when Jenny bought in an instant meal of some kind from Marks & Spencer and they both relaxed with a bottle of wine. Jenny liked to think her home was a haven for Jill, a place where she could completely unwind and be herself. Jill would sometimes call in there even while Jenny was out, to see her children with the nanny.

That evening they considered the sketch together and knew it wasn't right. The model on which the design had been drawn was typically long and thin, shaped like a stick insect: 'you're not built like that,' Jenny said to Jill. It looked impractical, too, for an autumn wedding, with a top like a bathing costume, fitted and then splaying into a huge, wide skirt. Very nice for a long, skinny woman getting married in mid-July, but not for Jill in late September.

Jenny saw that Jill was reluctant to go back and discuss it with Lindka Cierach, uneasy at the prospect of a confrontation, wanting everything to be all right and not having to rock the boat. 'But Jill,' said Jenny, 'it's your wedding and your dress. The designer wants you to be happy, too.'

'I'm not sure I can go back and tell her.'

'For God's sake, of course you can, just go and tell her what you want.'

Like Judith, Jenny was direct and plain-speaking and sometimes wished that Jill would stand up for herself more, was always trying to encourage her in the direction of self-respect. There were lines you didn't cross, of course, moments when she saw Jill's face setting and knew not to push any further.

At the end of the evening, Jill seemed determined to speak to Lindka. She must have gone home and tucked the sketch and the fabric away out of sight, perhaps to forget about them. That was where Jenny would find them after Jill's death when she was clearing out Jill's things at Gowan Avenue and came across the sketch and the fabric, stuffed into a bedroom drawer.

There had been similar discussions between Jenny and Jill about the location of the marital home and whether it would be in or out of London. Jill was ready to leave London and move to a mansion in Berkshire or somewhere.

She had given an interview once to the Money section of the *Sunday Times*, in 1997, in which she said she was 'insecure' in the centre and wanted to live among suburban people like herself. Now she had friends, such as Cliff and Gloria, who lived on the outer reaches of the Home Counties, though not quite in ordinary suburban circumstances.

Alan did not want to live in the country, he wanted to live in London, even closer to the centre, in fact; ideally, right on top of the hospital where he worked and to which he was often on call at all hours. Not unreasonably, he didn't want to have to make a long drive every time the pager went. A patient in labour probably wouldn't appreciate that either.

This was an issue between them, though the underlying issue was money. When Jill was feeling ballsy, as she sometimes was when she saw Jenny, she would say things like, 'Well, to be quite honest with you, I could point out that it's basically my money we're buying this property with anyway.'

Alan was at a stage in his career where his future was likely to be lucrative, far more lucrative than his current position. He was not doing badly, but he would do much better as his private practice developed and he made the most of his highly regarded specialisation in laparoscopy.

Jill shared many of the events in her life with an old and trusted friend, Brian Ellsbury, whom she had known since childhood in Weston. Brian was now living in south London where he worked as a classical pianist, composer and teacher. He and Jill would meet quite often, for coffee or meals. She told Brian all about Alan. 'He's got such excellent prospects,' she said. She told him how she had overheard a telephone conversation in which Alan had disclosed his salary, or what she thought was Alan's salary.

Jill told Jenny about this, too. 'Jill,' Jenny said, 'I work in the same hospital, I'm on the same grade, I know exactly how much he earns and it isn't that.' She felt a bit guilty saying this to Jill, but then she knew that Alan's prospects were excellent.

Alan was always a little uncomfortable with the subject of money, and Jill must have been, too, for opposite reasons. In fact, it was a taboo subject between them, never discussed until the matter of the mortgage arose, well over a year into the relationship.

The last thing Alan wanted was to be accused of being a gold-digger. It would almost have been better if Jill hadn't had money, like Alan. Alan had zero, or less than zero, with the accumulation of debts arising out of his separation. He was confident that he would rise above those debts in time, without help, but he worried what other people would think and imagine of his motives in being with Jill.

As you could guess by now Jill was careful with her money and, while she had some pension plans and investments and saved at least a third of everything she earned, she kept most of it in an instant access building society account. She imagined that, any day, she might be earning a third of what she was earning now, so saving that proportion of her income was a perfect symmetry.

The purchase of the London equivalent of a Berkshire mansion was obviously going to cost a lot more money. Amid the ongoing uncertainty over her contract and her future, Jill was afraid of taking on a big joint mortgage that might impinge on the lifestyle she was anxious to maintain – restaurants, champagne, shopping in Harvey Nichols and Harrods. She also wanted to buy a Jaguar XK8. She did not want to buy a big house and then have to leave it. She never wanted to downgrade.

Alan assured her that it would be all right soon. She realised it made sense living near his work, that she did not want to be sitting at home alone while he drove back and forth to St Mary's, so she agreed to live in London and they began house-hunting around St John's Wood and Maida Vale. They put both their houses on the market at the beginning of March.

Jill's house went into the window of Cowan & Rutter, the estate agent on the corner of Gowan Avenue and Fulham Palace Road, for £352,000. (By 2002, there would be houses in Gowan Avenue selling for nearly double that amount.) Almost immediately, there were three or four offers at the asking price. The estate agent proposed going to sealed bids.

Alan and Jill went away that weekend to Stapleford Park in Leicestershire, a hotel with a series of interior-designed rooms, each with an individual theme and designer, the Wedgwood room, the Tiffany room, the Zoffany room by Lindka Cierach – for a 'house summit', to decide what they could afford. They took with them a calculator, pens, paper and bank balances. Unable to declare their incomes to each other, they made a game out of it and wrote them down on a piece of paper, with what they thought the other earned. Alan underestimated Jill's and she overestimated his (so she obviously had misheard that telephone conversation).

They agreed a budget of around £1.5 million. The bids on Jill's home went in that Monday. The couple who won, Claire and Patrick Bullman, offered just under £10,000 over the asking price. They exchanged contracts on 13 April, and had agreed a moving date in mid-July with Jill. By 26 April the house was already theirs and there was no going back.

The Bullmans were related to Richard Hughes next door. Patrick's brother was married to Siobhan (they lived in Fulham too, in the next street) and Siobhan was the sister of Fiona, Richard's wife. The Bullmans were moving from round the corner, on Fulham Palace Road. Claire rationalised at the time that Jill's death was about her alone and had nothing to do with the house. She wanted to forget what had happened, which must have been quite difficult.

Jill and Alan continued house-hunting and discovered that many houses in that area, around St John's Wood, never actually came on the market, appeared in estate agents' windows or had boards go up in the front garden. Nothing so vulgar. The owner might call the agent and say they were thinking of selling, and the agent might propose a potential buyer. Or the agent might ring round some of the local homeowners occasionally to see if they were thinking of moving. All very discreet and dignified. That was how it was with the house that Jill and Alan were going to buy. The £1.5 million house on Warwick Avenue. It had never gone on the market.

On 26 April everything was proceeding as planned. The property had been surveyed, the mortgage was a week away from clearance and they were a week away from exchanging contracts, signing off life insurance, making wills – Jill had never had a will. Alan had also accepted an offer on his home in Chiswick.

Then it all evaporated. Only the sale of Gowan Avenue was committed. The rest of it just fell away. Alan was asked if he still wanted to continue with the purchase of Warwick Avenue. Of course he couldn't afford to, and even if he could have done, he wouldn't have moved there. He couldn't imagine living in the family home they had bought together, alone.

Wedding, house, BBC contract, work, travel . . . everything was happening at once. It was a crazy time and Jill was getting quite stressed with it all. She went to Rio for *Holiday* in the week following their house summit. She had only just got back from Brazil when she got a call to say her brother Nigel was in hospital with a blood clot in his leg, a deep-vein thrombosis apparently caused by the long-haul flight he had taken on his recent holiday to Thailand.

The holiday had been Jill's gift to Nigel and Vanessa, a belated twentieth-anniversary gift which Nigel had been reluctant to accept. Vanessa had no qualms about it – they hadn't had a good holiday in ages, and Jill was insistent. Jill had called her a couple of times and told her that she had to persuade Nigel. In the end Vanessa had said, 'Look, if you want to celebrate twenty-one years of marriage . . .'

It had been five-star all the way, lovely hotels, and even if the place in Koh Samui had been a bit too posh – a bit too mind your ps and qs – they'd had a fabulous time. Then Nigel's leg had started to swell and swell.

Jill could not believe it when the story of Nigel's blood clot was pursued by the *Sunday People*. The paper knew all the detail – how the holiday had been her gift. There was extra detail, too, Nigel being stretchered from the plane, which was not true at all. Nigel thought it was funny, but Jill wanted to know who had told the *Sunday People*. Who had betrayed her.

She retraced her conversations about it. She called Gill Capewell, her old friend from Radio Devon whom she had spoken to at length the day before, mentioning Nigel's illness. She had been asking Gill what it was like being an older mother. Did she get tired? Now she phoned back and asked her whether she had told anyone. She hadn't.

Jill had first heard about the *Sunday People* from her agent, Allasonne Lewis, who had been called by a journalist asking if it was true about Nigel and the holiday. Ally had called Jill straight away. Jill had been beside herself with anger. Ally had never known her so angry. Jill barked at Ally. 'Who called you? What did they say? Just repeat that? I don't believe it!' she said.

Less than half an hour before Allasonne's call Jill had been talking to her friend Suzanne Yates about Nigel on her mobile in the back of a Niven car provided by the BBC. 'Perhaps it was the Niven car driver,' Ally suggested.

'No way,' said Jill.

She called Suzanne back and more or less accused her of leaking the story. Suzanne was very upset and vehemently denied it. She immediately wrote to Jill to say how hurt she was. Jill replied with an apology and said she realised her old friend could not have betrayed her. The mystery of the leak was never solved but Jill continued to be a little crazed by suspicion.

Jill was furious too, around this time, with her second agent,

Kate Moon, with whom she hoped to be doing more business in the coming months, because she needed the money – or thought she did – and because she had new opportunities in the wake of leaving BBC News. Working for news restricted the range of non-broadcast work you could do. All those lucrative corporate jobs, hosting conferences, fronting corporate videos, making personal appearances and endorsements. Although Jill had done all these things over the years, they had always been limited by working on news. She could hardly appear in a video for Esso, for example, and then appear on the news announcing a story about oil pollution.

Jill had been with Kate's agency, Speakeasy, long before she met and went over to Jon Roseman. She had met Kate, in fact, when she was first in London, living with Judith. Jill had not left Kate when she joined Jon. Jon was supposed to handle all Jill's broadcast work and share the rest with Kate, which was confusing and annoying sometimes, for Kate and Jon, when they were both approached for the same job with Jill and made separate offers on her behalf.

Kate had told Jill more than once that she was free to leave her, but Jill did not want to burn her bridges. It always amused Eamonn Holmes that Jill had two agents. 'If she is so lacking in ambition,' he would say, 'how come she has two agents?'

Celebrities, long-term and fleeting, had day rates for jobs, the rate they went out for, which were important measures of their worth and current standing. A *Big Brother* house guest might have a brief moment of opportunity to capitalise on their passing fame with personal appearances, before returning to obscurity. Their price might be high. The day rate hovered in the thousands and it depended on the job and the client too, of course. Jill had gone out for £10,000, but more usually it was half that amount and it fluctuated.

Jill, like others, was always interested in the rates for her fellow celebrities. What was Carol Vorderman going out for? Anthea Turner? They were, almost all of them, always looking over their shoulders at the opposition. Jill liked Kate to notify her every time she was requested by a client. Whatever the price for the job, and whether she could do it or not, she wanted to know about it. Kate used to send her reams of faxes, dozens of them, outlining every single client inquiry about Jill.

Early in 1999, when she was about to leave news, Jill told Kate to put up her rate to see what happened. She had limited availability until later in the year, but it was just to see if the men in suits wanted her, and how much they wanted her. The men in suits loved her, of course: she was a very marketable woman, as Kate well knew. What the clients wanted was serious journalists that looked good, too. That was Jill.

As it happened, there were few bites at Jill's proposed higher rate, and they lowered it again, brought it back down closer to earth. That was okay, they were just trying it out.

There was a new opportunity, however, with Grattan, the clothing catalogue, for their Cutting Edge range, in which a celebrity endorsed a wardrobe of clothes designed in their style. Cutting Edge had been after Jill for ages. Now she was free of news and available to participate.

Kate arranged a meeting with the Cutting Edge men in suits over lunch at Claridge's. It was, Kate said to Jill beforehand, not really a business meeting, more a get-to-know-each-other-occasion, a prelude to talking turkey. Everything seemed fine, during lunch and afterwards.

Jill was away working for much of the following fortnight, early March. Kate had not called her, saw no need to call her. Then Jill called Kate. She was, in Kate's words, apoplectic. She was taking it away from Kate, she said, she didn't want her to handle it any more.

'Why?' asked Kate. 'What have I done?'

'Basically, because I haven't had any calls from you to ask me how I felt about it.'

Jill complained that the meeting had been all about her and what she was doing, and nothing to do with the business. Kate thought that had been the whole point of the meeting.

'No,' said Jill, she just thought Kate was in it for the money.

Kate was very hurt. 'If that's the way you feel about it, I'm sorry I didn't ring you, but you were away.'

'Roseman's called me,' said Jill. 'They called me every other day. I'm cherished with Roseman. They cherish me.'

'Well, I'm sorry,' said Kate. 'Bloody well give it to Roseman, then, but if you think I'm in it for the money, then you've forgotten who I am.'

Kate had never been a big or ostentatious agent. She had known Jill for over ten years and there had never been so much as a cross word between them. She had never been so upset by someone she represented. The Cutting Edge deal was potentially worth many thousands and seemed perfect for Jill with her love of clothes and her own image, her own aspirational style. Kate had never before realised that Jill needed to have her hand held. That was obviously an oversight. Kate wrote to Jill and said how hurt she had been to be accused by Jill of greed. Jill called and apologised and Kate said if she still wanted to take the deal to Roseman, she could. 'No, no,' replied Jill. She wanted to keep it with Kate. She was sorry, she said. It was just that she was so used to being looked after every step of the way.

There were further discussions and another meeting. Kate was careful to keep Jill informed, hold her hand and briefed her for the last time two weeks before her death when it was still progressing. Kate could not forget the unpleasantness between them and it stayed with her long afterwards, so that she would cry while describing it to me a year later.

Jill talked to one or two people about her blow-up with Kate and it seemed to them that she felt Kate had used the Claridge's lunch, Jill's precious time, as a social occasion rather than a business meeting. They had obviously got their wires crossed about the purpose of that lunch, since that was broadly Kate's intention in the first place. Jill felt Kate was basking in her limelight just a little.

When other extra bits and pieces of work came through, Jill would speak of them in terms of the new home she and Alan were buying together. 'Well, that'll pay for a sofa,' or 'That'll redecorate a bedroom.' She seems to have been anxious about money and the commitment they were making. She evidently wished she could have got back from Bob Wheaton the £35,000 she had contributed back in the early 1990s when he had bought his house by the river in Maidenhead.

Bob bought a boat and Jill sometimes said she had paid for that boat, which was not true at all. Bob had bought the boat with his own money and could have repaid Jill's money too, if she had asked for it. After Jill's death, when the police came calling, Bob would show them his bank balance to prove it.

In fact, so far as Bob was concerned, the issue had been settled in July 1998, when he and Jill had spoken about the money and she had asked him for a letter, which he gave her, confirming the amount of £35,000 and their arrangement that if he sold the house or if he died, the money would be repaid. He was none too happy after Jill's death, when stories about the 'unpaid debt' appeared in the newspapers. He was asked to make a new agreement with Jill's family to repay the money, which he did.

Bob and Jill were still in touch, all through the drama over her BBC contract, and last spoke a week before she died. He could tell she was having a stressful time of it, even though she sounded like a woman on her way. That was how she had always seemed to him: a woman who knew where she was going. Until she ran into a wall over the *Six* and lost direction. Then she feared she might lose everything.

When she left Jenny at Harrods that March lunchtime after the try-out fitting for the wedding dresses, Jill went back to the BBC to meet Jane Lush and Peter Salmon – alone, which Jon Roseman was far from happy about when he heard.

There had been another confrontational meeting a week earlier, in the basement bar of the Halcyon Hotel in Holland Park, a popular venue with some BBC executives. Peter Salmon had not been present but Jane Lush had been there, along with Jill and Jon and another BBC executive, Angie Stephenson, who had been charged by Peter Salmon with the task of making Jill's contract work.

As Jon remembered it, Jane and Angie had produced a list of programmes which Jill could do over the next year. He had looked at the list and seen that it included what he considered to be Carol Vorderman's cast-offs and something else which just said 'new series', not even a title or a description. What was that supposed to be?

Jane Lush explained that it was a current affairs series being planned to replace another current affairs series, *Here and Now*.

There wasn't a title and there wasn't a format either. 'Well, what is it then?' Jon asked.

'It's in development.'

'Yes, but what is it?'

'Jon, it's in development.'

Jon was trying to work out how much of the year all this would occupy, and it didn't look like very much to him. He could feel Jill practically tugging at his trousers trying to signal him to back down. Jon was still hoping Jill might consider ITV after their meeting there with David Liddiment.

ITV would respect Jill and give her what she wanted. Jane Lush was saying, 'Well, name one ITV programme Jill would be proud to be doing. Go on, Jon, just name one programme . . .'

He remembered shouting, telling them that this deal was short-changing Jill. He was sure Jill was going to dump him any minute, but he really believed what he was saying and was only acting for her.

Jill was on the phone to Jane the next morning, apologising once again for Jon's aggressive stance. Jane felt more optimistic suddenly that Jill would stay with them and that they could make a contract. She still didn't know what Jon was up to and what was happening with ITV, so at the same time the BBC was checking its bottom line position with lawyers, looking at the possibility of compelling Jill to stay if she decided to go. That didn't seem viable, unless she actually walked away in the middle of a series.

They were lucky that Jill was willing to meet them alone. Without Jon there, the discussion in Peter Salmon's office was much easier, and Jill seemed committed to staying. By the time Peter met Jon three days later, he had conceded she would remain at the BBC. Now it was just a question of finding the right range of programmes and tacking on an extra year, which Peter conceded in return. That would have tied Jill to the corporation until April 2001.

Jill finally signed the contract in mid-April. Jon kept it sitting on his desk, for the hell of it. It was still sitting there on Monday the 26th. He still thought it was a crap deal, a pretty mediocre bunch of programmes, but it was the best he could get at the time. Even Peter Salmon would agree it was not the greatest package, but it was good enough. Jane Lush, who had helped to piece it together, thought the contract had more than achieved its purpose, filling in the gaps left by *Holiday* and the news and preserving Jill's continuous presence on peak-time television. It assured her immediate future.

'You can't do all this,' Ally Lewis said to Jill as the ideas and their details poured into the office in faxes and e-mails. Jill sent Ally some flowers after Ally sat up until three one morning trying to make a coherent list of all the offers.

The contract included an element of serious programming: two editions of *Panorama* and that proposed replacement for the current affairs series *Here and Now*. There was *Crimewatch*, which Jill continued to regard – or now regarded, in the absence of the news and *Holiday* – as her core programme; a *Crimewatch* spin-off, *Trail of Guilt*, which was essentially just voiceover work; *Summer Holiday*, from the *Holiday* stable, which involved studio presenting but no travel; a series on royal weddings, to coincide with the wedding of Prince Edward and Sophie Rhys-Jones in June 1999, which Jill and Alan would have attended as guests; hosting *Celebrity Proms* and co-hosting the BAFTAs with Michael Parkinson; some National Lottery shows; a new entertainment programme (a one-off to begin with) called *Thanks a Million*; a new live programme called

The Search; some editions of *Songs of Praise* (surprisingly, given Jill's expressed wish not to be associated with churchy matters); and a series called *Mysteries* (formerly presented by Carol Vorderman) which Jill had been unsure about because it involved an exploration of the supernatural, which made her uneasy.

In the end, Jill could not jump to ITV. There were enough changes going on in her life already. She was a BBC person at heart, a conservative person, and naturally fearful that a radical change might be disastrous.

Jill went down to the West Country in late March and met Jack at the hospital in Bristol, where he had been taken by Uncle Ken for a check-up on his eyes. They returned to Backwell and went for a pub lunch with Esme, where the wedding was the chief topic of conversation. A cab came to take Jill back to BBC Bristol for a voiceover. They waved her off as she went, the last time Esme and Ken would see her.

That weekend Jill and Alan went to Winchester, stayed in one of those Johansson's hotels overnight and moved on to Chichester to test-drive a TVR, as a possible new car for Alan when Jill got the Jaguar XK8, which she planned to do soon on a leasing arrangement. There had been talk of him inheriting her BMW, which was now nearly five years old, but they decided they should both have something new. In just a few weeks Alan would inherit the BMW after all and begin using it routinely, as a connection to Jill.

They were back in Weston, briefly, at the beginning of April collecting Jack to take him to Nigel and Vanessa's home near Bristol for an Easter lunch. Alan noted that Jill did not go to her mother's grave. He noted too that she never wanted to stay in

Weston now. They were always day visits, pleasant but brief. She had commented on the bleakness of Weston after filming there not long before for *Holiday*, as if she had only just noticed herself, after all these years.

The following week there was a meeting with the editor of *OK!* and on the same day Jill recorded the appeal for the Kosovan refugees, from a script she had been sent in advance. Ally had briefed her by fax, according to the producer's instructions, to be at TV Centre for noon for 'three minutes to autocue and one and a half minutes for radio. Clothes: casual not overdressed, friendly and soft, no hard shoulders.' Jill then went on to a meeting for *Panorama* and from *Panorama* to a *Holiday* voiceover. The Kosovo appeal was broadcast the following day, while Jill was doing a photo shoot for the forthcoming BAFTA awards.

She had just completed another photo session for a *Radio Times* cover, to launch *Antiques Inspectors*, wearing a two-piece leather suit, trousers and jacket, all zips and pockets, a designer version of bikers' leathers, standing, with parted legs and folded arms, in front of the Aston Martin that featured in the series. Jill loved the outfit, the *Avengers*-style Purdy pose, and thought the pictures sexy in a discreet way. Not quite as revealing as her earlier leather-clad cover for the *Radio Times*, but not very *Antiques Roadshow* all the same, not very Hugh Scully, whom Jill hoped to replace when he gave up presenting the programme.

The cover would appear on the newsstands just a few days before her death, with a seven-o 'Vroooooom' emblazoned across it and further pictures inside. In truth, the cover did not look much like Jill at all. It was not that she was trying to be someone she wasn't, it just looked like somebody else.

Quite a few people would tell Jill that they didn't think much of those pictures. Kate Moon's colleague Hilary told her she loved them.

'I'm so glad,' said Jill, 'because nobody else does. My father hates them, Alan hates them, everybody hates them.'

'Ah,' said Hilary, 'they're just not used to you looking like that. At least you've got them there to show the grandchildren. To show them that Granny had it once.'

Jill laughed. 'Good one, Hilary,' she said. 'As you get older and lose it, it is always nice to look back and think, once I had it.'

The day after the Kosovo appeal was broadcast, Jill and Alan went skiing at Courchevel in France, with an anaesthetist colleague of Alan's, David Lomax, and his wife Sally. They were away for four nights and returned on 12 April and on the 13th Jill wore the jacket from that cover shot to the end-of-series party for *Holiday*, which was also her leaving party. She had been given the jacket and trousers to keep, and she told Jane Lush it was the first time in all these years she'd ever had a freebie. Jane and Fenia Vardanis read an 'Ode to Jill' which they had written as a tribute to her. Jane and Jill promised to meet up for dinner in a couple of weeks with their partners. The arrangement was just a phone call away.

On the Friday before her death, Jill flew in from Dublin after a filming session for *Antiques Inspectors*. She spoke to Alan two or three times as she came in from the airport and Alan returned from St Mary's. They were both converging on Chiswick, arriving within two or three minutes of each other. They stayed in with a takeaway from Fatboys down the road. Alan went back to St Mary's later to deliver a baby, returning home in the early hours.

It was a slow and lazy Saturday. Jill called into Gowan Avenue briefly, they pottered about, did some chores, got dressed up to go to the Royal British Legion Ball at the Natural History Museum, which Jill was co-hosting with the news presenter Alastair Stewart. Jill had been on the organising committee, but had not actually been to any of the meetings and was completely unprepared. Luckily, Alastair handed her a script as she arrived.

Jeffrey Archer was there, too, and did his usual auction routine, bullying and cajoling the guests to part with their money, selling off a first dance with Jill, together with a signed copy of her *Radio Times* cover. 'Bloody good sport she was, too,' Jeffrey remembered, coming up on the stage, standing there while he did his thing. 'She was sold to a very nice chap, a doctor.' He recalled them leading the dancing, 'A waltz, it was,' he thought. Jeffrey went home soon after. Didn't give it a second thought.

Alan remembered Jill being engaged in conversation as they came off the dancefloor by a man of about his own age, whose seemingly boundless admiration for Jill was matched by his detailed knowledge of her past. Alan was used to those kinds of approaches by now but this one was different, inappropriate, somehow, all that awareness of Jill's past. He was glad he was there to protect her.

When it was time to go, they went round the room and said many goodbyes and left to take their arranged car home. But the car wouldn't be ready for half an hour. It seemed silly to go back in again, so they sat there, just the two of them, in this brightly lit room, like a storeroom almost, waiting for the ride home.

They looked at each, then, as if, 'Do we really want to be here?' They didn't, of course, but they were stuck. So they waited in near silence. It was very still after the hubbub of the ball, like a halfway place, not quite out and not quite home.

Sunday, Alan was up and out early for golf with David Lomax tee-ing off at eight in Stoke Poges Jill following him later a drink at the clubhouse and then back to David and Sally's home for lunch with talk of skiing and weddings among other things until about four when Alan and Jill drove home in a mini convoy of their separate cars and settled down and watched the broadcast of the first programme in the new series of *Antiques Inspectors* after which Alan's parents phoned to say how much they had enjoyed it and then Alan and Jill chatted a while about the week before them what are you doing tomorrow what time are you likely to finish what shall we do in the evening OK I'll cook what about Tuesday anything you fancy doing more talk about the wedding the music Claridge's did you really need three meals in three hours and that kind of thing and then to bed. Sleep. And Alan was up first in the morning and Jill made his breakfast while he got ready and she was going back to bed for a while when Alan left at about half seven and they said nice things to each other before he went out the door and they did not see or speak to each other again after that.

Jill was alone then to think about the day ahead between phone calls about being a lady who lunches about her fax machine and the cartridge it needed and the fish she would buy for supper at the shop on Fulham Road and the wedding the house the mortgage her career her friends her colleagues her family and the things she'd done and the places she'd been and her mother and Alan and the children they hoped to have . . . she could think about it all and may have done or might have done had she known in the hours she had left to live.

Seventeen

Jill's death was not just a private event, not simply a source of personal grief to those who knew her. It was in the nature of her celebrated life that she would be celebrated in death too, by many thousands of people who had never known her, who imagined or felt they did from her appearances on television, from the photographs and articles in magazines and newspapers.

As Alan said, it was an odd bereavement, in the sense that he never had to tell anyone Jill had died. The Prime Minister and the Queen both knew and wanted or felt obliged to make some public expression of regret at her loss. Alan received a handwritten letter from Tony Blair. Jack received a letter from Prince Charles. Her death was mentioned in Parliament. It was mentioned everywhere.

Many of those people grieved too, touched by the suddenness and the shock of her murder, in the middle of her life with so much happiness still to come. No doubt, as with the death of

Princess Diana two years earlier, which was equally sudden and shocking, many people grieved for themselves, for past personal bereavements of their own which remained with them, or for their own mortality, which would always be with them.

They had lost another icon too, a familiar and warm presence in their lives. That part of their lives which looked outwards for satisfaction or escape, or out of curiosity, to the remote, intriguing and appealing world of the celebrated, in all its various forms. Jill was a modern icon. Not because of the greatness of her achievements, which did not advance science or medicine or politics or philosophy or art, though they were great to her, and rightly so. She was an icon of popular culture. She was popular. People liked her. They liked seeing her on television. She was good at being on television and she looked good, and that was all there was to it. Almost.

She embodied something too and reflected back to people something of themselves. Beneath being famous she seemed, and indeed still was, ordinary. A very English ordinariness. Not the new metropolitan England of diversity and social change, but the middle England that was conservative and unchanging. The bulb in the middle of Hamish Campbell's bell chart, that commonest of denominators and biggest of groupings, Jill was both part of that and soared away to represent it. You could turn on the television and there she was, reliable, cheerful and always there.

For the BBC, Jill was a conduit in its noble mission to educate, inform and entertain. An inevitable byproduct of that very public job was that the BBC also made her famous, showed her the pleasures of being famous by which she was seduced. The BBC wanted Jill to be famous, which is why it paid her so much money to do what she did, and why it wanted her to be on television all the time. It divided her too, just as the BBC itself was divided, torn between the sobriety of news and the lightness of popular programming. Asking the impossible, that she be all things to all people, letting her believe for a while that was possible.

Famous for what? people would ask. For being on television? As if it were nothing; as if television itself was meaningless and shallow and not the dominant culture and medium of the age, the BBC not still its chief protagonist.

Jill died, apparently, because she was famous, because she sought and enjoyed public attention; because the BBC required it of her; because we watched the programmes and bought the newspapers and magazines. Her killing was an aberrant expression of that attention, but it was still part of it. Barry George might have pulled the trigger, but her death arose out of a wider complicity in the business of celebrity.

I could tell you a hundred stories of the aftermath from among those people who knew Jill and received the news in different ways at different moments on that day and reacted to it, in a hundred different ways.

Jill's father Jack was at home in Weston when the phone went and it was his neighbour, Doreen, asking, 'Have you got the news on?'

Jack saying, 'I haven't got any news or television on. Why?'

Doreen saying she had something terrible to tell him, and telling him what it was, and Jack saying, 'Are you sure? What are you saying?'

'I broke down,' Jack told me. 'I couldn't help it. I just collapsed in the chair here.' It was his chair, the chair he always sat in, by the front window. Around him were many photographs, of his family and especially of Jill, souvenirs of Jill, her trophies and awards. He could barely see them, but he knew they were there.

Cliff and his PA Roger were on tour in Scandinavia, on a plane to Copenhagen, Roger with ten missed calls on his phone when they landed, unable to access his voicemail, hearing the news in a call to the hotel room, telling Cliff, who went ahead and appeared on stage that night, Roger giving him a big punch, saying, 'Now, you have to get on with it. You'll be all right. You'll be able to smile.' Which he was, to his own amazement, when the adrenaline started pumping and carried him through. Showbusiness.

At the BBC, Tony Hall called a minute's silence in the newsroom and then they started talking about how it would be handled on the *Six* that night. People got very jumpy about the wider possibilities of danger and there was concern for the security of the presenters and the next day for Tony Hall himself who was the subject of threats and taken from his home for a week, to live in the company of armed police officers.

Elsewhere at the BBC, Peter Salmon, Alan Yentob, Jane Lush, Seetha Kumar and others sat around in a state of shock, someone saying, 'What do we do?' Peter and Alan first thinking of running *Fasten Your Seatbelt* at Disney as a tribute because there wasn't time to do more, Jane arguing that there was time, that she could do it, suspecting that Peter and Alan thought she was too upset, too emotionally involved to do a good job there and then. Jane winning the argument, the meeting finally deciding to make a full tribute programme, clearing the schedules, people who knew Jill well spinning hurriedly through hours of videotape footage of her, in which she was painfully alive, to use as clips in the programme. The programme still being finished as the BBC1 balloon went up, so that they had to run the balloon twice before the tribute programme was ready to broadcast. Just under ten million people watched that programme.

Bob was alone on his boat, having only just arrived when the phone rang and it was Janey, his new partner, not so new by then, who relayed the news. Bob lay on his bed for a while and then Janey joined him and began fielding the many calls seeking public comment from him, which he resisted, deciding instead to compose a formal statement for release.

Judith Dando was driving home that day, moving home to Bristol from France, crossing on the ferry, not bothering to retune her radio as she arrived in England (as her family feared she would), deciding then not to call in at Jill's on the way home as she had said to Jill she might, going straight to Backwell instead, knowing something was up when she called in and found her parents' home empty, arriving at her own home around 6.30, her sister turning up. 'Hello, how are you, how was the journey?'

'Fine.'

'Have you seen mum?'

'No.'

'Have you seen Hilary?'

'No.'

'Ah, have you heard the news? There's been some really bad news. I think you'd better sit down.'

With her daughter to look after, Judith went into coping mode and did not break down until two days later, while making a complete balls-up of trying to cook spaghetti and sauce for her boyfriend.

The family all got together soon after and they were all there in the sitting room at Ken and Esme's and one of them, maybe Nigel or Vanessa, though Judith was thinking the same, said, 'It feels like you're playing a part in a soap opera, and you're going to get to the end of the episode and it'll be, "Well, thank God for that, now we can get back to normal."' That was how it felt. But it was far from normal. It was very, very weird.

Suspicion and paranoia began to set in among Jill's friends and family and colleagues as they wondered who might have killed her and why. Somebody they knew, perhaps. Somebody they had just passed in a corridor of the BBC. Alan, Jenny, Judith cast around for possible suspects. What about this person, what about that person? Reaching into the recesses of their memories, trying to recall any threat or fear Jill might have felt or expressed. It was amazing, you could find a motive for everyone if you really thought about it.

Then there was Jill in the chapel of rest in the basement of the undertaker's in Weston. Judith seeing her there, thinking, God, that glamorous life she was leading, and here she is in this basement, with the traffic going past on the main road. How can you leave people in these places, even if they are dead?

Jill returned to Weston, as she would not have done for her wedding. The Baptist Church at Milton was being rebuilt, so the funeral was held at Clarence Park Baptist Church across town from the undertaker's. The service conducted by Roger Collins, the former minister at Milton, who had led the service at Jill's mother's funeral thirteen years earlier. He wrote the address for Jill, as he had for Jean, focusing on the Jill from Weston who had remained unspoilt and did not 'scorn the base degrees by which she did ascend'.

Weston people lined the streets and stood still and silent in respect, some had flowers which they threw as the hearse passed, evoking memories of the funeral of Princess Diana.

Afterwards Jill was buried in her mother's grave. The graveside screened off from public gaze, just Alan there, with Jack and Nigel and Vanessa and Esme and Ken and Judith and Jenny and her husband Ed.

And now, just as Jill had once gone there to talk to her mother, so friends and relatives would come to talk to her, conversationally, telling her some of the things that went on, things she would not have believed.

She would not have believed, for instance, that an academic institute would be established in her name, as it was the following year when the Jill Dando Institute of Crime Science was inaugurated at University College, London. It was Nick Ross's idea, which he introduced during early discussions about the formation of an appropriate charity in which to invest Jill's memory, something that would carry her name in perpetuity.

The charity became the Jill Dando Fund and created a symmetry of bereavement in its involvement of many of the people who had been closest to Jill, drawing them together in a constant round of meetings and functions. There were two tiers of people. The trustees: Alan, Nigel, Jenny, Nick Ross, Sir Cliff Richard, Abel Hadden, the Countess of Wessex and the Metropolitan Police Commissioner, Sir John Stevens. The management committee: Judith, Jane Lush, Allasonne Lewis, Seetha Kumar, Robin Williams, Anastasia Baker, Michael Dobbs, Belinda Hadden, Sarah Mason, another friend, and Donald Steel, the chief press officer of the BBC.

There was a loop, and not everyone was in it. Some people were out of the loop such as Bob Wheaton, Jon Roseman and others, old friends such as Pete Baylis and Gill Capewell, who felt, through nobody's fault, isolated in their bereavement, and were glad to make contact later and have each other to talk to and share their feelings. Even Jill's family sometimes felt distanced from events in the aftermath, with their focus on the celebrated Jill and the involvement of the other celebrated or high-powered people who had known her.

I went to one of those Jill Dando Fund events, a recording of a television programme, *Song for Jill*, at TV Centre. There was a reception afterwards and I could not help noticing that Jack and Nigel and Vanessa and others had gravitated to the outer edges of the throng, as if it were the West Country and the centre of the room was London. Those tensions had existed in Jill's life and did not diminish in death.

As is inevitably the case, in any group, even, or especially among the bereaved, there were minor disagreements within the fund. Not everyone thought a crime science academy was the best way to remember Jill. Though no one could think of a better idea, and it did go forward with a consensus.

Nick Ross thought, because it had been his proposition, that he would be the most appropriate person to chair the fund and was surprised when Alan and others thought that Alan would be more suitable, as the man whom Jill had been going to marry, the chief protector of her memory. It was probably what Jill would have wanted too.

There was keen discussion about the policy and direction of the fund and the speed at which it was moving, which Nick sometimes found too slow. But there was general awareness of the need to get it right, for the launch and later, during the fund-raising.

With the Institute as its goal and after discussions with UCL, on its launch in March 2000 the fund-raising target was set at £5 million in twelve months. It seemed ambitious at the time, but the intention was to aim high, far higher than the amount that was actually needed. Crime science was not an easy concept to get across to people. Later, with its objective in sight, the funding target was repositioned at a more realistic level. Just over £1 million was raised and this was more than enough to get started and to employ the first UK director of crime science, Gloria Laycock, whose background was in the Home Office. The fund was able to persuade the government to provide further financial support, and some organisations which had donated to the appeal were willing to provide ongoing assistance. HSBC, for example, gave £100,000 and provided offices, and the Home Office agreed to pay Gloria Laycock's salary for the first three years.

The launch of the Institute was marked by a lecture from Gloria Laycock, who seemed dynamic, and clever. She articulated in her speech what crime science was all about, so that it made sense – to me, at least – and seemed valuable and important: a broad-based endeavour which would draw together all kinds of people – sociologists, designers, criminologists, architects – focused on improving ways of reducing and detecting crime. Social study would result in practical solutions. If it worked, then it would certainly honour Jill's memory, not let her down.

Not letting Jill down, for Alan, also meant not breaking down, especially not in public. He became perhaps slightly driven in his determination not to show his emotions. We spoke together quite regularly for a long period of time and he always seemed the same, cautious and contained.

He told me about flying to Nice, going virtually straight from court one day during the trial, to participate in the celebrations for Cliff's sixtieth birthday and joining the other guests on Cliff's private cruise, which was later featured in *OK!*. He mentioned being uncomfortable, sitting next to the editor of the magazine at a meal. It was not until later, and not initially from Alan, that I heard there had been an onboard wedding during which there had been hymns, some of the same hymns that had been played at Jill's funeral, 'How Great Thou Art', 'Amazing Grace'. Alan became visibly upset and was probably embarrassed, though perhaps it did him good.

The cruise was to plague him later in another way because he had met a young woman actress, Helen Hobson, who had been Cathy to Cliff's Heathcliff during his stage show. Helen was a Weston girl of origin, or if not quite Weston then not far off. They saw a little of each other afterwards and became friends, and Alan found himself back in the papers. Dando fiancé finds new love, or some such story.

But there was no big romance. As Alan had told his mother when she called to inquire after reading about it, 'If and when anything happens, you'll be the first to know, and not from the papers.' Later, while I was writing this book, Alan sent me an e-mail telling me to disregard Nigel Dempster's proclamation in the *Daily Mail* of his forthcoming engagement. 'I don't know why I feel compelled to correct this story,' he wrote, 'and please forgive me if you were sensible enough not to have read it in the first place.'

It was funny during the trial. Every time an unknown woman turned up with Alan at the court, Jenny Higham on one occasion, Allasonne Lewis on another, I would be asked if that was Alan's new girlfriend. Usually by a reporter, once by a court usher. Not so funny for Alan though, who has years of this ahead of him, as he attempts to make a life for himself without Jill.

He was different after the trial, lighter in his mood and more relaxed. He said he hadn't expected the trial to be an ending, just as well, but it was only afterwards he had realised what a milestone it was. He knew it might sound like control freakery, he said, but he was aware of a feeling of wanting to move on which he had kept at bay in the run-up to and during the course of the trial.

There had been talk of milestones early on; all those fixed dates that then lay ahead, plans they had made together. Others had been aware of those dates too and tried to help him through them. He had spent the day of his wedding – the wedding that would have been – 25 September 1999, at Cliff's home, with Cliff's friends and his friends, Jenny, Mark, who would've been his best man.

It had not been a formal occasion, everyone brought some food they had prepared. Gloria Hunniford described how they all started singing later, when they were clearing up the dishes, singing along to Cliff's greatest hits.

Alan said when I saw him after the trial that he knew you could only control your thoughts so much and he tried not to torment himself with all those 'what if' scenarios. That previous evening he had come home from work and gone out alone for a walk by the river near his home. The sun had been setting, it was still hot and the tide was high. He was wandering along, aware that I was coming the next day and perhaps it was that thought that had started him wondering . . . thinking, I wouldn't have been walking alone along the Thames on 27 July 2001. I wonder what I would have been doing. But, he said, you can't spend your life thinking like that.

*

Acknowledgements

This book emerged out of the co-operation of many people who were close to or knew Jill at different stages of her life. None of them, I am sure, ever imagined that such a book would be either necessary or desirable. Almost everyone had some doubts as to the value of the book and their own contribution to it. They hoped, I think, to document and celebrate her life and accepted that part of the narrative would be an account of her death.

There would have been no book without the support of Alan Farthing, Jill Dando's family: father Jack, brother Nigel and his wife Vanessa, cousin Judith, aunt and uncle Esme and Ken; her best friend Jenny Higham; her BBC colleague Jane Lush; Abel Hadden.

I am further grateful, for interviews and other assistance, to Jeffrey Archer, Sven Arnstein, Anastasia Baker, Peter Baylis, Roger Bruce, Hamish Campbell, Stephen Cape, Gill Capewell, Brian Cathcart,

Judith went to Jill's grave on special occasions, to be close to her in a way, although she did not really think Jill was there. Though they were quite different in their personalities there was a similarity between them too, in their age, their appearance and their outlook. It seemed to me that Judith carried something of Jill with her. Some part of Jill that lived on in her cousin.

Judith said she had been scared in the first few nights after Jill's death. Scared at the thought that Jill might come back to see her. She was sure that if she was going to come back then she would come and see her. The thought made her nervous, even though it would only be Jill. Lying there alone in bed, waiting for signs, almost expecting Jill to speak. Which she didn't, of course. It taught Judith something about faith and belief.

'It might sound twee,' she said, 'but being Jill she would have come back and said, "It's all right, mum's here and everything's fine, don't worry about me."'

That was what she would have done. And the fact that she didn't confirmed something for Judith. This was it. This was all there was.

Roger Collins, John Crockford-Hawley, Michael Dobbs, Helen Doble, Brian Ellsbury, Andy Gathercole, Philip Gathercole, Belinda Hadden, Tony Hall, the staff of Hammersmith and Fulham Archives and Local History Centre, Martin Hawkins, Eamonn Holmes, Gloria Hunniford, Liz Johnston-Keay, Jonathan Keeping, Ingrid Kelly, Jan Knott, Seetha Kumar, Allasonne Lewis, Martyn Lewis, Ashley Lovell, Sally Magnusson, Martyn Maxey, John McVicar, Kate Moon, Andy Page, Helen Phelps, Andrew Ray, Sir Cliff Richard, Jon Roseman, Nick Ross, Peter Salmon, Alison Sharman, Fran Shisler, Donald Steel, Zoe Taylor, Fenia Vardanis, the staff of Weston Reference Library, Bob Wheaton, Robin Williams, Nicholas Witchell, Kate Woodward and Suzanne Yates. It was impossible to speak to everyone Jill knew (and still to produce a book this side of the next millennium) and I am sorry if anyone feels left out.

As a gesture of thanks to all contributors, I have agreed to make a donation from the sale of each book to the Jill Dando Fund. The fund would be pleased to receive further donations (made payable to 'Jill Dando Fund') at PO Box 321, London W1A 6JD. Further information is available on its website, www.jilldandofund.com.

Thanks are also due to the former deputy editors of the *Sunday Times Magazine*, Rosemary Collins and Dorothy Wade, and to the editor, Robin Morgan, for his generosity in tolerating my absence; to my agent, Georgina Capel; to my editor, Alan Samson; to my two excellent transcribers, Heather Wood and Caroline Bach-Price.

I've been grateful for the encouragement and interest of a number of people, in particular Jamie Bruce, Andy Dore, Jayne Dore, Tim Hulse, Dominic Lloyd, Tim Lott, Anthea Mason, Steve Mason, Allan Nazareth, Ashok Prasad, Vij Prasad, Chris Williams and my parents, Pat and George Smith.

A thousand thanks, above all, to my partner, Petal Felix, for her enduring wisdom, for carrying the family while I worked and for her unfaltering support.

David James Smith
davidjamessmith@hotmail.com
May 2002